MW00800382

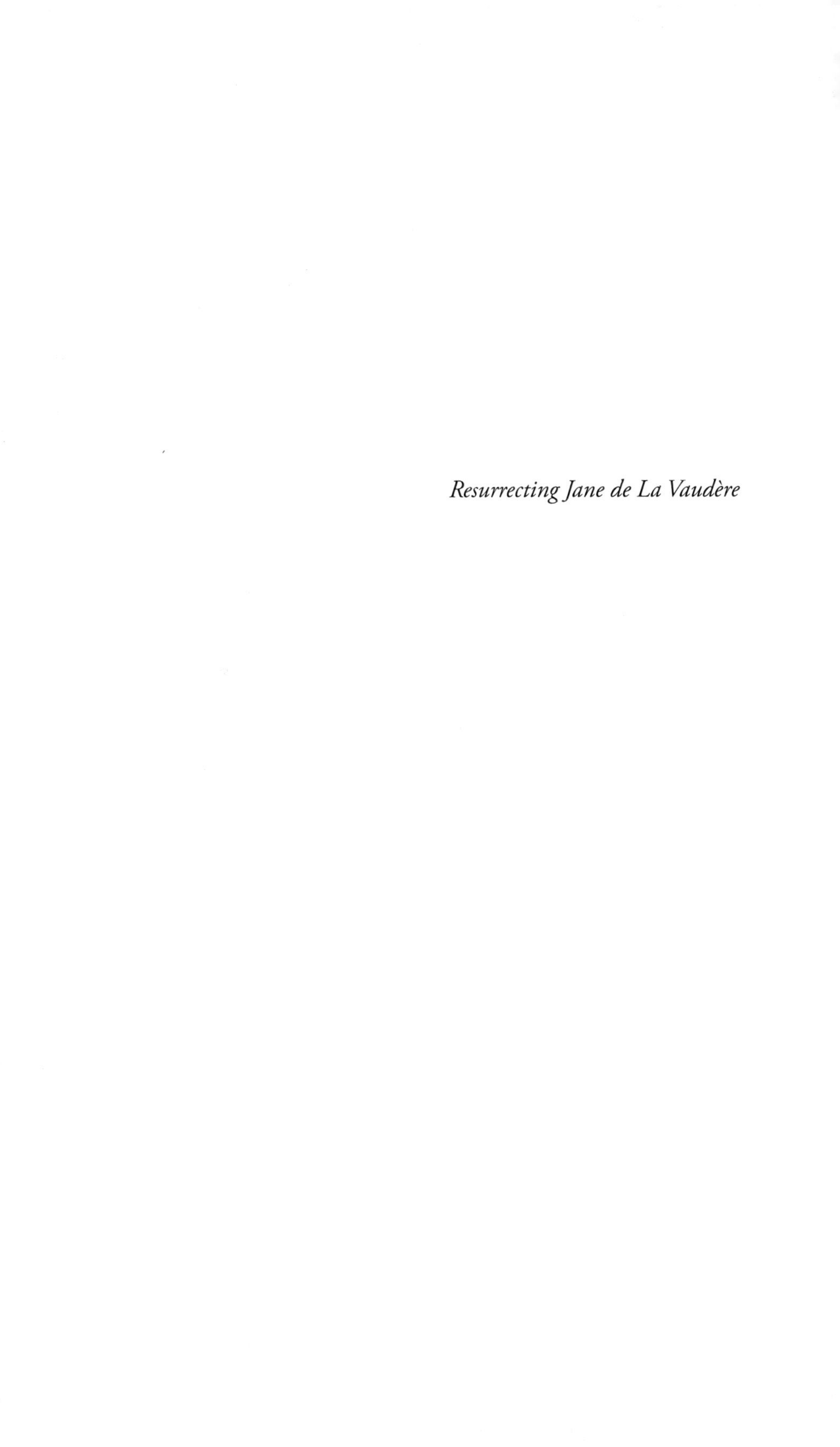

Resurrecting Jane de La Vaudère

Resurrecting Jane de La Vaudère

Literary Shapeshifter of the Belle Époque

SHARON LARSON

The Pennsylvania State University Press
University Park, Pennsylvania

Frontispiece: Jane de La Vaudère, image from *Le carnet de la femme*, October 15, 1906. Photo: author.

Library of Congress Cataloging-in-Publication Data

Names: Larson, Sharon, 1979– author.
Title: Resurrecting Jane de La Vaudère : literary shapeshifter of the Belle époque / Sharon Larson.
Description: University Park, Pennsylvania : The Pennsylvania State University Press, [2022] | Includes bibliographical references and index.
Summary: "Examines the life of French writer Jane de La Vaudère (1857–1908), exploring how she adapted her persona to shifting literary trends and readership demands, which captured public curiosity and advanced her sales"—Provided by publisher.
Identifiers: LCCN 2022038405 | ISBN 9780271094441 (hardback)
Subjects: LCSH: La Vaudère, Jane de, 1857–1908. | Women authors, French—Biography. | Plagiarism—France—History—19th century. | Feminism—France—History—19th century. | LCGFT: Biographies.
Classification: LCC PQ2623.A9 Z76 2022 | DDC 848/.809—dc23/eng/20220927
LC record available at https://lccn.loc.gov/2022038405

Printed in the United States of America
Published by The Pennsylvania State University Press, University Park, PA 16802–1003

The Pennsylvania State University Press is a member of the Association of University Presses.

It is the policy of The Pennsylvania State University Press to use acid-free paper. Publications on uncoated stock satisfy the minimum requirements of American National Standard for Information Sciences—Permanence of Paper for Printed Library Material, ANSI Z39.48–1992.

TO JENNIFER,

WITH ALL MY LOVE

CONTENTS

ILLUSTRATIONS

Except where otherwise indicated, all photos are by the author.

ACKNOWLEDGMENTS

This book was born, as most creative endeavors are, of human connection and exchange. At a coffee shop in Providence, Rhode Island, at the annual Nineteenth-Century French Studies conference, I shared with a colleague some captivating discoveries that I had made about La Vaudère. When I mentioned that I was contemplating editing a volume of scholarship on Decadent women writers, her advice was transformative: "Sharon, why don't you just write your own book about her?"

Of the variety of sources that informed my research, the most worthwhile were often other humans, and the kindness of strangers (cemetery groundskeepers, museum directors, car connoisseurs) led to my most notable discoveries. Archival work can be a solitary and isolating endeavor, and researchers can easily spend days absorbed in dusty annals in library basements obsessing about the dead and rarely interacting with breathing beings. The friendships that grew out of this project were a happy surprise. Over the course of my research, I met three people who have an association with La Vaudère: Michael Scrive, a family descendant; Anne-Charlotte Rousseau, the current owner of the Château de La Vaudère; and Pierre Naudet, a resident and amateur historian of Parigné-l'Évêque. Michael, a distant cousin of La Vaudère and avid enthusiast of the Belle Époque, was a goldmine of information about the Scrive family. He shared pictures from family albums, reconstructed an exhaustive family tree, and deciphered her distinctive and angular handwriting. The research for this book owes much to his kindness and fondness for La Vaudère (whom he affectionately calls "Tante Jane"). Despite having no familial relation to La Vaudère, Anne-Charlotte welcomed me to the château property multiple times and put me in contact with community members from Parigné-l'Évêque. She gave me a tour (in her Ferrari convertible) of village points of interest: the city hall, the local cemetery, and the retirement home named after La Vaudère's grandsons. Her passion for automobiles shaped the final chapter and inspired me to further scrutinize a rare photograph of La Vaudère seated behind the steering wheel of a car. I appreciate her generosity and hospitality that made many of my discoveries possible. Toward the completion of my research, I corresponded with octogenarian Pierre Naudet, La Vaudère's most indefatigable advocate in Parigné-l'Évêque. He has repeatedly reached out to city council members, local librarians, and regional journalists to bring La Vaudère the recognition that she has long deserved. In 2021, he organized a local exhibit on La Vaudère for the *Journées du patrimoine* and convinced the city council to designate a square in her name. I am thankful for my written exchanges with Pierre and for his efforts in helping to revive La Vaudère's name. This book is dedicated in part to Michael, Anne-Charlotte, and Pierre, and to their gratifying conversations, warmth, and friendships. In sharing their personal perspectives and visions of La Vaudère, they have helped to inspire and shape the structure of this book until the very last pages.

Friends and colleagues have provided generous feedback on the manuscript while juggling school closures, childcare, and virtual teaching. I am indebted to Anne O'Neil-Henry, Heidi Brevik-Zender, Margot Irvine, and Elizabeth Emery for their helpful comments on chapters in progress. I am deeply grateful to Rachel Mesch for her multiple readings and our extended dialogue about La Vaudère's slippery feminist positions. The great sleuth Melanie Hawthorne shared her best research tips and archival leads and was the first to encourage me, over lattes, to write this book. I am obliged to mentor and friend Gretchen Schultz and take comfort in having her continued support over the decades.

Others kindly responded to emails and phone calls from afar. Embalmment experts Anne Carol and Dario Piombino-Mascali helped me make sense of the "mummies" housed on the Château de La Vaudère property. Mathilde Huet visited Parisian archives on my behalf when travel was not possible, and Alain Maury regaled me with childhood stories about Parigné-L'Évêque and La Vaudère's daughter-in-law. Michael Garval examined a "photo truquée" of La Vaudère and pointed out the telling signs of Photoshop *avant la lettre*. Courtney Sullivan shared her expertise on a rare Liane de Pougy novel and its caricatural depiction of La Vaudère. Thank you all for providing the momentum to take this book to the next stages.

This project depended on hands-on archival research and travel to and throughout France over multiple summers. The College of Arts and

Humanities and the Provost's Office at Christopher Newport University provided the financial and logistical support that facilitated the research and writing phases. Upon my return stateside, Kendra Boileau and Josie DiNovo from Penn State University Press walked me through the different phases of this project and answered my endless questions along the way. Their support was invaluable.

My dear friends Rocío Gordon and Clay Howard have offered unwavering personal and professional support over the years. I only hope that I have been able to return the favor. I express my gratitude to Jessica, Abe, and Ada ("Ada, je t'aime!"), and to my parents for their logistical support (dog sitting) and emotional support (sending pictures of the dog). More seriously, their steadfast love, humor, and positivity are infectious, and for that I am grateful. And finally, I send eternal love and appreciation to Jennifer, who spent precious vacation hours meticulously proofreading, and to Harper, who kindly shared her workspace with me and my intolerable puns. My greatest joy while writing this book has been to see our sweet families of humans and canines coming together as one.

Introduction

In 1898, French writer Jane de La Vaudère (1857–1908, née Jeanne Scrive) appeared before a judge and demanded a divorce. Armed with correspondence between her husband and his mistress, she claimed that her husband's neglect and reckless spending had forced her to rely on writing to support her son. For the widely published author, this argument was strategic: in casting her literary production as an expression of maternal self-sacrifice, La Vaudère averted accusations of domestic neglect typically directed at female intellectuals. Her pursuit of financial justice and autonomy from her husband ultimately prevailed and the judge ruled in her favor. La Vaudère extended this skillful negotiation of personal convictions and social norms to her writing, where she balanced transgressive and conservative narratives while continually shaping her mutable and alluring public image.

La Vaudère published more than forty novels, plays, and volumes of poetry, and hundreds of her editorials, short stories, and serial novels appeared in periodicals throughout her career. She always remained relevant to the times, adapting to the trends of Decadent, Naturalist, and Orientalist fiction, or integrating topical or provocative subjects like feminism, divorce reform, or the nascent automobile industry into her texts. Today, like other prolific female authors of her time, she remains relatively unknown, despite the controversies—and ensuing renown—that were once associated with her life and writing. She had a reputation as a plagiarist, and nearly all of her novels and short stories contain passages from previously published works. She was both the plaintiff and defendant in several lawsuits for theft of creative property that involved prominent contemporary figures. In 1907, she claimed to be the original author of the *Rêve d'Égypte* mummy pantomime, whose notorious Moulin Rouge production featured a kiss between Colette and her lover Missy de Morny that ended in uproar (and increased publicity). As reflected in the titles *Les demi-sexes* (1897), *Les androgynes* (1903), *Le harem de Syta* (1904), and *Sapho, dompteuse* (1908), La Vaudère's fiction often depicted subversive sexualities and betrayed a preoccupation with nonnormative versions of womanhood. Like many of her fictional characters, La Vaudère broke from traditional standards of femininity. Following her divorce, she continued to enjoy her ex-husband's family estate, the Château de La Vaudère, which had also been the inspiration for her pen name. Despite her personal and professional independence, La Vaudère's relationship with contemporary feminism was complicated. Her texts advocated for gender equality in education and marriage, and she once referred to herself as a "féministe farouche" but spent years critiquing organized movements and their agendas.[1] She adopted misogynistic fin-de-siècle discourses that characterized women as malevolent manipulators whose ultimate downfall (ostracization, death) represented satisfying justice for bourgeois readers. Her unconventional lifestyle and corpus attracted the attention of her peers, and she was consistently parodied in literary periodicals, newspapers, and *romans à clef*.

Until now, there has been no monographic study devoted to La Vaudère's life story and collective works. *Resurrecting Jane de La Vaudère* attempts to remedy this neglect and examine how she molded and adapted her persona to shifting literary trends and readership demands, branding a controversial image that captivated public curiosity and advanced her sales. In the last decades of the nineteenth century, when La Vaudère came of age as a writer, women were publishing at record numbers. This trend can in part be explained by a series of educational reforms in France that gradually increased girls' access to education, literacy, and new professional possibilities. The Press Law of 1881 loosened censorship restrictions, and advances in printing technology boosted the publishing industry and gave rise to a plethora of new periodicals. Women such as La Vaudère contributed poems, editorials, and *feuilletons* to newspapers and magazines in unprecedented numbers.[2] Several anthologies about women writers appeared in response to these new trends, and critics attempted to classify and make sense of the evolving gender demographics of the writing profession.[3] Some of these anthologies were relatively reverent in their discussion of women authors, and others were more vitriolic in their analysis, taking issue with those who broke from conventional gender roles in their own lives or depicted "unsavory" themes in their texts. La Vaudère's name appeared in both types of collections.

Readers may be tempted to ask why a plagiarist such as La Vaudère deserves our attention. To dismiss La Vaudère is to miss a crucial opportunity to examine how one of many women writers of the Belle Époque navigated the demands of a bourgeois readership and cultivated a complex writer's persona to attract and profit from media attention. As this book demonstrates, La Vaudère's sales relied on her chameleonlike adaptability to evolving literary and social trends. The diversity of her collected works attests to her shapeshifting throughout her career. From her sentimental verse poetry to her salacious Naturalist, Decadent, or erotic Orientalist fiction, the contents of La Vaudère's *œuvre* exemplify her continual transformation and instinct for the literary market. Consequently, the challenges of documenting La Vaudère's life begin with her persona, which she incessantly shaped and reworked in interviews, advertisements, and photomontages. These original sources are some of the few that remain from her lifetime and play a crucial role in mapping out her biography and professional trajectory. They also point to the paradox inherent in trying to "pin down" La Vaudère, whose slippery positions manifested themselves not only in divorce court (described above) but also in opinion pieces about contemporary women's issues. In editorials, for example, she advocated for women's sexual fulfillment and reforms to divorce laws, yet countered any explicit identification with feminist movements by parodying well-known activists and denouncing their agendas as impractical. Ultimately, she transcended classification by inhabiting multiple genres (poetry, short stories, plays, novels, editorials), literary movements (Naturalist, Decadent, and Orientalist fiction), and social questions (feminism, marriage, divorce, education) to deftly appeal to readers' interests. Her plagiarism facilitated this malleability. As one critic marveled, "Toute l'œuvre de Jane de la Vaudère a ce caractère double, ou, pour parler en pédant, cette *dualité* difficile à saisir, et attirante comme tous les mystères."[4] In the context of this fluidity, La Vaudère's plagiarism points to an element of her savvy self-construction. Mummy-like, she wrapped herself in a patchwork of voices and drew from a myriad of discourses to preserve her persona from the artistic and social demands placed on women writers.

In fact, mummies are central to this study, in literal and metaphorical form. The burial chapel at the Château de La Vaudère contains the embalmed corpses of three of La Vaudère's family members, their faces on display under a glass plate. In late nineteenth-century France, the practice of embalming provided affluent families like La Vaudère's the possibility of preserving the body of a deceased loved one. Methods relied on chemical compounds, evisceration, and dehydration to impede the natural process of decay. Through artificial intervention, embalmers indulged the idea of immortality and a way for the body to live on but in an altered form. They reworked and transformed the corpse, removing organs and applying various balms, herbs, and chemical substances until the final product was a mere shell of the original. The mummified body moved beyond the confines of time to be available to future generations. In many ways, mummies are simultaneously dead and alive, bearing traces of both the original and new, undergoing perpetual recontextualization. La Vaudère's plagiarism functions in the same way, transforming an original text into a modified format, molding what came before into a new shape in the quest for literary immortality. More broadly, the château's mummies are a poignant reminder of the call for preservation that is at the heart of this study. With the loss of her papers, neglect of her literary *œuvre*, and unawareness of her unique biography, La Vaudère's legacy has suffered near erasure and decomposition. This monograph hopes to reverse this process.

LA VAUDÈRE'S ARCHIVAL ABSENCE

There are no archives devoted exclusively to La Vaudère. Nearly all of her manuscripts, contracts, and general correspondence have disappeared. A small selection of her letters and legal documents have been preserved, but these materials are dispersed throughout collections in Paris and Le Mans, requiring both luck and resourcefulness to locate. There is no evidence that La Vaudère's materials were ever saved, purchased, auctioned, or donated collectively. This lacuna is especially surprising considering the frequency with which she published in France, as well as in German-, Spanish-, and Portuguese-speaking countries where her most popular works appeared in translation. Locals in Parigné-l'Évêque have long speculated about the fate of La Vaudère's belongings, and some recall hearing that her papers were burned by her in-laws in retribution for the shame that her writing and lifestyle brought upon the family. The likelihood that the entirety of her manuscripts, letters, contracts, and personal library was destroyed in such dramatic fashion seems small. Nonetheless, the absence of a single, comprehensive archive indicates that a surviving relative—perhaps her sister or son—did not believe that her papers were worth preserving. The disappearance of her materials may be a clue about the final years of her life and may verify evidence of tension with at least one family member. Her notary files, housed in the Archives nationales in Paris, indicate as much.[5] From her deathbed, La Vaudère amended her will to bequeath her own portrait to her sister Marie. However, Marie rejected the bequest, claiming she had no need for it. It may be that La Vaudère had a sense about her impending invisibility, both within the family and literary history. Her tongue-in-cheek gesture irritated Marie, whose refusal of the portrait was equally symbolic (and perhaps foretelling of her intentions for La Vaudère's archive). The amendments to La Vaudère's will also implicate her friend and writer Théodore Cahu, whom she acknowledged for managing a selection of her manuscripts. As I discuss in more detail in chapter 1, there are no traces of the manuscripts in question in Cahu's archives, and they have since disappeared. La Vaudère's remaining papers—other manuscripts, letters, related ephemera—were likely left to her immediate family. In the end, it was La Vaudère's surviving relatives who had the last word, and to this day her name remains absent from the family grave in Paris's Montparnasse cemetery.

This book seeks to bring order and cohesion to La Vaudère's scant and scattered archival catalogue. It compiles a diverse selection of materials and leads for future research and includes library references and call numbers when applicable. At the end of this book, readers will also find an exhaustive bibliography of La Vaudère's publications across genres and media. In assembling all available pieces, I offer the first detailed profile of La Vaudère that includes important elements from her childhood, marriage, and writing career. I also consider her reception by her contemporaries, whose depictions both shaped and perpetuated her notoriety. In turn, La Vaudère exploited disparaging media coverage to construct a provocative writer's persona—a marketing strategy that ultimately led to more publicity and sales. What other people thought about La Vaudère—and how she co-opted these narratives—is an important part of her selling power. This book therefore gives equal weight to "authoritative" sources like civil records and notarized documents and "unofficial" sources like editorials, *romans à clef*, and book reviews. In his work on Belle Époque dancer Cléo de Mérode, Michael Garval emphasizes the value of informal, secondhand accounts for contextualizing celebrity: "Serious reporting can clarify important details. But spurious journalism can be more broadly revealing. Like caricatures, parodies, or apocryphal 'biographies,' such fanciful evidence plunges deep into the imaginary, offering insights into the star's larger impact and place within the history of fame."[6] To complement written accounts, I also consider rumors and anecdotes that still circulate today in the village of Parigné-l'Évêque. Inevitably, the diversity of these materials has produced conflicting perspectives and information, testimony to the breadth of La Vaudère's renown. These contradictory accounts can be traced to La Vaudère as well, who often lied about her age or embellished childhood stories for interviews. I posit that these contradictions and their points of intersection inform our understanding of La Vaudère's evolving celebrity and skillful fluidity. This study does not privilege certain materials over others or rank their accuracy or value. Instead, it examines them critically and in relationship to one another to build a holistic, complex portrayal. Collectively, the materials illuminate how La Vaudère navigated and negotiated readership demands, marketing strategies, and a public image.

Given La Vaudère's limited archives, the research for this project involved creative problem-solving and an open mind. France's national library, the Bibliothèque Nationale de France (BnF), contains a large selection of La Vaudère's published works and an occasional letter, and served as a good point of departure for the general details of her life and works. To piece together the basic elements of her biography, I consulted archives in Paris (the Archives de Paris and the Archives nationales) and Le Mans (the Archives départementales de la Sarthe) that house "official" records such as legal registers, notarized documents, marriage certificates, and contracts. While these collections verified major biographical junctures—her birth, marriage, and divorce—they did not convey the nuances of her relationships with contemporary writers nor how she navigated the growth of her celebrity. To cast a wider search net, I visited a range of specialized collections in Paris, some off the beaten path: the Société des gens de lettres (SDGL), the Archives de la Préfecture de police, the Archives de l'assistance publique-hôpitaux de Paris, the Bibliothèque-musée de l'Opéra, the Bibliothèque Marguerite Durand, the BnF's Département des arts du spectacle, the Service historique de la Défense, the Institut historique allemand, and the Société des auteurs et compositeurs dramatiques (SACD). I also traveled to the Abbaye d'Ardenne outside of Caen to consult publishing records at the Institut mémoires de l'édition contemporaine (IMEC). Some of these collections were dead ends, but others housed hidden gems that informed new perspectives of La Vaudère's place in French literary history. To supplement the archival research, I considered her coverage in the contemporary press (interviews, photos) and reviews of her works in literary periodicals or anthologies, many of which have been digitized by the BnF and are accessible online. Other pieces of information came by random strokes of luck through booksellers' and collectors' websites selling the rare La Vaudère letter. Geneanet, a French website for genealogy enthusiasts, was a useful starting point for tracing La Vaudère's ancestry and identifying family names for supplemental archival research.

LA VAUDÈRE'S LITERARY ASSOCIATIONS AND RECENT SCHOLARSHIP

In the last few decades, while considered a minor genre of obscure authors, the Decadent novel has elicited renewed interest among nineteenth-century scholars and the general public alike. Though La Vaudère's corpus reflects a wide and diverse range of literary production, her name is commonly cited among a small group of Belle Époque women writers like Rachilde, with whom she shared an interest in the moral and sexual pathologies typical of Decadent fiction. But La Vaudère's habitual association with Rachilde denies the heterogeneity of her corpus, which encompasses a multitude of genres beyond the confines of Decadent literature. Rachilde herself seemed to recognize this: in her reviews for the *Mercure de France*, she instead compared La Vaudère to women writers Camille Pert and Daniel Lesueur.[7] Like La Vaudère, contemporaries Pert and Lesueur privileged woman-centered themes in their popular novels and underscored tensions between a woman's social (i.e., marital and maternal) duties and her quest for emotional and sexual fulfilment.[8] However, La Vaudère stands out for the remarkable fluidity of her public image and constant adaptability to a variety of literary genres (Decadent, Naturalist, Orientalist, erotic fiction). In many ways, regardless of Rachilde's attempts at classification, La Vaudère cannot be placed. Nonetheless, her name has recently benefited from her association with Decadent literature, and the genre's revival has presented an opportunity to finally showcase its otherwise marginalized writers. Decadent scholarship has found momentum in the work of Jean de Palacio, whose publications have brought to light the aesthetic and thematic trends of the fin de siècle. Unfortunately, Palacio has been dismissive of La Vaudère's literary merits and has argued that she holds minimal interest for nineteenth-century literary studies.[9] The inclusion of La Vaudère in his well-regarded scholarship has nonetheless brought attention to her name and paved the way for alternative perspectives of her literary, cultural, and historic value. Where Palacio has failed, feminist scholars may take over and bring to light figures like La Vaudère who maneuvered and exploited the contradictory expectations placed upon the Belle Époque woman writer.

There is little information available about the literary or artistic circles that La Vaudère frequented. Her memberships in organizations like the Société des gens de lettres (SDGL) and the Société des poètes français (SPF) provided her access to a diverse group of authors and ample opportunities for networking. We know from internal documents and newspaper blurbs that she often attended SDGL and SPF meetings and dinners alongside renowned and prolific writers, both male and female, as well as those who were in the early stages of their careers. More specifically, she maintained strong professional ties to writer Théodore Cahu throughout her career, and her last-minute addition of him to her will suggests that their artistic relationship likely extended to friendship (if not more). With the exception of Émile Zola, whose *Pour une nuit d'amour* she adapted for the stage, La Vaudère's collaborative projects involved writers of popular literature or marginalized genres (such as Félicien Champsaur, Gaston Derys, or Cahu) that did not share the artistic prestige of the father of Naturalism.[10] Many of the writers who wrote laudatory pieces on La Vaudère (Cahu, Champsaur) fell into these categories, as did those who parodied her in their fiction (such as courtesan Liane de Pougy and gay dandy Jean Lorrain, whose texts I discuss in chapter 2). These literary intersections suggest that La Vaudère moved in circles with artists who defied social conventions or were on the fringes of elite artistic groups. She does not appear to have belonged to any community of women artists, nor to have collaborated or networked with other popular women authors of the period (like Camille Pert, Daniel Lesueur, Rachilde, Georges de Peyrebrune, or Marcelle Tinayre). With one or two minor exceptions, her name, like Rachilde's, was notably absent from *Femina* and *La vie heureuse*. These women's magazines regularly featured articles on contemporary women writers like Lucie Delarue-Mardrus, Anna de Noailles, Lesueur, or Tinayre, whose paths La Vaudère had certainly crossed at literary readings or conferences. However, *Femina* and *La vie heureuse* endorsed a model of femininity that integrated Belle Époque modern womanhood with the conventional bourgeois values of the domestic sphere. Colette Cosnier and Rachel Mesch attribute La Vaudère's exclusion from the magazines to the risqué and salacious themes of her texts; neither she, nor Rachilde for that matter, fit the magazines' image of the respectable woman author.[11] And yet La Vaudère's conflicting, noncommittal views on gender roles led to ostracization from feminist circles as well: Marguerite Durand's newspaper *La fronde* went so far as to condemn her as an antifeminist.[12] Too audacious for respectable women writers and too conservative for leading feminist activists, La Vaudère courted contradictions and eschewed any one political narrative. As we shall see repeatedly through this study, La Vaudère was and remains deliberately difficult to classify.

The interdisciplinary fields of gender, literary, and cultural studies have witnessed a growing commitment to recovering neglected marginal writers of the past and salvaging their stories and works. Nineteenth-century France in particular has appealed to feminist scholars across disciplines who have written extensively on evolving discourses on sexual and gender difference.[13] Female figures such as Marie Krysinska, Gisèle d'Estoc, Georges de Peyrebrune, André Léo, and Marc de Montifaud have elicited recent attention in academia and publishing.[14] La Vaudère's works have earned her references in studies on gender transgression in Decadent literature, and a selection of scholarly articles address her writing in particular.[15] She has gained increased visibility through the digitization of her works on Gallica, a digital library run by the BnF that is available to online readers from around the world. An assortment of her novels and short stories have recently been translated by Snuggly Books, a publisher specializing in Decadent and Occultist fiction, and are now available to Anglophone readers for the first time. French author Lyane Guillaume, who specializes in historical and documentary fiction, is also preparing a work on La Vaudère that reimagines her life in the Belle Époque.[16] A scholarly study devoted to her life and works has been long overdue. As La Vaudère's renown and readership begin to expand across disciplines and genres, this monograph emphasizes the deft shapeshifting inherent to her writing and public image. With a particular focus on the plagiarism and diversity of literary styles that characterize her *œuvre*, as well as the transgressive and bourgeois narratives of womanhood that she carefully constructed, I hope to show the uniqueness and value of La Vaudère's literary production. While La Vaudère is in many ways exceptional, I also encourage readers to consider her as representative of the skillful social, artistic, and ideological negotiations demanded of the woman writer during her time period.

STRUCTURE AND LAYOUT

Resurrecting Jane de La Vaudère interweaves biography and literary study. To give context to the discussions that follow, the first chapter is devoted to a detailed profile of La Vaudère's life. To this day, there exists no extensive biography on Jane de La Vaudère. Though condensed chronicles of her life are scattered throughout the Belle Époque press or today's limited scholarship, these abridged accounts are often fragmentary or erroneous and underscore the need for a detailed life history of La Vaudère—and Jeanne Scrive. The title of this chapter, "The Makings of a Biography," is an intentional double entendre that draws attention to the process of biography. This chapter also provides an important foundation for the larger book and allows readers to trace the development of La Vaudère's complicated persona and feminist positions alongside critical moments in her personal life. Chapter 1 serves as a complement to chapter 2, "Becoming Jane de La Vaudère," which examines the clichéd representation of La Vaudère's persona in contemporary fictional works and the press. In considering her own agency in these seemingly one-dimensional constructions, chapter 2 also brings to light La Vaudère's marketing tactics, which exploited a troubling reputation in order to sell more books. I draw from the work of Mary Louise Roberts and argue that La Vaudère's varied performances of womanhood exposed the arbitrariness of gender codes and exemplified the mutability of her persona. It may be tempting to view chapters 1 and 2 as foils: whereas chapter 2 considers discursive, ideological, and subjective depictions of La Vaudère's works and public image, chapter 1 pieces together "hard" facts (dates, addresses, finances) from "authoritative" archival sources (notary files, birth certificates, court documents). Both chapters, however, encourage critical interpretations and readings of primary sources, including La Vaudère's own interviews, which exhibit her tendency to exaggerate or lie to maintain a certain persona. As Arlette Farge reminds us, archival documents should not be taken for granted as decisive bearers of "truth" but as a foundation for further interrogation: "Qu'on entende bien: à de rare exceptions près, le document, le texte ou l'archive ne sont pas la preuve définitive d'une vérité quelconque, mais butte témoin incontournable dont le sens est à bâtir ensuite par des questionnements spécifiques."[17] The elements of La Vaudère's life that I have uncovered in these chapters open the door to new and evolving understandings of a woman writer's agency in crafting a multidimensional and marketable persona.

Chapters 3 and 4 are connected by the common theme of plagiarism. As some critics had already discovered during her lifetime, La Vaudère was a frequent plagiarist. Today, with the help of plagiarism software, we can identify hundreds of passages in La Vaudère's fiction that were lifted from nineteenth-century literary and scientific texts. Chapter 3 reads the trends of plagiarism through a feminist and postmodern lens. In examining her plagiarism of Guy de Maupassant's Sicilian travel memoirs and his novel *Notre cœur*, I demonstrate how La Vaudère's novel *Les demi-sexes* reappropriates masculine discourses on femininity, exposes their precariousness, and proposes new models of womanhood, all through the subversive act of copying. As we will see throughout this study, La Vaudère's plagiarism facilitated her fluid movement between the diversity of discourses (i.e., medical, feminist), narrative structures, and literary genres that defined her *œuvre*. In an ironic reversal, chapter 4 considers La Vaudère in a new role: as a victim of plagiarism. The 1907 production of *Rêve d'Égypte* brought Colette and Missy added fame and notoriety, but La Vaudère claimed (rather convincingly) that their piece was based on her own Egyptian pantomime *Le rêve de Mysès*. Though her legal case was eventually dropped, La Vaudère published a novella version of *Le rêve de Mysès* a few months later with titillating erotic content and nude photographic illustrations intended to recall the Moulin Rouge scandal and boost sales. In light of the couple's plagiarism, La Vaudère's revisions point to an ongoing, intertextual exchange and exemplify her calculated marketing of nonnormative female sexuality. In a strange twist, this chapter is informed by discoveries that I made while visiting the small burial chapel at the Château de La Vaudère that houses the embalmed remains of her relatives. For the larger project, I consider the "mummified" corpses at the château to be a metaphor for the possibility of La Vaudère's own artistic immortality and the resurrection of her story.

La Vaudère's feminism is contradictory and inconsistent, both radical and conservative, but always engaged with contemporary campaigns and debates. Chapter 5 deciphers the ambivalence of La Vaudère's feminism in relation to organized feminist movements. More specifically, it considers her strategies for promoting female sexual and emotional fulfillment while clinging to some traditionalist views of womanhood, a tactic that many activists also employed. To tease out the nuances of La Vaudère's brand of feminism, I have divided this chapter into three sections and consider her engagement with contemporary feminist movements, her critique of marital conventions and divorce laws, and her adoption of spiritist conceptions of gender difference. Finally, in the book's concluding chapter, we return to the present day to consider La Vaudère's lasting legacy at the Château de La Vaudère and how she is remembered in the village of Parigné-l'Évêque. The point of departure for this section is a photograph from *Le carnet de la femme* of La Vaudère seated behind the steering wheel of a car. Though we cannot confirm that La Vaudère was a pioneer female motorist at the turn of the century, she regularly incorporated automobiles into her writing and often linked the expanding car industry to the modern woman. In a notable coincidence, Anne-Charlotte Rousseau, the current owner of the Château de La Vaudère, is an aficionado of vintage automobiles and is one of only a handful of women to compete in international rally racing. This chapter examines the history of the Château de La Vaudère, its lineage of autonomous women, their cars, and the emancipation afforded through driving.

The resources that informed this book have been widespread and varied, ranging from rare archival documents from the nineteenth century to personal connections formed more recently. Through the extensive nature of this research, which spans the parameters of time, media, and genres, we can better recognize the literary and historical importance of authors like La Vaudère and the avenues that they open for interdisciplinary study. These discoveries have shown why it is critical for stories like La Vaudère's to be studied and shared and have brought important attention to a dynamic woman writer whose contributions to fin-de-siècle literature have unjustly been forgotten. Though her gravestone remains unmarked, it is my hope that this book may serve as a headstone of sorts, with her story finally engraved in its pages.

CHAPTER I

The Makings of a Biography

My attempt to correct the erasure of La Vaudère's name from French literary history begins with the recovery of her biography. We will see La Vaudère's professional trajectories unfold in the subsequent chapters, but the biographical details in these pages provide crucial points of reference in understanding Jeanne Scrive's strategic transformation into Jane de La Vaudère.[1] The contents of this chapter are informed by a patchwork of legal documents, overlooked letters, and press clippings. These archival records shed light upon the circumstances of La Vaudère's upbringing, marriage, and divorce and the events that likely inspired the feminist themes in her corpus. As nineteenth-century artifacts, the records document a woman writer's success and notoriety in a male-dominated field inhospitable to female intellectual activity. By filling in the gaps of La Vaudère's biography, we can locate the important landmarks of her professional arc and the strategies that she employed to build and exploit her growing celebrity. Through the construction of a persona, networking with established peers, and the skilled manipulation of the press, La Vaudère exemplified the strategic navigation of a self-sufficient woman and author. Despite a series of traumatic episodes in her life—the loss of her parents at a young age, the collapse of her troubled marriage, and the alienation from her immediate family—this biography underscores La Vaudère's continued resilience, agency, and drive in personal and professional domains. To highlight the stages of her development as a writer and the marketing of her evolving persona, I have scrupulously included details from various aspects of her life. Considering that La Vaudère's manuscripts have disappeared and that very few of her letters have been conserved, this chapter privileges newly uncovered details of her life that are essential to reviving her story. It is my hope that these archival discoveries may serve as leads for future research and facilitate additional scholarship on La Vaudère and her family members.

JEANNE SCRIVE: THE EARLY YEARS

Jeanne Scrive was born on April 15, 1857, to Gaspard-Léonard Scrive (1815–1861) and Barbe-Elisabeth Weigel (1822–1870) in their Paris home at 13, rue d'Enfer.[2] Like most civil records housed in the Hôtel de Ville and the Palais de Justice, her birth certificate was destroyed during the Paris Commune in the spring of 1871. As required by the Loi du 12 février 1872, which ordered the restoration of the birth, death, and marriage certificates lost during the insurrection, Jeanne's birth records were reconstituted on April 16, 1875, likely in preparation for her marriage. A certificate was also re-created for her baptism, which took place on June 2, 1857, at the Paroisse Saint-Jacques du Haut-Pas, a Catholic church located near the family home.[3] Gaspard Scrive's mother, Sophie Debonte (1787–1878), was listed as the godmother, and Barbe Weigel's brother-in-law, Louis Loew (1828–1917), was chosen as Jeanne's godfather. Barbe was from a Protestant family (her father is buried at the Protestant Sainte-Hélène cemetery in Strasbourg), and she chose the Protestant Loew to represent her side of the family in the Catholic ceremony. The designation of Sophie Debonte as Jeanne's godmother anticipated the central role that she would play in her granddaughter's life. When the young Jeanne lost her father at age four and her mother at age thirteen, Sophie Debonte assumed the triple role of godmother, grandmother, and legal guardian, and she remained an influential figure until her death in 1878.

Jeanne's mother, Barbe Weigel, was born in Strasbourg, and her father, Jean-Jacques Weigel, was a notary and city councilor. Barbe's brother, Léon Weigel, married a wealthy Argentinian whose maternal aunt, Juana Manuela Gorriti (1818–1892), was one of her country's most celebrated women writers. Barbe's sister, Mathilde Weigel, was married to Loew, a magistrate who presided over the criminal chamber of the Court of Cassation and was an important factor in the overturning of Alfred Dreyfus's wrongful conviction. Jeanne's father, Gaspard Scrive, was a distinguished military surgeon from a prosperous bourgeois family in Lille. Throughout the nineteenth century, the Scrive family name was associated with the booming textile industry in northern France, and a number of buildings and historic markers in the region still bear the name.[4] In Lille, Gaspard served as both a surgeon and professor at the city's military hospital before relocating to Paris and holding a teaching position at the Val-de-Grâce hospital. Over the course of his career, he published a number of scientific texts in which he applied his combined medical and military expertise to treating patients in France and Algeria. During the Crimean War (1853–56), he served as chief medical officer and was awarded the prestigious order of Légion d'honneur. His work with wounded soldiers, as well as those stricken with cholera and typhoid, inspired a number of his publications, which addressed developments in anesthesia and hygiene.[5] In 1861, when Jeanne was four years old, Gaspard died at the Val-de-Grâce hospital of an illness that he had contracted while serving overseas.[6] To this day, he is remembered for his pioneering work using chloroform as anesthesia during the Crimean War.[7]

Barbe and Gaspard were married in 1841 in Strasbourg. On February 16, 1848, they had their first child, Frédéric, who died three months later and was buried at the Sainte-Hélène cemetery. On May 28, 1849, Marie was born in Strasbourg, and eight years later, upon their father's return from the Crimean War, Jeanne was born in Paris. We know very little about this time in Jeanne's life, save for a few anecdotes that she shared with the press later as an adult, which she may have fabricated or exaggerated to elicit her readers' compassion.[8] In these accounts, La Vaudère mentioned her fragile disposition as a child, the result of a premature birth that earned her the nickname "princesse Criquette," a playful reference to the pantomime character who fell from a nest and broke his paw. Not uncommon for upper-class families at the time, Gaspard hired a young wet nurse to strengthen and nourish Jeanne during her infancy. After her father's death, it appears that Jeanne spent her preadolescence in Paris at the family home with her mother and sister. On November 8, 1870, her mother died in their home on the rue de Vaugirard, leaving Jeanne, age thirteen, and Marie, age twenty-one, orphaned. Marie was already a major under French law, and Jeanne's legal guardianship was conferred to her grandmother Sophie Debonte on April 18, 1871, by the Justice of the Peace of the Canton de Sceaux, outside of Paris.[9]

From this point, Jeanne lived with Sophie Debonte at 83 bis, rue Notre-Dame-des-Champs in Paris. As an adult, La Vaudère portrayed a childhood shaped by her grandmother's eccentric and devoted presence. In 1906, the mysticism periodical *L'écho du merveilleux* interviewed

La Vaudère about her interest in the supernatural. With nostalgia, she recounted her grandmother's influence and her claims to converse with the dead when Jeanne was a child: "Dès ma plus tendre enfance, j'ai été bercée par des récits extraordinaires. La grand'mère qui m'a élevée—car j'étais orpheline—assurait que les morts nous entouraient, qu'elle les voyait, qu'elle s'entretenait avec eux."[10] La Vaudère recalled witnessing a related phenomenon herself, in her grandmother's home, when a dining room table rose from the ground and hovered in the air.[11] While La Vaudère has been known to embellish for the press (see chapter 2), what emerges from this story is the tender image of a female guardian who remained influential for the impressionable Jeanne beyond her death in 1878. Under a more critical lens, this anecdote also reveals Sophie Debonte's role in the marketing of La Vaudère's persona in her adult life. By 1906, La Vaudère had published a number of occultist-themed works, and a personal narrative about a grandmother who communicated with the dead would attract readers eager to understand how these childhood experiences played out in her fiction.

Shortly after moving in with her grandmother, Jeanne attended the Notre-Dame de Sion Catholic school a few buildings down at 61, rue Notre-Dame-des-Champs. The Notre-Dame de Sion Congregation was created in 1843 by the brothers Théodore and Alphonse Ratisbonne. Inspired by its founders' own religious conversion, its primary mission was to introduce Jews to Christianity. In 1853, the motherhouse was established on the rue Notre-Dame-des-Champs, a section of which served as a boarding school for Catholic girls. Théodore Ratisbonne envisioned this "pensionnat" as a "famille dont la supérieure est la mère; une école de sagesse où, par les soins des sœurs parfaitement unies entre elles et subordonnées à l'autorité principale, la piété et les vertus solides sont cultivées dans les âmes; un sanctuaire de la science, où rien n'est omis de ce que peut comporter le programme le plus complet."[12] The "supérieure" was Marie Émilie Lagarmitte, or Mère Marie Émilie, who was originally from Strasbourg and oversaw the operations of the convent school. Her sister, Mère Marie Jean-Baptiste, was also active in the congregation and both shared a direct lineage with Jeanne: they were the first cousins of her late mother, Barbe. With her sister, grandmother, and cousins in close proximity, Jeanne was continually surrounded by family members at Notre-Dame de Sion, despite having lost her parents.

The turbulent years of 1870 and 1871 coincided with La Vaudère's arrival at the school and drastically affected the functions of the Paris convent. During the Franco-Prussian War (July 1870–January 1871), the building and school remained open and housed a temporary military hospital that treated hundreds of wounded soldiers.[13] The motherhouse was not spared from the unrest: on the night of January 11, two bombs struck the dining hall and caused severe structural damage.[14] Months later, when the violent uprisings of the Paris Commune (March–May 1871) spread to the rue Notre-Dame-des-Champs, community members were urgently relocated to Grandbourg, an affiliated residence in the nearby commune of Evry. During the remaining months of the Commune, this house served as a refuge for "les neophytes, les quelques élèves de nouveau rassemblées et presque toutes les religieuses" and shielded them from the descent of insurgents and national soldiers at the doors of the Paris site.[15]

Though the institution's archives from this period are limited and no official registers remain, the collection does contain a source that offers a rare glimpse into the daily happenings of the Notre-Dame de Sion community: the nuns' daily journals.[16] Jeanne and her family members are only referenced a handful of times, but the timeline of these entries gives us a sense of how the political unrest in the city affected the functions at the school. On November 12, 1870, during the Siege of Paris, the nuns noted, "Marie et Jeanne Scrive viennent occuper le rez-de-chaussée de Béthanie [a residence on the premises], qu'on met à leur disposition." This entry was written just four days after their mother's death and was likely referring to Jeanne's initial arrival at Notre-Dame de Sion. On April 12, 1871, in the height of the civil unrest, La Vaudère's grandmother wanted to leave for Grandbourg where her granddaughters had likely been evacuated. However, the political chaos made travel impossible: "Elle doit y renoncer, il faut un passeport de la Préfecture pour sortir de Paris, et la foule est si grande qu'elle ne peut parvenir à s'en procurer," a nun recorded. If Jeanne had indeed relocated to Grandbourg, the journal indicates that she may have been back in Paris on May 11, shortly before the Commune's infamous "Bloody Week." On this day, her grandmother arrived at the Béthanie house to be with one of her granddaughters, though it is unclear if this was Jeanne or Marie, who was twenty-one at the time.[17] Following this date, there is no additional mention of the Scrive family in the convent's journals.

The unrest and violence of 1870–71 surely marked the young Jeanne, and though there are no official records to confirm the dates of her residency, accounts from other sources suggest that she spent the remainder of her adolescence at the convent. According to her brief biography in the *Figures contemporaines tirées de l'Album Mariani* (1902), La Vaudère left Notre-Dame de Sion in 1875 when she was married.[18] The irony that La Vaudère, whose novels depicted homosexuality, adultery, and orgies, received her education in a Catholic convent was not lost on the biographer. Underscoring the humor of this paradox, the author emphasizes Jeanne's precocious curiosity, which caused alarm at the religious institution and was suggestive of developing immoral penchants: "Sa fantaisie, oscillant entre la douceur rêveuse du mysticisme claustral et les séductions de la vie mondaine qu'elle brûlait de connaître, scandalisa parfois les bonnes sœurs, et la découverte d'un journal quotidien (écrit derrière le pupitre, d'une plume un peu trop frondeuse) faillit la faire expulser de la sainte maison."[19] The author also remarks in a footnote that La Vaudère's first significant poems were penned in the early years at the Notre-Dame de Sion. Though this portrait seems to sensationalize La Vaudère's notoriety as an adult (a phenomenon I examine in detail in the next chapter), it underlines the influence that Catholic education and the years at Notre-Dame de Sion had on the aspiring writer. Many of La Vaudère's novels and short stories feature female characters who reflect upon the influences of their religious instruction on their personal development. These fictional works include particulars—names, timelines, family situations—that coincide with La Vaudère's own lived experiences. Her 1903 novel *L'expulsée*, for example, is devoted entirely to convent life and depicts the implementation of the Law of Associations of 1901 and its consequences for religious institutions. The text's fictional congregation—reminiscent of Notre-Dame de Sion—is forced to close, and La Vaudère depicts the perspective of its students and nuns with great compassion.[20]

MARRIAGE AND A NEW NAME

On April 29, 1875, two weeks after her eighteenth birthday, Jeanne married Gaston Crapez under the "régime de la communauté de biens réduite aux acquets."[21] According to this model, spouses maintain individual possession of their respective properties prior to marriage and enjoy common ownership of assets that are acquired once legally joined. This type of contract likely appealed to the newlyweds and their families because it guaranteed a continued proprietorship and direction over a long lineage of inherited wealth and properties. When the marriage certificate was drafted, Gaston, age twenty-six, was living with his mother on the Château de La Vaudère land. The château, which was built in 1830, had been passed on to Gaston's mother and would soon be in his name. At age eighteen, Jeanne's living situation was less clear, though her marriage contract may help elucidate conflicting accounts.[22] According to her portrait in *Figures contemporaines tirées de l'Album Mariani*, Jeanne remained at Notre-Dame de Sion until this union. However, both the marriage certificate and contract state that she was living ("de fait" or *de facto*) in Le Mans at 5, rue Erpelle (the address of her sister Marie and Victor Dauvais de Gérardcourt) but legally residing ("de droit" or *de jure*) at her grandmother's address in Paris. Le Mans was in convenient proximity to Gaston's residence in Parigné-l'Évêque, which may explain how she met her future husband. There were four witnesses to the marriage: Dauvais de Gérardcourt, two mutual friends of the newlyweds, and a cousin of Gaston's. Gaston was represented by his mother, his grandmother, and a proxy for his father, each of whom was implicated in his financial portfolio. Jeanne, still a minor under the Code Civil, was represented by her grandmother and Dauvais de Gérardcourt, to whom Sophie Debonte extended full legal authority in the preparation of the contract.

Given the nature of the contract, each spouse supplied an inventory of his or her personal possessions prior to the union.[23] Jeanne declared an inheritance from a deceased relative and the remaining balance from her grandmother's guardianship account. In addition, she shared titles with her sister to various stocks and bonds, as well as properties in Lille, Clamart, and greater Strasbourg. Gaston's assets included partial ownership of properties throughout Parigné-l'Évêque, as well as a gift of twenty thousand francs from his mother, Estelle Emmanuelle Huet, to be made available upon her death. Gaston's family endowed him with full ownership of the La Vaudère property, but with two stipulations. First, Gaston's mother would be allowed continued use of the château's east wing—including six bedrooms spanning the second and third floors—and reserved space in the stable for her transportation needs. Second, she demanded full control over the burial chapel on the château property: "Madame Crapez se réserve encore le droit exclusif pendant sa vie d'entretenir comme bon lui semblera la chapelle placée à proximité du château, de sorte que le futur époux donataire n'y aura aucun droit pendant la vie de sa mère."[24] As we will see in further detail in chapters 4 and 6, the chapel is an integral part of the property's history. Today, it houses six of La Vaudère's immediate family members and in-laws, including the embalmed bodies of Sophie Debonte, who died in 1878, and Estelle Huet, who died in 1900. In accordance with the terms of the contract, Gaston's mother maintained full authority over the chapel maintenance and enjoyed continual access to the property until her death. Through the details provided by this marriage contract, some of them seemingly inconsequential, we can begin to construct an image of life at the La Vaudère property and its influence on the newly married Jeanne Crapez, who would soon craft a persona inspired by her current surroundings.

Just shy of nine months later, on January 26, 1876, Jeanne gave birth to Gaspard Victor Fernand Crapez ("Fernand") in Le Mans. According to the birth records, Fernand was born at 95, rue du Bourg Belé at Gaston's (and presumably Jeanne's) home.[25] At this time, it is unclear if Jeanne and Gaston had spent any significant amount of time at the Château de La Vaudère, and Fernand's birthplace suggests that they continued to frequent at least one other property in Le Mans. Little is known about the next few years of Jeanne's life, before she began publishing regularly and attracting the attention of the press. While archival material from the period following Fernand's birth is scarce, newspaper articles and letters provide glimpses into Jeanne's—and La Vaudère's—coming into writing. In his lengthy profile in a 1904 issue of the *Revue illustrée*, Théodore Cahu notes that before turning to verse in the 1880s, La Vaudère explored the artistic mediums of painting and sculpture.[26] According to the nearly identical portrait in *Figures contemporaines tirées de l'Album Mariani*, she purportedly exhibited in the prestigious Paris Salon, yet there are no traces of her involvement in its catalogs or records.[27] Nonetheless, these two accounts suggest that La Vaudère made a deliberate shift from the visual arts to literature. By the late 1880s, this shift had fully materialized. On March 23, 1889, the newspaper *Le Figaro* announced the publication of a new collection of poetry, *Les heures perdues*, by a poet named "Jane de La Vaudère": "Un début à remarquer et un livre à lire."[28] La Vaudère's career had been launched.

The year 1889 thus marked the inauguration of her professional persona and Jeanne Crapez, née Scrive, became Jane de La Vaudère. The pen name "Jane de La Vaudère" allowed her to play with the unstable boundaries of nationality and class, as well as those separating her "true" identity from an authorial construction. The anglicization of a common French name (Jeanne to Jane) added a note of international sophistication and intrigue. "Jane" carried a boldness that the softer "Jeanne" was lacking while remaining somewhat faithful to La Vaudère's birth name.[29] In a similar fashion, "Jane de La Vaudère" was not a complete break from her status as a married woman. Though she eliminated her husband's surname from her writer's identity, she replaced it with the name of his family property (La Vaudère).

The addition of the particle "de" suggested an elite or noble lineage, and with its succession of rich vowels, "Jane de La Vaudère" certainly had a more pleasant ring than "Jane Crapez." Furthermore, "Crapez" could inevitably be associated with *crapaud* or "toad" in the French imagination. More importantly, "Jane de La Vaudère" points to a fusion of identities, a collage of Jeanne Scrive, Jeanne Crapez, and a newly imagined authorial image. From her earliest professional days, La Vaudère's pen name muddled the borders of the "real" and "imaginary" and, through this ambiguity, created a space for her to gradually contest clichéd and one-dimensional conceptions of the woman writer. By the time La Vaudère divorced in 1898, her pen name had evolved into a well-established part of her literary persona, independent of her husband and his property. Reverting back to "Jeanne Scrive" was not a professional or public option. Nonetheless, likely in an attempt to distance herself from her husband, she briefly explored other pseudonyms. In 1898, under the hybrid name "Jean Scrive," La Vaudère cowrote a popular Japanese-themed operetta with Félicien Champsaur entitled *Les trois mousmés*. The spectacle premiered shortly after her divorce, and journalists failed to link the masculinized version of her maiden name (from Jeanne Scrive to Jean Scrive) to La Vaudère. This is the only known instance in which she adopted a masculine pseudonym or reverted to her maiden name. She soon returned to her initial pen name, and the literary press, to my knowledge, never reported on her divorce. Jane de La Vaudère was able to construct and maintain her original persona without interruption.

In the early years of her career, La Vaudère published a number of poetry collections that critics embraced and that signaled creative momentum: *L'éternelle chanson* (1890), *Minuit* (1892), and *Évocation* (1893). By the time her second volume of poetry appeared, La Vaudère had made a significant impression. The periodical *Le gaulois* welcomed her poetic vision as "un réveil et un cri de joie dans la nuit," lauding *L'éternelle chanson* and estimating that it would launch her professional success: "Elle avait débuté par *Heures perdues*, un volume que seuls quelques lettrés avaient goûté; mais voici qu'on en parle, et maintenant tout le monde veut lire *L'Éternelle Chanson*."[30] The prediction rang true, and the poetry collection earned her important recognition from the Académie française. Though it did not choose her for its Archon-Despérouses poetry prize in 1891, the Académie noted in its report that her *Éternelle chanson* was "chantée avec beaucoup de grâce" and deserved special acknowledgment among the forty-nine submissions it considered.[31] During this period, she also considered other genres such as theatre and short stories, and published her first of many novels, *Mortelle étreinte*, in 1891. Other novels and collections of short stories followed, and the incessant rhythm of her writing production remained steady until her death in 1908 (see her full bibliography at the end of this work).

Later in her career, when La Vaudère brought up these inaugural years, she emphasized her innocence and naïveté as a young poet, a stark contrast to the transgressive persona that she would come to embrace in the late 1890s. In a 1904 tribute to Victor Hugo, she recalled this early period and the influence that the Romantic poet had on launching her career. Prior to his death in 1885, Hugo had supposedly read the notebooks that she kept as a child and encouraged her to pursue her writing. "Victor Hugo guida mes débuts dans la carrière littéraire," she wrote. "Il voulut bien accueillir avec faveur mon premier petit cahier de vers, celui que, gamine, j'avais noirci au hasard de l'inspiration, célébrant les roses, les abeilles, les eaux chantantes [. . .]. 'Vous avez, m'écrivait-il, une âme de poète; vous avez, surtout, ce qui ne s'apprend pas, ce qui est un don de nature puissant et rare, l'enthousiasme du beau et la bonté.'"[32] Though impossible to verify, La Vaudère's anecdote conveniently positioned her as a protégée to a great master poet.[33] By 1904, the purity and innocence that first characterized her writing had drastically evolved. In retrospectively highlighting the Romantic—albeit, unsophisticated—themes of her early texts, she reminded readers of her benevolent intentions that gained the support of a revered male poet. However, as Melanie Hawthorne has shown, Hugo often wrote letters of encouragement to aspiring writers (including to La Vaudère's contemporary Rachilde). The sheer abundance of his letters that circulated in Parisian artistic circles thus diminished the gravitas of his praise.[34] In 1904, twenty years after his death, La Vaudère relied less on the content of Hugo's letter than on its symbolic weight, which served to highlight her aesthetic and professional development since its reception.

PROFESSIONAL INITIATIONS

With multiple publications and various works in progress, La Vaudère now qualified for membership in the influential Société des gens de lettres (SDGL). Founded in 1838 and still active today, this prominent writers' association promotes and defends the literary property rights of its adherents. In the nineteenth century, it protected its members from the unauthorized reproduction of the serial novel, an increasingly popular genre, in newspapers and journals. For La Vaudère, affiliation with the SDGL signaled an important symbol of recognition in literary circles and reiterated her commitment to professional authorship. As an active member, she maintained an ongoing correspondence with the SDGL and her letters make up an exceptional set of documents from her life that have been conserved.[35] These letters document the progression of La Vaudère's career, from her initial moments of self-doubt and inexperience to a solid command of her rights as a thriving author. From a logistical standpoint, they also help us fill in the biographical blanks regarding her activity within the society, her communication with editors, and her living situation.

In 1890, with the sponsorship of writers Georges Ohnet and Joseph Reinach, La Vaudère applied for membership in the SDGL. At the time, married women could not work or publish without the authorization of their husbands; in February 1891, Gaston provided a letter to the association granting his wife, "Madame Jeanne Crapez de la Vaudère," permission to join (fig. 1). La Vaudère was accepted by the association as an "adhérente," a symbolic declaration of her emergent professional autotomy that poignantly contrasted with her husband's required signature. Initially, La Vaudère had applied for the more distinguished status of "sociétaire." The committee, judging her two works of poetry (*Les heures perdues* and *L'éternelle chanson*) and novel (*Mortelle étreinte*) as evidence of her "inconstatable" talent, nonetheless ruled that three published works were not sufficient for the title of "sociétaire."[36] In exchange for her admission as an "adhérente," La Vaudère granted the SDGL full authorization over the reproduction of her works with participating periodicals. Though activity within this association was critical to her professional success as a writer, she demonstrated a surprising naïveté about her initial involvement. In a letter dated May 9, 1891, she requested information regarding the purpose of the society to which she had just been admitted: "Veuillez me renseigner sur les usages de la Société car je ne suis nullement au courant."[37]

Within a few years, however, La Vaudère maintained regular involvement with the SDGL and frequently called on its support in the reproduction of her short stories, poems, and novels in various periodicals. By March 1894, La Vaudère had published a total of five volumes of poetry and four works of prose, enough to be considered again for the next tier of membership. A selection of her works had also been on display at the Woman's Building at the World's Columbian Exposition in Chicago in 1893, garnering attention overseas for her expanding corpus. She reapplied for status of "sociétaire" with the support of Georges Ohnet and Paul Foucher. Recognizing that her

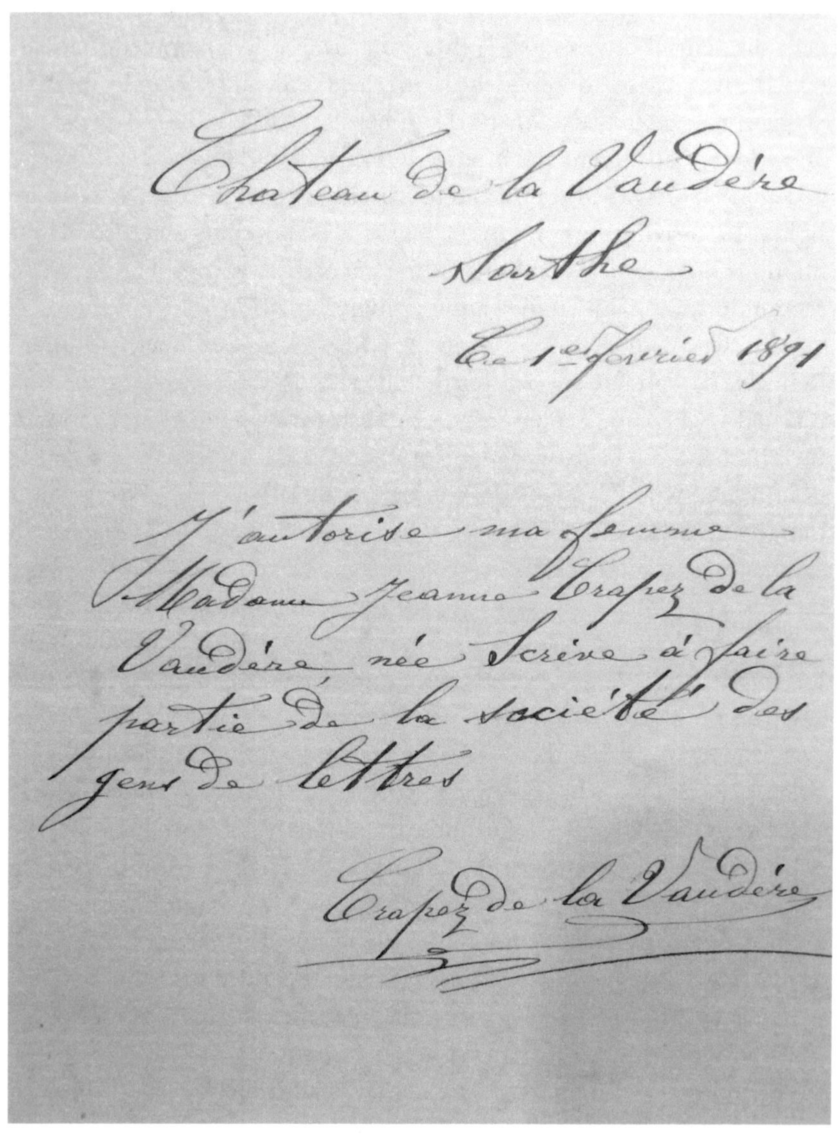

Chateau de la Vaudère
Sarthe
Le 1er Février 1891

J'autorise ma femme
Madame Jeanne Crapez de la
Vaudère, née Scrive à faire
partie de la société des
gens de lettres

Crapez de la Vaudère

FIG. 1 Gaston's permission letter to join the SDGL. Archives nationales, February 1, 1891, 454P/431, dossier Jane de La Vaudère.

"langage littéraire dépass[e] celui que nos statuts imposent," the committee, led by SDGL president Émile Zola, voted in her favor.[38] As a "sociétaire," La Vaudère was required to pay a membership subscription, could vote in general assembly meetings, and was eligible for financial support like pensions or monetary advances. Other institutions acclaimed her momentous creative productivity around this time: in 1897, the state awarded La Vaudère the honorary title of Officier de l'instruction publique for her literary contributions to French culture. In addition, it appears that her initiation into the SDGL paved the way for a valuable relationship with its renowned president, despite his imminent legal troubles. In a correspondence with Zola shortly after her acceptance, she proposed adapting a work of his fiction for the stage, to which he agreed.[39] In February 1898, following the publication of his inflammatory letter "J'accuse!" in defense of Alfred Dreyfus, Zola was prosecuted for libel. La Vaudère was in attendance at Zola's trial, likely in support of her cowriter and peer.[40] A few months later, when *Pour une nuit d'amour* premiered at the Grand-Guignol theatre, La Vaudère's name was associated with one of the great literary figures of nineteenth-century France.

La Vaudère remained active within the SDGL for the remainder of her life and frequently attended meetings and dinners for members at the restaurant Le Marguery (known today as Le Delaville).[41] As the attendance counts provided by the *Chronique de la Société des gens de lettres* consistently confirm, these gatherings placed La Vaudère among hundreds of the most prominent literary names—male and female—of the time. Though clearly a minority faction, women were becoming increasingly active in the SDGL, as evidenced by the committee elections in which La Vaudère participated. As of April 8, 1900, nine positions had opened up on the SDGL committee, and of the fifteen candidates, four were women (and many with masculine pen names): Henry Gréville, Daniel Lesueur, Camille Pert—and La Vaudère. For context, in the week preceding the election, the newspaper *Le Figaro* reported that of the eight hundred members of the organization, eighty were women.[42] The increasing female participation in the SDGL and the unprecedented number of female candidates signaled a new era for the organization. As one journalist predicted, regardless of the election outcome, "La cognée est entrée dans le tronc. L'an prochain, une branche au moins tombera."[43] The day before the election, all of the candidates gathered in one final attempt to secure votes from their fellow members. Of the female candidates, Daniel Lesueur appeared to garner the most support, though La Vaudère was "particulièrement acclamé[e]."[44] At the general assembly meeting the following day, a total of 221 votes were cast; candidates needed a majority count of 111 to be elected officer. La Vaudère received 20 votes. Although some of her female peers fared slightly better (Daniel Lesueur had 96 votes, Henry Gréville had 63 votes, and Camille Pert had 15 votes), all nine officers elected were men.[45] Nonetheless, the election marked a turning point in the SDGL and paved the way for Lesueur to become the association's first female vice president in 1908.

As an active member of the SDGL, La Vaudère benefited from its legal resources when discrepancies arose with editors over her property rights. The collection of letters held at the Archives nationales in Pierrefitte-sur-Seine illustrates her progressive self-advocacy amid the legal issues that she encountered in her profession. They document episodes when she fought to recover unreturned manuscripts from newspapers or pursued legal action against noncompliant editors who denied her appropriate compensation. These letters also elucidate everyday elements of La Vaudère's biography: based on their return addresses, the letters allow us to pinpoint where she was living during her career. The Château de La Vaudère appeared intermittingly throughout the years, but its presence overlapped with references to multiple locations in Paris, each in the affluent Faubourg Saint-Honoré neighborhood: 2, avenue de Messine (1891 to mid-1892); 39, rue la Boëtie (mid-1892 to mid-1897); and 9, Place des Ternes (mid-1905 until her death). To narrow down the timeline even further, other sources indicate that she was living at the rue la Boëtie as late as 1902 and the Place des Ternes as early as 1904.[46] With the château consistently in the backdrop, La Vaudère maintained a residency in Paris where she could navigate artistic circles and invest in her professional relationships. Though she did not divorce until 1898, it appears that she occupied each of these locations independent of Gaston, and her growing autonomy during these years corresponded with an influx of writing and professional success.

LA VAUDÈRE'S DIVORCE AND NEW BEGINNINGS

On March 7, 1898, La Vaudère was granted a divorce from Gaston. By the time of her court case, divorce in France had undergone many legal and social transformations. Ongoing debates were shaped by contemporary feminist discourses and evolving questions about civil status, sexual mores, and secularism. The conditions of La Vaudère's case in particular reflect the possibility of social and financial agency that divorce extended to women. For context, divorce was first legalized in France on the heels of the Revolution in 1792 in the spirit of Republican secular ideals. However, divorce was abolished in 1816 under the Bourbon Restoration, whose newly restored monarchy moved to reinstate conservative values and undo the work of its Republican predecessors. Though divorce would remain illegal until its reestablishment in 1884, the "séparation de corps" remained possible and provided spouses with an opportunity to maintain separate lives financially while remaining legally married. The "divorce question" continually resurfaced in public and judicial stages. After years of debate and numerous revisions, the Loi Naquet of 1884—named after its sponsor, Alfred Naquet—permitted divorce on the grounds of adultery, severe criminal sentencing (such as forced labor, deportation, or death), and "excès, sévices, et injures graves."[47] "Excès" referred to extreme violent behavior, while "sévices" included acts of cruelty that, though not life threatening, made marital life unbearable. "Injure grave," loosely translated as "serious insult," was exceptionally vague and therefore appealing to litigating spouses. While adultery, for example, was difficult to prove, the "injure grave" allowed for flexibility in presenting arguments to the judge, whose own personal views on marriage were likely to affect the verdict. Andrea Mansker argues that judges at the fin de siècle viewed divorce cases through a lens that scrutinized male honor and what she calls the "new republican husband."[48] Under this model, husbands who neglected their wives and refused to fulfill their conjugal duties—both emotional and sexual—were frequently found guilty of the "injure grave." This was the case for Gaston.

In an effort to discourage adultery or abandonment of the marital home, the Loi Naquet also prohibited divorced spouses who had committed adultery from marrying their accomplice. Unlike the original law of 1792, the newest legislation did not allow for divorce by mutual consent.[49] Divorce was a highly public affair, and court rulings were rumored to be chaotic and swift. The fourth chamber of the Tribunal Civil de la Seine, where La Vaudère's 1898 case was tried, was especially notorious for its dramatic divorce proceedings. Contemporaries such as the magistrate Charles Morizot-Thibault ridiculed the rapidity of the hearings, even citing a judge in 1898 who granted 294 divorces in one day.[50] In 1898, roughly 8,100 total divorces were granted in France, up from 5,482 ten years earlier.[51] Women were responsible for the majority of divorce requests: from 1884 to 1914, women filed between 53 and 60 percent of total divorce cases.[52] Nicholas White points out the transgressive nature of a female spouse's divorce request, an act that directly challenged conventional gender norms: "To pursue a divorce suit was in and of itself a contravention of the theory of gender separation, a challenge to men on their own home ground (which was, precisely, outside the home)."[53]

In 1898, a *jugement de divorce* was pronounced at La Vaudère's request. The Fourth Chambre of the Tribunal Civil de la Seine cited Gaston's infidelity and abandonment—an "injure grave"—as justification for granting her a divorce.[54] The ruling provides additional elements that shed light on the state of their relationship and La Vaudère's indignation in the face of her husband's betrayal and abandonment. In documenting one woman's appeal to the law to correct the emotional and financial wrongs inflicted by her husband, this *jugement de divorce* serves as an important cultural artifact from a period when more married women benefited from renewed legal protections. The details of the ruling, though lengthy, offer valuable information about La Vaudère's personal and professional situation:

> La femme Crapez a formé contre son mari une demande en divorce; attendu que, depuis plusieurs années, Crapez a abandonné le domicile conjugal et qu'il a toujours refusé de reprendre la vie commune, malgré les sollicitations réitérées de sa femme; qu'il est établi, en outre, par deux lettres produites à l'audience et qui ont été écrites en mil huit cent quatre vingt [*sic*] quinze (** et qui seront enregistrées en même temps que le présent jugement), qu'il a eu pour maîtresse une fille M. M., avec laquelle il vivrait encore actuellement; que Crapez, après avoir dissipé la dot de sa femme, n'a jamais subvenu aux besoins de celle-ci; que la demanderesse a dû, par son travail, se créer des ressources pour elle et son enfant; attendu que les faits ci-dessous constituent des injures graves envers la femme Crapez, et justifient son action en divorce contre son mari.

According to these claims, Gaston's wrongdoing extended beyond infidelity, and his definitive departure from the family home and refusal to support his wife and child suggested a realized desire to maintain a separate life from his family.[55] As the document confirms, La Vaudère was living at 39, rue de la Boëtie, while Gaston's address was listed as 59, boulevard du Montparnasse. It appears that La Vaudère's patience had worn thin, and despite multiple attempts over "plusieurs années" to persuade him to return home, she finally resorted to legal action and supplied proof of his transgressions.

The two letters that La Vaudère provided were dated three years prior and seem to have convinced the judge of Gaston's infidelity (not always an easy feat in divorce suits). The ruling does not specify whether they were written by Gaston or by his mistress. After speaking with various archivists and consulting collections in Paris on multiple occasions, I have been unable to locate the transcriptions of these letters and they were likely not conserved. Nonetheless, their mere mention hints at La Vaudère's outrage and self-assurance: despite the social scandal of divorce, she presented these letters in a court of law as an assertion of her legal rights. Though we do not have any information about Gaston's mistress "M. M.," the use of the pejorative term "fille" was typically reserved for a prostitute or a woman of questionable moral values. According to the ruling, Gaston's affair had financial consequences for his wife, and "fille" implies that he had depleted a significant amount of money—La Vaudère's dowry—on this woman. As the sole remaining breadwinner of the household, La Vaudère claimed that she worked by necessity rather than choice. By 1898, she had published a selection of poetry collections, as well as various short stories, novels, and plays, and her most productive years still lay ahead of her. In an effort to show fault of "injure grave" (in addition to adultery), La Vaudère used her working status to her advantage. It is noteworthy that in 1898, La Vaudère's son was twenty-two years old and had been an active infantryman for two years. Two weeks following this hearing, he earned the title of sergeant.[56] Nonetheless, by arguing that she was forced to work to support her son, La Vaudère distanced herself from the potentially injurious image of the female intellectual—often associated with domestic neglect—and shifted blame on her husband's abandonment. Through this narrative, she directed anxieties about the collapse of the gendered family structure away from the professional authoress and instead targeted the irresponsible spouse. A mother forced by necessity into the professional world to support her family was a self-sacrificing mother, driven only by a nurturing instinct to care for her child. Under this lens, La Vaudère's writing career was not just "acceptable"—it was commendable.

Swayed by her arguments, the court ruled in La Vaudère's favor. Gaston was ordered to pay his wife's legal fees and the court cost for the transcription of the two letters. The couple was also instructed to consult a notary for their financial disentanglement. The notary Pierre-Marie Moreau worked with La Vaudère and Gaston for a number of years, and the Archives nationales in Paris contains his records.[57] On December 27, 1898, La Vaudère's assets were liquidated and a sum of 145,910.10 francs was to be paid to her by her ex-husband. Unable to compensate her in cash, Gaston mortgaged his properties as collateral, and this guarantee of payment was recorded in the Bureau des hypothèques in Le Mans on January 11, 1899. The properties implicated in this agreement were located in Parigné-l'Évêque or the neighboring areas and included the Château de La Vaudère and its surrounding land.

In 1904 La Vaudère and Gaston returned to Moreau's office to prepare an "Obligation et reconnaissance de dette." At this time, six years following the divorce, Gaston had yet to pay any of the money that was due to his ex-wife. Additionally, because he had failed to manage his debt, he had accumulated 41,520.78 francs in interest. Nonetheless, La Vaudère lent Gaston an additional 42,500 francs to pay an external debt that dated from 1882 during the earlier years of their marriage. The total debt due to La Vaudère was now 229,930.88 francs, a considerable sum at the turn of the century and which forced him to continue to mortgage his properties. Perhaps due to the large amount, La Vaudère drafted a will in December 1904 that released Gaston from his financial obligations until her death: "Je donne et lègue à M. Gaston Camille Crapez, demeurant au château de la Vaudère par Parigné-l'Evêque (Sarthe) l'usufruit, sa vie durant, de la somme totale qu'il restera me devoir, lors de mon décès, en principal, intérêts et accessoires—Je désire que ma succession supporte, sans recours contre lui, les frais et droits de mutation auxquels ce legs donnera ouverture." Though he was given twenty years to pay his debt, La Vaudère's death in 1908 suspended any possibility of her enjoying the financial terms of her divorce. At this time, Gaston had still failed to reimburse her, and notarized records cited the sum of 251,610.85 francs—including interest—that he ultimately owed her.

Nonetheless, in 1904, the "Affectation Hypothécaire par M. Crapez au profit de Madame Scrive" provided La Vaudère with "tous les droits de passage et autres droits quelconques," allowing her continued access to the properties in question, including the Château de La Vaudère. While she likely continued to spend a significant amount of time at the château (many of her letters listed it as a return address), it was also cited as Gaston's primary residence in notarized documents of late 1904. Gaston had thus returned to the home—perhaps due to a rupture with his mistress—and the two ex-spouses likely encountered one another at the château. Having established both a persona and a career that would always be associated with the Crapez family property known as "La Vaudère," her divorce also had implications for her professional identity. In these notarized legal documents, she signed her name "Jane Scrive," a curious hybrid of her maiden name and the anglicized "Jane." This signature that blended her family origins and public persona is a symbol of the ever-shifting identities that she molded and negotiated throughout her life (examined in detail in chapter 2). Nonetheless, despite a legal break from the Crapez family, La Vaudère continued to write as "Jane de La Vaudère" for the remainder of her career.

THE WRITING LIFE

La Vaudère's divorce did little to slow down her writing, and she continued to produce novels, short stories, and theatrical pieces at a rapid rate. After publishing collections of Romantic-inspired poetry in the early 1890s, La Vaudère turned almost exclusively to prose and exhibited her literary versatility. She had an accessible style and a knack for page-turner storylines that attracted an expanding readership. Her growing fascination with the occult no doubt explains the apparitions and reincarnations found in her short-story collections *L'anarchiste* (1893) and *Les sataniques* (1897). A selection of her novels from the 1890s also explored many of the preoccupations of contemporary Naturalist literature, such as the fatalistic heredity central to *Le sang* (1898). She concurrently published a number of works that depicted nonnormative gender expression and sexual perversions, themes that were common to Decadent fiction. Provocative titles like *Les demi-sexes* (1897), *Les androgynes* (1903), and *Sapho, dompteuse* (1908) recalled the fin-de-siècle fascination with sexual and moral pathologies and attracted a wide array of readers. The early 1900s signaled a new period in her work with a series of Orientalist, highly eroticized novels that took place in the Far East. *Trois fleurs de volupté* (1900) and *Le mystère de Kama* (1901) were the first of nearly a dozen comparable novels to follow, many supplemented with titillating illustrations that exaggerated the sexual and moral "otherness" of Eastern cultures. Given her own penchant for drawing, La Vaudère contributed illustrations to her own novels and to those of her contemporaries, including Félicien Champsaur's widely read *Lulu, roman clownesque* (1901).[58] She was also active in the theatre scene and wrote a number of dramatic works, many in verse, which were performed in Parisian venues. La Vaudère's corpus stands out for the sheer breadth of its themes and genres and reflects her shrewd adaptation to fluctuating literary markets and movements.

As La Vaudère's name grew to be more commonplace, various editions of her works were made available in translation to international readers in the early 1900s. She frequently collaborated with other important names of the time, like writers Félicien Champsaur, Théodore Cahu, and Gaston Derys as well as the singer Jane Vieu, for whom she supplied verse lyrics.[59] Renowned artists like Charles Atamian, Théophile Steinlen, and Raphael Kirchner provided illustrations for a selection of her novels, which surely contributed to the surging sales of her works and the demand for multiple editions.[60] By the early 1900s, for example, *Les demi-sexes* (1897) had reached its twentieth edition, and the publisher Flammarion printed an astounding thirty thousand copies of *Les courtisanes de Brahma* and twenty-five thousand copies of *Le mystère de Kama*, *La mystérieuse*, and *La guescha amoureuse*.[61] Beginning in 1896, La Vaudère was a regular contributor to *La presse* and continued to publish editorials—sometimes weekly—with the newspaper until 1906. Prominent critics frequently reviewed her works, including fellow Decadent darling Rachilde, who praised La Vaudère's *Les sataniques* in an 1897 issue of *Mercure de France*.[62] Like many Belle Époque artists, La Vaudère commissioned both Félix Nadar and Alphonse Liébert for her portraits, joining ranks with celebrities Sarah Bernhardt, George Sand, Victor Hugo, Charles Baudelaire, Maupassant, and Victorien Sardou, who were all portrayed by the famous photographers.[63] The extent of La Vaudère's renown can also be measured by the frequency with which she was parodied in contemporary *romans à clef* and short stories. But La Vaudère's success did not come without its social and legal battles. She was denounced by the press as a plagiarist (and with reason) and was involved in a handful of lawsuits (as both plaintiff and defendant) over intellectual property rights. Surprisingly, given the abundance of copied passages that she incorporated in nearly all of her works, claims of plagiarism did not slow down her steadfast production or remarkable readership rates.

La Vaudère was her own best advocate. In January 1908, days before the staged reading of her play *Mlle de Fontanges* at the Théâtre Femina, she wrote a letter to the editors of *Le journal* demanding immediate publicity. This exceptional letter—discovered by a stroke of luck on a book collector's website—provides a glimpse into La Vaudère's assertive methods of self-promotion and the rivalry between women in a profession governed largely by men. Her vehement tone is especially noteworthy and was prompted by *Le journal* not respecting the terms of a contract in preparation.[64] "Faut-il écrire aux plus influents?" she threatened. "Donnez-moi leurs noms? Il est grand, grand temps de faire annoncer notre séance aux courriers des Théâtres!" She evoked the stipulations of the contract and her unwavering demands, flexing her negotiation skills. "Je suis prête à signer le traité avec le *Journal* pour un roman," she wrote, "en échange d'un article en première page et de l'insertion d'une scène de *Mlle de Fontanges*." For comparison, La Vaudère attached a recent clipping from *Le journal* to show that poet Jane Catulle Mendès had received generous amounts of publicity for a similar production at the Théâtre Femina.[65] "Voici une conférence de Mme C. Mendès qui a déjà été annoncée 4 fois!" she protested. Though La Vaudère intended to highlight the newspaper's arbitrary advertising practices, she did so at the expense of a female contemporary (and another Jane). The Théâtre Femina was located in the Hôtel Femina, which was also home to the publishers of *Femina*. Though the theatre's program showcased male playwrights, it shared an affiliation with the women's magazine. La Vaudère's choice to target a woman poet at this particular venue illuminates the scarcity of resources for women writers: in the fight for representation, turning on each other was a more realizable option than competing with male peers. Her strategy appears to have worked, and *Le journal* ran a detailed advertisement for *Mlle de Fontanges* on January 20.

DEATH AND SUCCESSION

Contemporary portraits of La Vaudère often commented on her frail and weak disposition, but when she died on July 26, 1908, at the age of fifty-one, very little was said about the cause of her death. According to her death certificate, she passed in her home at the Place des Ternes in the early morning. Two men who had no familial relation to her reported her death: Nicholas Mohr, retired, age fifty-six, and Georges Roux, "employé," age sixty-two. Neither man lived in close proximity to La Vaudère (Mohr lived on the rue de la Croix Nivert, and Roux lived on the rue des Saints Pères), and neither seems to have been part of La Vaudère's artistic circles.[66] In a lengthy obituary, the *Chronique de la Société des gens de lettres* reported that she succumbed to "une cruelle et longue maladie," confirming that she likely suffered from a chronic illness for a period of time.[67] The nature of this illness, however, remains a mystery, though a combination of clues from various sources may point to a possible explanation. Two months earlier, in May 1908, La Vaudère had responded to a query in *La critique indépendante* about the future of idealist and realist theatres. She explained in her letter that she was too ill to contribute to the debate and had been bedridden for three months.[68] Previously, on January 13, in a letter to *Le journal* regarding advertising prices for her works, La Vaudère had complained of being homebound due to a bout of pleurisy: "Je suis toujours très malade des suites d'une pleurésie et il m'est impossible de me rendre au Journal" (fig. 2). Pleurisy, a potentially severe condition in which the lung's membrane becomes inflamed, can be caused by a virus or brought on by other pulmonary illnesses or bacterial infections. There is no evidence to suggest that La Vaudère was plagued by a lung condition throughout her life, nor that she had contracted tuberculosis as a child due to her weak disposition. Nonetheless, the fact that this letter, in which she describes a persistent debilitated state, was written just months before her death is one of the only clues that we have about her physical health in 1908. Days prior to her death, the journalist known as "Butterfly" visited La Vaudère in her home and published an article depicting the writer on her deathbed. Without elaborating on the nature of her illness, Butterfly emphasized her physical agony, pale hands, and weak voice as she lay "étendue sur son lit de souffrance, ses beaux cheveux épars encadrant la face émaciée . . . doucement, elle agitait ses mains, deux mains pâles d'idole."[69] Though aspects of this portrait were certainly romanticized—in particular, La Vaudère's painful effort to recite her favorite poems—it provided a rare account of the symptoms of her illness and her physical state before passing.

As her only child, Fernand would inherit the entirety of La Vaudère's estate. However, days before passing, La Vaudère decided to make amendments to her will. Too sick to write, she dictated the revisions to surrounding friends. These changes involved five people: Alfred Belmontet Dailly, the ex-mayor of Saint Cloud; Théodore Cahu, a writer with whom she had previously collaborated; Georges Humbert Deturmény, a manufacturer; Lucie Routier, her housemaid; and Marie Scrive, her sister.[70] La Vaudère wished to bequeath works of art to friends and six months of wages (500 francs) to Routier. While the details of these final wishes seem incidental at first glance, the roles of Cahu and Marie are especially insightful about La Vaudère's personal and professional relationships at the end of her life. Of those mentioned, La Vaudère singled out Cahu in particular "pour le remercier de s'occuper de mes manuscrits qui lui seront tous remis." La Vaudère's manuscripts have otherwise disappeared, and this is the only clue we have regarding their possible fate. Moreau's records provided a list of the manuscripts that Cahu accepted, "dans le but d'exécuter les volontés" of La Vaudère.[71] These manuscripts make up only a fraction of her complete *œuvre* and, with the exception of *Le droit d'aimer*, are written exclusively for the stage. Though it is unclear what La Vaudère's wishes may have been,

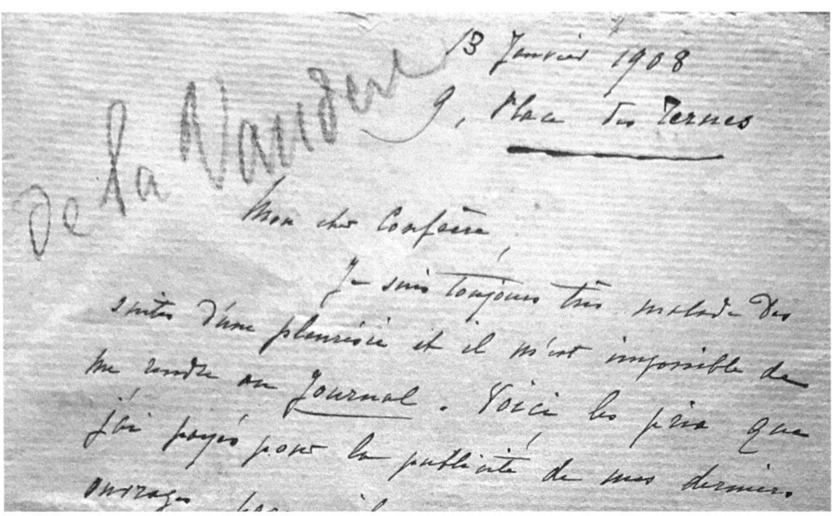

De La Vaudère 13 Janvier 1908
9, Place des Ternes

Mon cher Confrère,

Je suis toujours très malade des suites d'une pleurésie et il m'est impossible de me rendre au Journal. Voici les prix que j'ai payés pour la publicité de mes derniers ouvrages

FIG. 2 La Vaudère's letter referencing pleurisy. Author's collection.

she was likely in the process of submitting these manuscripts to theatrical venues to be considered for production.[72] Why she chose Cahu to take on this charge remains a mystery. Unfortunately, Cahu's archives have turned out to be dead ends, providing no mention of the manuscripts' existence. Moreover, only one of the titles mentioned was published posthumously: *Mlle de Fontanges* (Méricant, 1909), for which La Vaudère organized a theatrical reading just months before her death.[73] Cahu also worked with La Vaudère's son, Fernand, to update the necessary contracts with the SDGL regarding the continued reproduction of her works.[74] In 1911, Cahu served as a witness for Fernand's marriage—he was designated as an "ami" in the certificate.[75]

Marie Scrive, who was also added to La Vaudère's will in the final hours, responded less graciously to the bequest. Marie was to be given a portrait of her sister whose value was estimated at a mere fifty francs. While the four other designated individuals accepted their respective gifts, Marie "n'a pas cru devoir bénéficier de ce legs" and rejected La Vaudère's portrait. Though tucked away in the margins of the notary's report, this seemingly insignificant detail is suggestive of a possible rift between the two sisters at the time of her death. Given the value of her estate, La Vaudère's gift of her portrait seems an intentionally insulting gesture, though she also bequeathed portraits to Belmontet and Cahu, who readily accepted. However, Marie certainly had the last word in her refusal, a symbolic renunciation on her end of their familial ties. These traces of tension between the sisters may also hint at why La Vaudère's grave at the cemetery Montparnasse remains unmarked. Ten years later, Marie became the next and final family member to be buried there.

On July 29, La Vaudère's funeral service was held at the Saint-Ferdinand des Ternes church, followed by a procession and burial at the Montparnasse cemetery. The *Chronique de la Société des gens de lettres* reported that the services attracted a large number of people, but that "selon la volonté expresse de Jane de la Vaudère, aucun discours n'a été prononcé sur sa tombe."[76] La Vaudère's name was not inscribed on the family sepulcher (figs. 3 and 4). As announced by the large engraving "Sépulture des Familles Scrive et Dauvais de Gérardcourt," this plot joined two families. It had been the burial place of Pierre Scrive, La Vaudère's paternal grandfather; Gaspard Scrive, her father; Barbe Weigel, her mother; and Joseph Victor Dauvais de Gérardcourt, her brother-in-law. In 1918, it housed the last family member, Marie, who never had any children with Dauvais de Gérardcourt. Despite the absence of her name, there is no doubt that La Vaudère's remains are here. The Montparnasse cemetery office has verified on various occasions that she was, indeed, buried in the family plot.[77] In addition, the official registries have been digitized for the public and provide a helpful breakdown of the week of La Vaudère's funeral.[78] Why La Vaudère's name is missing from the sepulcher remains a mystery. Perhaps this was her desire, a product of modesty, just as she had forbidden any elaborate speeches at her grave. Or perhaps this was Marie's doing, a sort of symbolic erasure of a sister with whom she had clashed. It is not known whether Fernand or Gaston had any influence on this decision, as the sepulcher was originally managed by the Scrive family beginning in 1861.

In 1911, three years after La Vaudère's death, her son, Fernand, married Anne Marie Léopoldine Simonot in La Roche-sur-Yon in the Vendée department of western France. They had two sons, Alain Crapez, who was born in 1912, and Jean Crapez, who was born in 1914. Fernand then served as mayor of Parigné-l'Évêque from 1919 to 1935. La Vaudère's only grandchildren did not live long lives. At the age of twenty-two, following his military service in Africa, Alain died in Parigné-l'Évêque, most likely from an undisclosed illness. During the Second World War, Jean, age twenty-six, was killed by enemy fire in Orival, Normandy, while carrying wounded infantrymen to safety.[79] Like his great-grandfather Gaspard Scrive, Jean was pursuing military medicine as an "aspirant médecin auxiliaire," as indicated by the plaque above his tomb. In 1942, he was posthumously awarded the Croix

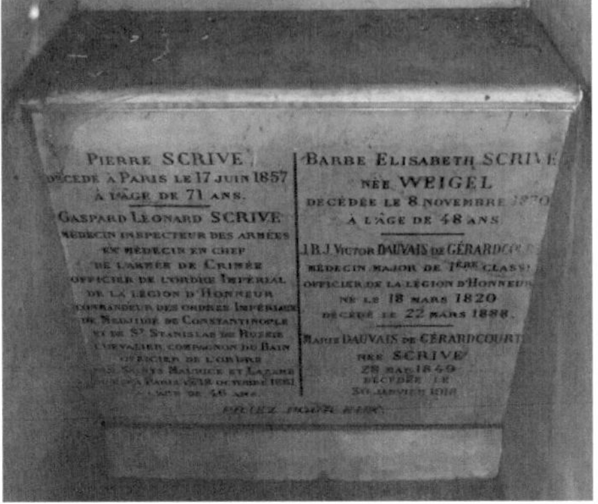

FIG. 3
The Scrive family sepulcher (exterior), Montparnasse Cemetery, Paris.

FIG. 4
The Scrive family sepulcher (interior), La Vaudère's name is absent.

de Guerre medal for rescuing and treating injured soldiers on the battlefield. Both Alain and Jean were laid to rest in the chapel on the Château de La Vaudère property. Though neither Alain nor Jean had children, the Crapez family name is well integrated into the community of Parigné-l'Évêque. In 1951, when Fernand drafted his will, he arranged to donate his estate to the commune of Parigné-l'Évêque with one condition: the town build a nursing home in commemoration of his two sons. Fernand died in 1953 and his wife in 1966, setting into motion the plans for the construction of the "Maison de Retraite Alain et Jean Crapez," which officially opened in 1973 and is still operating today. The road that leads to the nursing home, rue Fernand Crapez, bears its benefactor's name. In 1968, in preparation for carrying out Fernand's plans, the commune of Parigné-l'Êvêque sold the Château de La Vaudère property at auction to a man named Jacques Rousseau, Anne-Charlotte's father. The sale of the château marks an ending to La Vaudère's biography and a beginning of a new story to tell later in this book: that of Anne-Charlotte Rousseau, current owner of the property.

Like lost biography, the absence of La Vaudère's name from her burial site is emblematic of her disappearance from cultural memory. For over a century, La Vaudère's unmarked grave has denied her the possibility of pilgrimage, a reverential act of homage, recognition, and preservation. While the tombs of canonical writers Charles Baudclaire, Marguerite Duras, Simone de Beauvoir, and Jean-Paul Sartre have lured visitors to the Montparnasse cemetery, La Vaudère's final resting place, like her place in literary history, has been obscured. Only the dusty, fragile annals of the Montparnasse cemetery can confirm her presence in the family sepulcher, and under today's policy, only immediate descendants can make alterations to a family plot. La Vaudère's grave will likely remain unmarked for the foreseeable future. But this biography is a start in restoring her memory.

CHAPTER 2

Becoming Jane de La Vaudère

In 1904, for an issue of the *Revue illustrée*, La Vaudère provided a handwritten letter to the graphology specialist Albert de Rochetal (fig. 5). Through the popular pseudoscience of handwriting analysis, Rochetal's objective was to relate the written sample with the temperament of its author. In his evaluation, Rochetal's longwinded list of contradictory descriptors perfectly encapsulated the paradoxes and ambiguities at the heart of La Vaudère's public image. He characterized her handwriting as simultaneously "gigantesque, orgueilleuse, absolue, souple, serpentine, charmante et féroce, artistique, séduisante et caustique."[1] Given the metonymical function of graphology, Rochetal's comments extended to La Vaudère herself, whom he considered at once charming and ferocious, seductive and snakelike. Like many contemporaries writing about transgressive women writers, Rochetal searched for signs of La Vaudère's gender rebellion. "Au premier abord, l'écriture de Jane de La Vaudère est masculine: c'est un compliment," he noted. "Mais si l'on regarde attentivement, on remarque quelques traits que toute femme, surtout intellectuelle, commet inconsciemment."[2] For the graphologist, La Vaudère exhibited both masculine and feminine traits (*malgré elle*), and his concluding remarks accentuated the mystery and allure behind her hybrid persona: "Il y a des curiosités morphologiques bizarres, telles que ce J de *Jane*, qui se dresse, sphynx [*sic*]-énigme, et dont le charme étrange, fascinateur, m'obsède et me fait courir un frisson dans le dos."[3]

Like Rochetal, novelists, playwrights, journalists, and photographers portrayed La Vaudère across different artistic mediums and literary genres

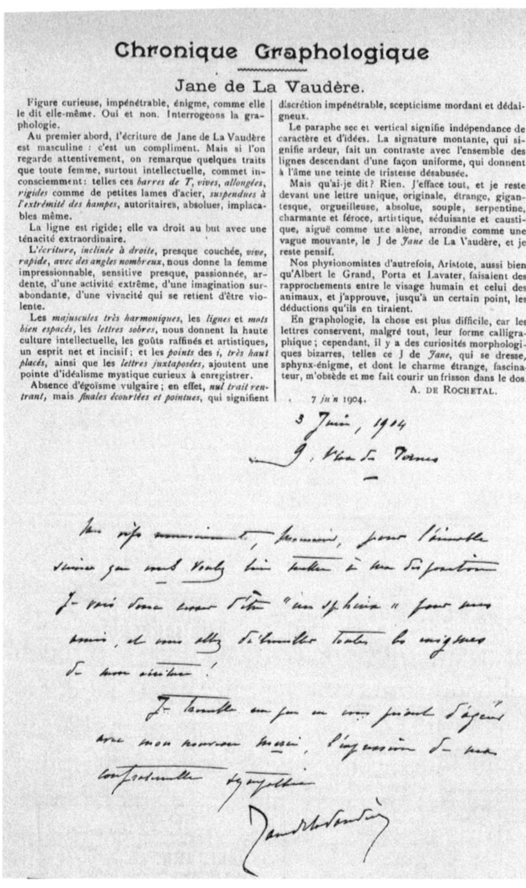

Chronique Graphologique

Jane de La Vaudère.

Figure curieuse, impénétrable, énigme, comme elle le dit elle-même. Oui et non. Interrogeons la graphologie.

Au premier abord, l'écriture de Jane de La Vaudère est masculine : c'est un compliment. Mais si l'on regarde attentivement, on remarque quelques traits que toute femme, surtout intellectuelle, commet inconsciemment : telles ces *barres de T, vives, allongées, rigides* comme de petites lames d'acier, *suspendues à l'extrémité des hampes*, autoritaires, absolues, implacables même.

La ligne est rigide; elle va droit au but avec une ténacité extraordinaire.

L'*écriture, inclinée à droite*, presque couchée, *vive, rapide, avec des angles nombreux*, nous donne la femme impressionnable, sensitive presque, passionnée, ardente, d'une activité extrême, d'une imagination surabondante, d'une vivacité qui se retient d'être violente.

Les *majuscules très harmoniques*, les *lignes* et *mots bien espacés*, les *lettres sobres*, nous donnent la haute culture intellectuelle, les goûts raffinés et artistiques, un esprit net et incisif; et les *points* des *i, très haut placés*, ainsi que les *lettres juxtaposées*, ajoutent une pointe d'idéalisme mystique curieux à enregistrer.

Absence d'égoïsme vulgaire; en effet, *nul trait rentrant*, mais *finales écourtées et pointues*, qui signifient discrétion impénétrable, scepticisme mordant et dédaigneux.

Le paraphe sec et vertical signifie indépendance de caractère et d'idées. La signature montante, qui signifie ardeur, fait un contraste avec l'ensemble des lignes descendant d'une façon uniforme, qui donnent à l'âme une teinte de tristesse désabusée.

Mais qu'ai-je dit? Rien. J'efface tout, et je reste devant une lettre unique, originale, étrange, gigantesque, orgueilleuse, absolue, souple, serpentine, charmante et féroce, artistique, séduisante et caustique, aiguë comme une alène, arrondie comme une vague mouvante, le J de *Jane* de La Vaudère, et je reste pensif.

Nos physionomistes d'autrefois, Aristote, aussi bien qu'Albert le Grand, Porta et Lavater, faisaient des rapprochements entre le visage humain et celui des animaux, et j'approuve, jusqu'à un certain point, les déductions qu'ils en tiraient.

En graphologie, la chose est plus difficile, car les lettres conservent, malgré tout, leur forme calligraphique; cependant, il y a des curiosités morphologiques bizarres, telles ce J de *Jane*, qui se dresse, sphynx-énigme, et dont le charme étrange, fascinateur, m'obsède et me fait courir un frisson dans le dos.

A. DE ROCHETAL.

7 juin 1904.

3 Juin, 1904

FIG. 5
Deciphering La Vaudère's handwriting. *Revue illustrée*, June 15, 1904. Source: gallica .bnf.fr / BnF.

in an attempt to capture her amorphous persona. Over the course of her career, her representations took many forms and perpetuated familiar and essentialist discourses on gender difference, female authorship, and the New Woman. The diversity of these narratives, which portrayed La Vaudère as meek and soft-spoken or as a disquieting threat to traditional gender roles, attests to the instability of her public image. Through the fluidity of a public image that Mary Louise Roberts would characterize as "disruptive," La Vaudère challenged the legitimacy and stability of dominant discourses about femininity and the woman writer.[4] However, while contemporary feminists like Marguerite Durand performed elements of hyperfemininity to distance themselves from the archetype of the New Woman, La Vaudère cultivated a troubling and transgressive persona and successfully boosted her sales.[5] One such instance can be traced to the letter that she provided Rochetal. Upon closer look, we note that she was the first to refer to herself as the enigmatic "sphynx" in Rochetal's portrayal: "Je vais donc cesser d'être 'un sphinx' pour vous aussi, et vous allez débrouiller toutes les énigmes de mon écriture."[6] Here, the lines between representation and self-representation blur, and the fragmentation of her persona destabilized the rigid categories of gender difference.

Throughout the decades, La Vaudère's iconographic transformations coincided with changes in the thematic and aesthetic content of her writing. When she moved away from the sentimental verse poetry of her early years to salacious short stories and Orientalist fiction, her public image grew increasingly disconcerting. Literary periodicals, newspapers, and various *romans à clef* emphasized her eccentric and troubling character or simply denied her literary merits. However, as media attention increased, so did her sales, and La Vaudère's "rebranding" signaled an astute awareness of evolving trends in the literary market and the value of curating her image. As she allegedly exclaimed about erotic literature, "Cela vous dégoûte. Et il n'y a pourtant que cela qui se vende."[7] La Vaudère capitalized on what Sharon Marcus has identified as the three interconnected and interdependent influences of celebrity culture: the media, the public, and the celebrity figure.[8] La Vaudère's methods of self-promotion provide a circular illustration of this system, with no evident point of departure. Aided by the press, La Vaudère crafted a persona that intrigued the public, and in turn, readers purchased newspapers that featured articles about her. These articles served as publicity for La Vaudère, and as newspaper sales increased, so did her book sales. To trace this cyclic relationship, the first part of this chapter examines contemporary representations of the evolving persona "Jane de La Vaudère," from the virtuous and banal poetess to the disquieting and renowned *bas-bleu*. I then consider La Vaudère's own self-construction and how she exploited media depictions that tended to exaggerate and demonize the subversive elements of her fiction and behaviors.[9] La Vaudère's fiction, once responsible for her troubling reputation, became a conduit to exploit and build upon her notoriety for her own gain. She was in many ways the mastermind in adopting discourses on nonnormative femininity that targeted women writers like herself, and in so doing, exposed their own precariousness.

It is important to note that La Vaudère presented herself as unequivocally female. In profiles of her work, it was not uncommon for critics to comment on her feminine charm, delicate features, soft voice, and angelic blond hair. Because of these conventional markers of femininity, the content of La Vaudère's fiction, with its effeminate dandies, predatory lesbians, and bisexual orgies, was even more disconcerting. The fact that such themes were both imagined and depicted by a woman of La Vaudère's disposition undermined the rigid binaries of gender (and genre) and exposed their instability. As Roberts has shown, "To play with gender norms by embracing both conventional and unconventional roles can be seen as a disruptive act. To present an image of woman that was internally contradictory was to reject all notions of the 'eternal feminine.'"[10] La Vaudère used these incongruities to her advantage. Because of the legibility of her femininity, she created sensation and buzz when she strayed from the conventions of her sex and wrote about sexual vice or gender confusion. The tension lay in the indeterminacy of La Vaudère's identity, and the public faced an uncomfortable uncertainty: was the "real" La Vaudère the demure and docile version, or the depraved and debauched? Which one was the act? To my knowledge, the press never directly commented on her personal life, neither before nor after her divorce. Her marketing relied on the indecisiveness of any "true" identity, and the confusion and disorder that it sowed worked to her advantage.

THE DUAL NARRATIVES OF JEANNE CRAPEZ AND JANE DE LA VAUDÈRE

Two opposing depictions of La Vaudère dominated the press throughout her career: that of an amiable and unassuming young woman with a romantic vision, and that of a debauched and unscrupulous *bas-bleu* set out to obliterate the gendered social order. Though the former characterization was frequently associated with her early years of poetry and the latter with her works of Decadent, Naturalist, and Orientalist fiction, La Vaudère eventually orchestrated the convergence of these two models during her most successful professional years. Initially, as she was first making a name for herself, benevolent critics limited their focus to her works of poetry. In the early 1890s, critical articles conflated discussions of La Vaudère's poetry with her feminine grace and charm. Many celebrated La Vaudère's works simply because they believed them to be a manifestation of conventional femininity. This praise may best be understood in the context of "gendered" literary genres of the period. With the constraints of French versification, poetry was considered an elite masculine domain, beyond the reach of a woman's creative and intellectual capacities. According to traditionalist critics, women who did venture into verse risked being overly effusive and lacking in originality.[11] As Jean de Gourmont explained in his work on contemporary women poets, "Vivre, de toute la puissance de son ressort physique, sans autre curiosité que le mécanisme de ses propres sensations, vierge de toute culture intellectuelle, telle me paraît être l'ambition de la femme poète."[12] Reviews of La Vaudère's earliest works reproduced these ideologies, for better or for worse. While most critics extolled her verse for its virtuous moral content (this would change drastically in the years to come), some denigrated it for its hackneyed themes and unoriginal aesthetic. Nearly all, however, linked her creative production to the same source: her womanhood.

In 1890, *Le Gaulois* printed a brief exposé on women poets that hinged on essentialist discourses associating womanhood with sentimentality and intuition. "En définitive, on peut dire que toute femme est née poète," it began, situating this natural aptitude for poetry in a woman's delicacy and sensitivity.[13] Accordingly, "la femme possède en elle-même une essence de tendresse et de rêverie qui la porte à voir toute chose au point de vue du sentiment et de la forme."[14] Nonetheless, the unnamed critic was aware of fin-de-siècle literary trends, "cette *influenza* de la littérature moderne," and their potential to contaminate virtuous poetic visions.[15] In his eyes, the young Jane de La Vaudère was the positive promise for what would come: "Tenez, voici justement une femme-poète qui sort de l'inconnu et apporte successivement deux volumes de vers, qui sont comme un réveil et un cri de joie dans la nuit. [. . .] L'auteur est une jeune et jolie femme, Mme Jane de la Vaudère, qui, sans prétention, sans pose, sans draperies savantes, se laisse aller à l'inspiration du cœur, vraie science qui dépasse, en fin de compte, celle des analyses cruelles et désenchantées."[16] The author presented La Vaudère as a fresh voice, an alternative to the morbidity and debauchery that plagued modern literary representations. The portrayal highlighted both her modesty and femininity ("une jeune et jolie femme") and praised her penchant for intuition ("l'inspiration du cœur") rather than intellectual inquiry. From this perspective, La Vaudère embodied the feminine ideal, and her poetry, though lacking in artistic ingenuity, exemplified an acceptable form of creative expression. However, the critic recognized a downside to La Vaudère's artistic reserve and noted that her humility, though inoffensive, cost her important media attention: "Il s'agit d'une femme que sa modestie et sa timidité éloignent de la presse."[17] Though intended to praise her modest self-effacement, this closing comment may have prompted the thematic and creative transformation of La Vaudère's persona in the years to come.

This was not the only review to juxtapose La Vaudère's early works with the pessimism of modern fiction. In 1892, a journalist known as Rubempré lauded her as the "la gracieuse prêtresse de l'idéal."[18] He cited her sonnets as a light-hearted distraction from the realities of the fin de siècle, "comme si elle voulait, en nous faisant regarder en haut, nous obliger à oublier toutes les vilaines choses d'ici-bas."[19] Others reaffirmed La Vaudère's delicate disposition and conventional beauty, and even as she began her transition to fiction, critics clung to the narratives inspired by her poetry. In a brief mention for the publication of her first work of prose, *Mortelle étreinte*, *La justice* nonetheless referred to the up-and-coming novelist as "le délicat poète" and added that "l'auteur a su conserver un grand charme."[20] Critics celebrated her poetry and paradoxically embraced its flaws and clichéd motifs, which they excused as the inevitable product of her womanhood. In his anthology *Les muses françaises*, Alphonse Séché noted that though her poetry "n'est jamais sans grâce," it was not without imperfections.[21] "Malgré tout on éprouve comme un regret que Mme Jane de la Vaudère écrivît si hâtivement," he wrote, "qu'elle se contentât trop facilement et qu'elle ne voulût pas bannir les rimes banales, les expressions sans reliefs, les images et les métaphores conventionnelles, lorsqu'elle eût pu, presque sans effort, ne livrer au public que des œuvres achevées."[22] Séché's critique of La Vaudère cannot be divorced from her gender. Echoing familiar characterizations of women writers, he claimed that La Vaudère wrote too quickly (suggesting inadequate reflection), lacked innovation, and resorted to commonplace poetic expression. For a (male) poet, these were significant points of criticism, yet the review applauded her "dons poétiques remarquables" and was generally positive.[23] For Séché, these deficiencies—expected and accepted consequences of normative femininity—excused La Vaudère from serious poetic contributions.

Until 1897, the themes in La Vaudère's works were relatively inoffensive to bourgeois values, and conservative critics were generally encouraging. After moving to prose fiction with *Mortelle étreinte* in 1891, she continued to publish novels and collections of short stories, each appearing more risqué than the last. She began to explore transgressive representations of gender difference and feminist themes that considered women as prisoners in marriages or as sexually unfulfilled. These ideologies grew more blatant—and brazen—in each subsequent text, with a continued momentum that reached its peak in 1897 with the controversial *Les demi-sexes*. The journalist Georges Sénéchal tracked this progression in five novels published between 1891 and 1897 and urged readers to consider them as a series: *Mortelle étreinte*

(1891); *Rien qu'amante!* (1894); *Le droit d'aimer* (1895); *Ambitieuse* (1896); and *Les demi-sexes* (1897). Sénéchal argued that the series as a whole represented "une étude très consciencieuse, très fouillée de la situation faite à la femme dans notre société moderne."[24] He began his analysis with *Mortelle étreinte* and *Rien qu'amante!* and noted that La Vaudère depicted "la femme comme une absolue victime" who must endure the consequences of her social position.[25] Next, Sénéchal turned to *Le droit d'aimer* and *Ambitieuse*, in which he detected "un commencement d'insurrection" and growing agency in its female protagonists: "La femme exploite à son tour, dans son intérêt, les sentiments qu'elle a su faire naître, encourager, exalter."[26] Accordingly, as La Vaudère's female characters became increasingly active in shaping their lives, they did so at the expense of those around them, turning to manipulation, seduction, or deceit to realize symbolic revenge for their treatment in earlier novels.

It is not a coincidence that as La Vaudère's voice shifted, so did her portrayals in the media. In 1897, with *Les demi-sexes* and *Les sataniques*, La Vaudère evinced a new thematic interest in unconventional sexual mores and gender expression that she would explore in some form for the remainder of her writing career. These titles stood in strong juxtaposition with La Vaudère's early works, and in particular, her collections of poetry, which tended to engage with Romantic themes and were overly sentimental. Critics who condemned these new volumes also denounced La Vaudère's shifting themes and contributed to two opposing narratives that were emerging in the press. With provocative titles like *Les androgynes* (1903), *Le harem de Syta* (1904), and *Sapho, dompteuse* (1908), La Vaudère became an easy target for conservative critics who denounced her work as immoral and profane and scrutinized her womanhood. La Vaudère's shift from a more "feminine" style of writing—one concerned with sentimental reflections on nature or romance—to one that valued transgressive sexualities was certainly a trigger for the critical backlash. Perhaps what was also at stake were the gendered codes of literary production, given the ease at which this meek poetess made this transition.

LES DEMI-SEXES AND NEW SUCCESSES

Though La Vaudère had begun to reimagine heteronormative relationships in her fiction before 1897, the progression of these ideas reached its pinnacle with *Les demi-sexes*, a novel about female sexual pleasure and clandestine ovariectomies in fin-de-siècle Paris. Typical of Decadent fiction, the work privileged representations of sexual pathologies and unconventional gender expression. For an outraged Sénéchal, the novel embodied "la révolte poussée à son extrême limite," where women no longer had to answer to "toutes les obligations, divines, sociales et humaines."[27] His discussion of the text lacked the empathy that he had extended to La Vaudère's earlier female protagonists, the helpless victims of neglectful lovers and gendered double standards. Instead, he condemned the women of *Les demi-sexes*, the "cerveaux féminins déséquilibrés" that refused the gendered social contract.[28] While Sénéchal's tone had drastically shifted in his discussion of this novel, La Vaudère's ideology had not, and her message had been consistent in the five books that he considered. What had changed, however, was her approach to disseminating this message: no longer defenseless victims, female protagonists were powerful and merciless in their demands for emotional and sexual fulfillment. As the novel's title indicates, this model of feminism pointed to a break from normative femininity and a blurring of gender difference, a theme explored regularly in Decadent fiction. La Vaudère had once been praised for not following the trends of modern fin-de-siècle literature and for remaining faithful to the sentimental paradigm of past decades. However, as she seemed to have "caught up" with the developing poetics of the present day, critics condemned her shift to more transgressive representations.

Financially, La Vaudère's decision to follow the thematic course of modern fiction was the right one. *Les demi-sexes* marked a major turning point for her career, and book sales climbed sharply in response to media attention. Booksellers could not keep the novel on their shelves. Newspapers reported that the book had particular success among bourgeois women, and journalists sensationalized the dangers of her novel falling into the wrong hands. One critic wrote, "Jane de la Vaudère a piqué au vif la curiosité du public avec son roman *Les Demi-Sexes*, dont quatre éditions ont été enlevées en quelques jours. Toutes les femmes lisent ce volume, dans lequel le rare talent du romancier les initie à certains coins ignorés de la vie de Paris."[29] Some of La Vaudère's peers saw an opportunity to benefit from the novel's success, and the playwright Henri Fransois obtained La Vaudère's permission to adapt it to the stage.[30] The controversy associated with her novel surely contributed to its popularity, and journalists recognized the power of this paradox. As B. Bauer, a critic for *La presse*, noted, "On se défendit d'avoir lu les *Demi-Sexes*, ce qui procura au livre un grand nombre d'éditions!"[31] In tapping into a new literary niche, La Vaudère had found a way to reinvent her image and boost her sales, all while abandoning writing traditionally coded as "feminine."

Conservative critics like Han Ryner responded in kind. For him, La Vaudère was just one of many "amazones" invading the literary scene at the turn of the century. And yet, she had earned herself an entry in his 1899 sensationalist anthology *Le massacre des amazones*. The work opened with an unabashed declaration of a crusade against the woman writer: "Qu'est exactement l'ennemi que je vais combattre? Qu'est-ce qui constitue le bas-bleu, amazone de la littérature? Je le saurai mieux après la guerre."[32] Ryner devoted the pages that followed to a study of two hundred contemporary "bas-bleus," pejorative parlance for the woman writer and a prominent figure in the nineteenth-century cultural imagination. Caricaturists and writers frequently portrayed the *bas-bleu* as a threat to the structure of the family and gender order because she abandoned her domestic duties for intellectual pursuits.[33] As the cliché dictated, Ryner characterized the "bas-bleu" as a woman stripped of her femininity, an "apparente androgyne qui repousse son rôle naturel et, naïvement ou perversement, fait l'homme."[34] Accordingly, the *bas-bleu* rejected her "natural" or maternal responsibilities and was instead masculinized by her cerebral interests: "Ce qui constitue le bas-bleu ou l'amazone, c'est qu'un léger développement de ce qui semble viril en elle lui fait croire qu'intellectuellement elle est un homme."[35] Of the two hundred women writers scrutinized in the work, Ryner devoted a chapter called "Les cygnes noirs" to La Vaudère and Rachilde. This classification cemented La Vaudère's cultural affiliation with the infamous cross-dressing Decadent writer, whose novel *Monsieur Vénus* (1884) had faced charges of pornography and had been censored in Belgium. Not only was La Vaudère guilty by association, but she had crossed over into the territory of the unfeminine and subversive *bas-bleu*.[36]

Ryner centered his section on La Vaudère around her shift to a provocative style of writing. He opened with an apostrophe, addressing La Vaudère with the condescending "tu" and highlighted the juxtaposition of her earlier poetry collections with two recent works of fiction: "Voici Jane de la Vaudère, couveuse des *Sataniques* et des *Demi-Sexes*. Tu as changé de teinture, gamine. Tu fis jadis des strophes très blanches, oh! si blanches: en rayons d'étoiles, disais-tu; en verre filé, je m'en souviens. Et la liste de tes livres m'apprend que tu restes honorée d'un accessit à l'école où les singes verts récompensent les vieux enfants. Un de tes recueils innocents fut 'mentionné par l'Académie française.'"[37] Ryner characterized her previous verse as charming and innocuous, the product of her innocence as a young woman poet. In the early years, La Vaudère had been complicit with the stylistic expectations of the stereotypical woman poet, and Ryner gladly reduced such tropes to spiders' webs and beams of starlight. La Vaudère may not have been a great poet, but for Ryner, her works had been morally acceptable.

By 1899, La Vaudère had regrettably become, in Ryner's eyes, a "cacographe et pornographe."[38] Her short stories in *Les sataniques*, whose title evokes Barbey d'Aurevilly's celebrated collection *Les diaboliques* (1874), led Ryner to disparage her move to prose and to question her creativity and inventiveness. "Aujourd'hui, le poète manqué s'imagine écrire en prose," he wrote. "Notre ange raté se déguise en démon et imite un titre de Barbey d'Aurevilly."[39] Though Ryner had approved of La Vaudère's unoriginality as a (female) poet, her shift to prose took the form of Decadent fiction, whose themes of gender nonconformity, sexual vice, and malevolent femininity were unsuitable for the conservative critic. Ryner anchored his condemnation in claims of unoriginality (La Vaudère "se déguise" and "imite"), and accused her of plagiarism (and rightfully so). While claims of plagiarism are part of a larger pattern that I examine in detail in the next chapter, it is worth noting here that Ryner specifically targeted the moral and sexual transgressions that she depicted in her fiction. La Vaudère was following a fin-de-siècle trend, and while she had once reproduced clichéd visions in her verse, her "imitation" of her male peers struck Ryner as farcical and naïve: "J'avoue d'ailleurs que, parfois, elle y met un peu plus de bonne volonté. Seulement, voilà, elle a beau faire: elle ne sait pas, la pauvre petite."[40] Ryner dismissed La Vaudère's ostensibly salacious stories as sheer imitation, a fad, and condescendingly reduced her writing to a failed attempt to keep up with the (male) masters. As such, he diminished the threat of her gender transgression as a woman writer and concluded in one final blow, "Ça n'est pas un cygne; c'est une oie."[41]

In response to the publication of *Le massacre des amazones*, La Vaudère wrote an editorial for *La presse* in which she defended women writers and contested the strict gender norms that Ryner endorsed. In doing so, she also promoted a more fluid model of sexual difference and gender expression that was characteristic of the themes of Decadent fiction. In other words, she acknowledged Ryner's critique and doubled down: "S'il y a des femmes peintres, sculpteurs, écrivains, médecins, avocats, il y a des hommes couturiers, blanchisseurs, fleuristes, corsetiers, cuisiniers, bonnes d'enfants. . . . L'antagonisme est complet en cette agonie de siècle et de mœurs; n'était le vêtement, il serait difficile souvent de . . . distinguer."[42]

Through the hyperbolic opposition of "hommes" and "bonnes d'enfants," La Vaudère highlighted the arbitrariness of gender codes and endorsed limitless possibilities for working men and women across all professions. Gesturing toward a modern vision of gender performativity, she insisted that the sole discernible difference between a man and a woman executing the same work lay in their clothing. While Ryner condemned the *bas-bleu* for her perverse androgyny and encroachment on male spaces, La Vaudère responded with a fluid vision of sexual and gender difference in this "agonie de siècle et de mœurs." She added, "Il me semble que, comme dans toutes les civilisations un peu décadentes, le génie artistique et surtout littéraire de la femme s'est beaucoup développé en France."[43] Instead of countering Ryner's attacks with an emphasis on her inherent femininity, La Vaudère embraced narratives that linked modern decadence, female intellect, and the breakdown of distinct gender norms. As a writer of Decadent fiction (and classified alongside Rachilde in Ryner's anthology), she proudly owned her role in this causality, co-opting his portrayal to draw further attention to her own gender transgressions as a woman writer—and *bas-bleu.*

In 1903, La Vaudère continued exploring Decadent themes with her novel *Les androgynes.*[44] Illustrated by Maurice Neumont, the work tapped into fin-de-siècle anxieties about gender ambiguity and was a showcase of cross-dressing opium addicts, cabaret performers, prostitutes, and pimps. Brian Stableford, whose recent translation series pairs *Les demi-sexes* and *Les androgynes* in a single volume, argues that the latter was "obviously written as a companion-piece to *Les Demi-Sexes* [. . .] and blatantly intended as a bid to repeat the specific scandalous success of the earlier novel."[45] Predictably, critics highlighted the indecent content of the novel while nonetheless linking it to inevitable sales, which marked a notable shift from Ryner's commentary four years earlier. The *Revue du cercle militaire* called *Les androgynes* "un livre étrange, audacieux, terrible" but concluded that "*Les androgynes* compteront certainement parmi les romans sensationnels de l'année; il sera lu, relu et discuté."[46] *Le journal*, with a zealous use of exclamation marks, provided its own selection of tantalizing details for curious readers and emphasized the novel's contemporary relevance: "Le plus grand succès du jour! Jane de la Vaudère, en un admirable roman plein d'actualité et de passion, a flétri les dégénérés de la vie parisienne, ces fins-de-sexe de notre décadence, opposant au vice morbide et démentiel la frissonnante magie de l'amour vrai. Le volume, curieusement illustré, contient des peintures troublantes d'orgies, d'ivresses, de voluptés et de cauchemars!"[47] In painting present-day Paris as a stimulating site of decadent debauchery and gender confusion, the passage suggested a sensationalist urgency and social responsibility to read *Les androgynes* that likely appealed to a diverse readership.

Les androgynes was an immediate success, and in April 1903 La Vaudère planned for a theatrical adaptation to further promote a work "qui soulève en ce moment des polémiques si passionnés."[48] While unclear if this production ever took place, the literary and social sensation of *Les androgynes* was once again indicative of La Vaudère's adeptness at exploiting popular trends of the literary marketplace. Just a few months later, in an obvious nod to La Vaudère, Jean Lorrain parodied the marketing savvy of a self-described feminist author in a play for *Le supplément* called "Mme de Larmaille, féministe."[49] The piece ridiculed the protagonist's attempts to boost her sales with salacious novels like *Les hermaphrodites*, whose title was a clear allusion to La Vaudère's *Les androgynes*. A second reference in the play confirmed that Lorrain was familiar with La Vaudère's reputation and its influence on her profits: "Il y a une Mme de la Crapaudère qui fait des livres antiphysiques. Oh! alors, ça, c'est de la vente sûre dans tous les lycées et dans tous les pensionnats."[50] As suggested by the origin of her name (a fusion of La Vaudère's married and pen names), Mme de la Crapaudère was a clear stand-in for La Vaudère. Her "antiphysique" works—those against nature—recalled the themes of gender transgression and sexual deviance found throughout La Vaudère's writing. As a testament to the growing expanse of her celebrity, La Vaudère had become a target of parody. And like Lorrain claimed, she was cognizant of the selling power of scandal and uproar. The very content of *Les androgynes* demonstrates this awareness: the novel's preoccupation with the literary milieus of fin-de-siècle Paris, though highly satirical, serves as a *mise-en-abyme* for the calculated construction of La Vaudère's public image. In a self-referential moment, Jacques Chozelle, the novel's spokesman for Decadent poetics, remarks, "En ce temps de réclame à outrance, il faut se créer une personnalité presque inquiétante pour sortir des rangs, et cela s'use vite, car les *imitateurs* abondent."[51] La Vaudère had indeed created a "disquieting" persona and she did so precisely through imitation. Her swift maneuvering between genres depended on her capacity to mimic thematic and aesthetic trends and assume the corresponding role of Decadent, Naturalist, or Orientalist novelist. As Mary Louise Roberts has shown in her work on the feminist journalists at *La fronde*, mimicry may serve as a subversive act to expose the artifice of essentialist ideologies of femininity and rigid binaries.[52] Through her repeated imitation, La Vaudère contested popular tropes of the woman writer while exploiting an ambiguous authorial image. The next step in this trajectory was a series of erotic Orientalist novels.

ORIENTALIST AND EROTIC FICTION

Following the success of *Les demi-sexes*, La Vaudère continued to write erotically themed fiction that titillated bourgeois readers and critics alike. In 1900, she published *Trois fleurs de volupté*, set in Java, the first of a series of novels that took place in the Far East. Often based on fictionalized accounts of historic or folkloric figures, these works portrayed the customs of countries including India, Japan, and Egypt through an Orientalist lens that accentuated practices of gratuitous violence and unbridled sexuality.[53] Of the near dozen novels of this genre, many took place during ancient times and described in meticulous (and often plagiarized) detail scenes of torture, murder, human sacrifice, rape, incest, prostitution, and orgies. To add a visual thrill, several novels included illustrations of the most provocative settings and people, such as the exotic interior of a harem or a nude prostitute in a seductive dance. Many of these representations were likely based on La Vaudère's imagination or colonialist depictions that she had read or reproduced from others' works. Though La Vaudère alleged to have traveled significantly, there are no surviving passport records to substantiate this, and we know that she was prone to exaggeration. Nonetheless, she often appeared in various "oriental" costumes to promote a forthcoming Orientalist novel or theatrical piece (figs. 6–8).[54] Based on problematic clichés that reinforced colonial narratives, her publicity images were intended to attract potential readers who would be receptive to her works' caricatural content. La Vaudère's Orientalist iconography was thus rooted in a series of performances and appropriations of femininity and otherness that exemplified the continued fluidity of her persona.

The rise in Orientalism in La Vaudère's works coincided with significant European colonial expansion and the Paris Exposition Universelle of 1900, which included pavilions representing a selection of French colonies. These exhibits, visited by millions, emphasized the exoticism of non-Western cultures and often featured musicians and dancers in traditional dress, playing on stereotypes about the colonized Other. La Vaudère capitalized on this display of Orientalism with a new series of novels that fed these fantasies. The timely publication of *Trois fleurs de volupté* was also certain to evoke French dancer Cléo de Mérode and her famous (and inauthentic)

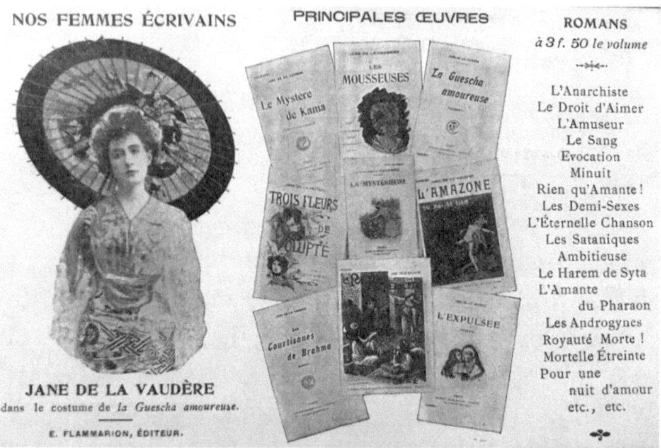

FIG. 6 Postcard advertisement for *La guescha amoureuse*. Author's collection.

FIG. 7 La Vaudère in Orientalist costume. *Revue illustrée*, June 15, 1904.

FIG. 8 La Vaudère in Orientalist costume. *Revue illustrée,* June 15, 1904.

"Cambodian" dance that she debuted at the Exposition. This spectacle had been inspired by her earlier interpretation of Javanese dance, a recording of which was also shown at the Exposition of 1900.[55] Mérode had modeled this dance on illustrations from a book depicting Javanese dancers, which meant that her "Cambodian" dance was one iteration in a series of imitations and appropriations. Both of Mérode's dances were wildly popular with the Exposition crowds yet represented a clichéd, reductionist vision of Javanese and Cambodian cultures (which she also conflated). Visitors marveled at her beauty and allure yet were quick to recognize the inauthenticity of her "Cambodian" performance.[56] To capture her signature dance, Mérode posed in her "Cambodian" costume for celebrity photographer Léopold-Émile Reutlinger (fig. 9), and images from this series

FIG. 9
Cléo de Mérode in "Cambodian" costume. Photo: Reutlinger. Source: gallica.bnf.fr / BnF.

began circulating as postcards across the globe. Mérode's "Cambodian" dance became her trademark both domestically and abroad, and contracts required that she include it—and her costume—in her shows.[57]

The frontispiece of the 1900 edition of *Trois fleurs de volupté* featured a photograph of La Vaudère's face superimposed on Mérode's iconic costumed body from Reutlinger's series (fig. 10). Though increasing in popularity at the time, photomontage was an imperfect technique, and we can see where the shadows of La Vaudère's jawline and the angle of her face do not properly align with the neckline. It also appears that sections of the headpiece were added to conceal the differences in La Vaudère's forehead and hairstyle.[58] In many ways, the inconsistencies of the photo are reminiscent of La Vaudère's plagiarized texts, where she weaved together passages from others' works into a disjointed collage of styles and voices. Through this photographic technology, La Vaudère merged her visual persona with that of the dancer and capitalized on Mérode's rapidly expanding iconography.

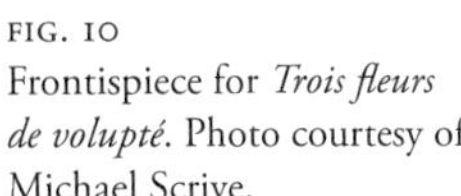

FIG. 10
Frontispiece for *Trois fleurs de volupté*. Photo courtesy of Michael Scrive.

As Michael Garval has shown, Mérode was not just any star. By the late 1890s, she was considered the most widely photographed performer in France (and perhaps the world), and her burgeoning fame was driven by a rise in mass visual culture (postcards, celebrity photography) and a series of scandals that eroticized her public image. Like many female dancers and singers, Mérode's body was scrutinized as an object of desire. Rumors that she was both the mistress of Belgian King Léopold II and the model for Alexandre Falguière's nude statue *La danseuse* fueled her reputation as a courtesan. But these controversies also propelled her fame, and this was something that La Vaudère understood firsthand. The technique of photomontage thus allowed La Vaudère to appropriate Mérode's erotic and exotic public image through a pastiche of narratives and identities. The frontispiece thus encapsulated a sequence of cultural (mis)appropriations, from Mérode's enactment of Javanese and Cambodian cultures (based on colonialist representations) to La Vaudère's co-opting of the dancer's visual celebrity. Ultimately, La Vaudère made a bold claim in this merging of visual personas. By affixing her face to Mérode's body and signing her name to the collage of fragments, La Vaudère equated her public image with the dancer's and declared herself a literary counterpart.

Trois fleurs de volupté was one of many in the genre to be simultaneously lauded and condemned for its erotic content, a paradox that undoubtedly led to more sales. In an acclamatory article entitled "Une princesse d'art," Félicien Champsaur commended La Vaudère's persistent poetic vision that survived her shift to prose. To demonstrate her enduring skill and appeal and inspire readers to purchase her work, he reproduced one of the novel's most suggestive passages in full, promising that "tout le roman [. . .] enveloppe et scintilla aussi joliment."[59] The most titillating parts of the chosen passage depict a sensual dance of three young women that eventually leads to an orgy. This section, a sample provided for everyday readers of *Le journal*, read as follows: "Elles se poursuivent et s'enlacent, se butinent et se pâment, se fuient et se reprennent, lèvres à lèvres, les seins tendus et mêlés. Une sueur fine fait briller leur corps ambré qui se lasse et s'énerve sous les caresses. Enfin, elles s'étendent, les membres déclos, la fleur secrète de leur chair offerte au bien-aimé."[60] The exaggerated eroticization of Javanese culture may have been shocking for some, but it also boosted book sales and increased La Vaudère's international renown and readership. In a 1901 review of *Le mystère de Kama* appearing in London's *The Saturday Review of Politics, Literature, Science, and Art*, a bewildered critic found the prevalence of nudity in the novel excessive, even for *French* literature. "Never, in any French novel, have we come across so much uncovering," the critic wrote, conceding, nonetheless, that "the monkeys alone are respectable."[61]

As La Vaudère's notoriety spread across the channel, it continued to build momentum within the Hexagon. Critics frequently supplemented their reviews with statements about her intended audience or warned when a novel "n'est pas fait pour être mis entre toutes les mains."[62] La Vaudère earned a mention in Louis Bethléem's *Romans à lire et romans à proscrire* under the unequivocal category "romans à proscrire en vertu de la morale chrétienne."[63] Yet while her transition to erotic Orientalist fiction earned her such sensationalist labels as "l'inquiétante Jane de la Vaudère," the ensuing media attention, deemed negative by some, worked to her advantage.[64] One critic commended her innovative and original depictions of sexual vice that broke from the well-read works of contemporaries Paul Bourget and Georges Ohnet: "Au milieu de tant de publications qui ressassent les mêmes banales aventures d'adultères plus ou moins bourgettistes et ohnettistes, un tel livre éclate et vibre de vie ardente, de robuste couleur, de brûlante nervosité, et se compare aux pâles et chêtives [*sic*] productions de la littérature contemporaine."[65] Later, in 1907, the year before her death, *Le journal* announced the publication of *Les prêtresses de Mylitta*, one of the last novels in the genre. However, unlike the ones that preceded it, this novel was illustrated with nude photography. La Vaudère was applauded for the remarkable popularity of her book, as measured by the twenty thousand copies that were printed to keep up with public demand. *Le journal* linked these sales to the images featured throughout the novel, suggesting that the nude models were its main selling point: "C'est qu'il est merveilleusement illustré par le nu photographique d'après les plus jolis modèles parisiens."[66]

In the last year of her life, La Vaudère published three works of fiction that were supplemented with photography "d'après nature," erotic photos that ostensibly illustrated the storyline as it unfolded: *Les prêtresses de Mylitta* (1907), *Le rêve de Mysès* (1907), and *Sapho, dompteuse* (1908). While many books throughout her career featured suggestive illustrations, the eventual progression to photographic nudes was indicative of La Vaudère's espousal of an increasingly sensationalist persona. These works were representative of the photo-literary genre that was popularized in the late nineteenth century (particularly from 1880 to 1910) and suggested evolving marketing tactics on La Vaudère's part in the latter years of her career. In his exhaustive study on the development of photoliterature, Paul Edwards emphasizes the selling value of photo-illustrated fiction at the turn of the century: "Présentée au lecteur comme un atout, l'illustration photographique apparaît sinon comme la raison d'être des romans, du moins comme partie intégrante de leur manière de narrer. [. . .] Il s'agissait avant tout, pour l'éditeur, de réaliser de grosses ventes."[67] However, while the photo-illustrated novel appealed to editors looking to increase their sales, its aesthetic value was controversial among the intellectual elite. In 1898, twenty-four writers participated in a survey initiated by André Ibels for the *Mercure de France* on the role of photography in fiction. Zola was adamantly against integrating photography into literature and warned that potentially salacious images risked overshadowing the aesthetic value of a text: "On tombera tout de suite dans le nu."[68] Ibels echoed Zola's concerns about what he saw as photoliterature's unavoidable shift toward eroticism and voyeurism. Certainly, not all photoliterature featured erotic images. However, Charles Grivel suggests that the "roman 'leste'" and the "récit 'parisien,' distractif et libertin" particularly lent themselves to photographic illustrations that, in turn, depicted the provocative content of their texts.[69] Erotic photography in fiction tended to highlight the female body: "Le roman que nous décrivons consiste moins à raconter une histoire qu'à retourner sous tous les angles ce qui fait l'objet principal, sinon unique, de son attention: *la femme*, ou plutôt sa séduction, ou plutôt son impossible soumission."[70]

With their photographic content, La Vaudère's three works were particularly eye-catching to a public already enticed by the photo-literary genre. However, through their erotic themes and depictions of the naked female body, these texts inscribed La Vaudère in a genre defined less for its aesthetic merit than its sexual provocation. Furthermore, her association with nude photography went beyond the pages of her fiction. For example, in as early as 1902, La Vaudère provided the preface to C. Klary's *La photographie du nu*, a selection of photographs and essays defending the artistic merits of nude photography. La Vaudère's name appeared centered and in bold font on the work's cover, and given her growing notoriety, her contributions were intended to provide both an intellectual and provocative perspective. Her preface, however, focused more generally on the aesthetic exactitude of photography without addressing the nude content of the collection. Nonetheless, through her association with this work, La Vaudère made a conscious effort to boost her sales and deliberately encouraged a narrative that further demonized her.

La Vaudère's continued ability to capitalize on the erotic was no secret in the literary world, even beyond her death. In 1911, two journalists who signed their columns "Les Treize" (Léon Bailby and Fernand Divoire) commented on the recent upsurge and popularity of erotic fiction. Bailby and Divoire offered one simple explanation for these literary trends by evoking La Vaudère. "On s'est étonné souvent du développement prodigieux pris, de nos jours, par la littérature érotique et pornographique," they observed. "Quel mot plus cruel à ce sujet que celui de Jane de la Vaudère, cette charmante femme écrivain, appartenant par sa naissance et son éducation à un milieu des plus honorables, et qui s'écriait, peu de temps avant de mourir: 'N'est-ce pas? Cela vous dégoûte. Et il n'y a pourtant que cela qui se vende!'"[71] In citing her respectable family lineage in a discussion of pornographic literature, the journalists confirmed the power of paradox and conflicting narratives that La Vaudère exploited.

While she was publishing novels at a nearly semiannual rate, La Vaudère was also building her persona through other artistic mediums. In 1901, Félicien Champsaur published *Lulu*, an illustrated clown novel that boasted two hundred "dessins de maîtres" by distinguished artists such as Jules

Chéret, Auguste Rodin, and Félicien Rops.[72] La Vaudère was listed among these renowned contributors and signed her name to three illustrations in the section entitled "Apothéose des Modernités."[73] In these pages, Champsaur described the clownesse's iconographic celebrity in the boulevards, stores, and music halls in the capital city. In a remarkable *mise-en-abyme* of her own trajectory, it seemed suitable that La Vaudère would illustrate Lulu's rise to fame as an emblem for feminine "modernités." Her illustrations corresponded to three particular representations of Lulu at the peak of her fame, in the art world or by the press, in advertisements and photographs. What is most notable about La Vaudère's contributions, however, is that they coincided with Lulu's salacious or transgressive depictions as a sexual being, a cross-dressing lesbian, and a New Woman riding a bicycle (figs. 11–13). Of the two hundred potential illustrations that supplemented Champsaur's novel, it was no coincidence that La Vaudère's name was associated with these three distinct representations. The corresponding text for each image reflected the magnitude of Lulu's celebrity and subversive allure, which was exploited for commercial purposes and poster advertisements.[74] Perhaps this felt familiar to La Vaudère, who provided a voyeuristic visual component that brought this modern, sexual woman to life before the reader's eyes. While the themes of unbridled female desire and gender ambiguity were not new to La Vaudère (figs. 11 and 12), her sketch of Lulu's bicycle advertisement ("Cycles Lulu," fig. 13) marked an important espousal of a clichéd figure of unsettling womanhood in the French cultural imagination. Clad in her bloomers ("culotte bouffante") and zipping down a hill, Champsaur's cycling Lulu was both an emblem of modern femininity and a source of anxiety about the breakdown of the gender binary. At the turn of the century, many bourgeois women relied on the increasingly popular bicycle for mobility and independence. Doctors, journalists, and caricaturists weighed in on the dangers of cycling for women, citing increased risks of hysteria, masturbation, domestic neglect, and a general loss of feminine grace and refinement. In providing the corresponding illustration to *Lulu*, La Vaudère appropriated a narrative about women, mobility, and emancipation that foreshadowed her depiction of women and automobiles (which I discuss in the final chapter). It is especially noteworthy that this was a poster advertisement, a drawing of a drawing, which underscored the elements of imitation and performativity essential to La Vaudère's self-marketing. La Vaudère's illustration, with her name distinctly sketched across the bottom, embodied the savvy manipulation of her own iconography and evolving celebrity.

FIG. 11
Illustrating female eroticism in *Lulu*.

FIG. 12
Illustrating cross-dressing and sapphism in *Lulu*.

FIG. 13
Illustrating the New Woman in *Lulu*.

Given the structural hybridity of *Lulu*, La Vaudère's artistic presence in the novel is one expression of a larger textual—and visual—collaboration with Champsaur that benefited her professional development.[75] Part of this exchange manifested itself intertextually. Consistent with La Vaudère's penchant for plagiarism (see chapter 3), multiple phrases from *Le mystère de Kama* (1901) and *Les androgynes* (1903) were lifted directly from *Lulu*.[76] Furthermore, La Vaudère's short story "Le vernissage," which appeared in the collection *Les mousseuses* (1901), included a playful reference to Champsaur and *Lulu*. As though in dialogue with La Vaudère, Champsaur responded with a positive review of the volume, whose modern Parisian women were reminiscent of his illustrious protagonist: "*Les Mousseuses*, compliquées, cruelles et charmantes, trouvent encore des péchés inédits après tant de criminelle et d'adorable science. [. . .] Jane de la Vaudère s'est attardée à la grâce érotique de ces petites Lulu, de ces sourires clownesques."[77] For sensational works like *Les mousseuses*, La Vaudère had perhaps drawn inspiration from Champsaur's professional path. In 1900, La Vaudère wrote a detailed article for *Gil Blas* commending him for his recent novel, *Poupée japonaise*. She complimented his alluring and audacious portrayal of Japanese culture and emphasized the erotic appeal of his work for women readers: "Romancier à la mode, le favori de la mondaine curieuse aux caprices ardents inassouvis, il est celui que les amantes heureuses ou délaissées lisent en souriant, en soupirant, en pleurant aussi de volupté lasse et renaissante, les nerfs secoués d'un invincible désir."[78] As with her own literary production, La Vaudère acknowledged the marketability of erotically themed fiction. She inflated the titillating elements of Champsaur's novel and encouraged female readers to experience their own sexual awakening through its pages. In so doing, she roused contemporary anxieties about female readership that linked solitary reading with hysteria, nymphomania, masturbation, or romantic fantasies (à la Emma Bovary).[79] As a reader of Champsaur's work, La Vaudère implicated herself in her description of female desire. Intrigued readers were left wondering if she was speaking from personal experience. La Vaudère would contribute her illustrations to *Lulu* just a few months later.

PHOTOJOURNALISM AND LA VAUDÈRE'S VISUAL PERSONA

In her work on Belle Époque photojournalism, Elizabeth Emery examines the trope of the "at-home" interview. Growing in popularity in the 1890s, journalists, accompanied by a professional photographer, would visit a writer or artist in his or her home and offer a rare glimpse into their intimate life. From 1892 until 1904, the *Revue illustrée* published a series of at-home photo-interviews with celebrity figures that presented "private life as a function of their work."[80] During these visits, interviewees gave tours of their private spaces and belongings to bolster their public perception. They maintained full authority over the sort of information that would be shared and eventually disseminated about the private space of the home. Emery notes, "The photo-interview, with its use of direct discourse and reliance on writers to lead reporters through the home, gave them more flexibility to express themselves. Unlike photographs, in which writers appeared as small objects seemingly determined by the objects around them, such interviews recast writers as agents; they acted on the objects, collecting and arranging them in order to create a space in tune with their aesthetic sensibility."[81]

In June 1904, the *Revue illustrée* published one such exposé on La Vaudère. The article was written by Théodore Cahu, who would cowrite *Confessions galantes* with La Vaudère the following year and to whom she would bequeath her manuscripts from her deathbed in 1908. As a professional colleague and likely a personal friend, Cahu penned a piece that was unsurprisingly acclamatory.[82] He provided enticing summaries of her recent Orientalist works and included lengthy excerpts. Overall, the feature read more as a publicity opportunity or biography for La Vaudère than an unprecedented peek into the life of an enigmatic author. In fact, it differed significantly from the typical "at-home" interviews associated with the journal. For one, despite a visit to La Vaudère's Paris home, the article contained no direct quotes from its subject (though we can assume an interview took place). Cahu claimed to visit La Vaudère "dans son bel appartement de la place des Ternes," but the photographs that accompanied his text lacked the intimacy promised by the "at-home" interview.[83] Most of the images in the spread were either advertisements that featured La Vaudère in "original" Orientalist costume or painted portraits that had been reproduced. With the exception of two images of La Vaudère seated among Orientalist furnishings that I discuss below, we have very little sense of her home space. To complicate matters further, though his visit had supposedly occurred in her Parisian apartment, Cahu devoted more detail to the Château de La Vaudère and provided an image of the exterior of the property. Regrettably, the captions did not specify which of the two interior photos had been taken at the château (where she continued to sojourn after her divorce), and which had been taken in her Paris apartment. Nonetheless, these images—some of the few we have of La Vaudère—allow us to further locate how she constructed her celebrity through a multilayered iconography. The photographs and paintings that supplement Cahu's piece are remarkably diverse in tone and subject matter. Two familiar and contrasting themes emerge: the mystifying and eccentric La Vaudère, whose subversion of gender norms is contrasted with the virtuous and docile La Vaudère, the embodiment of normative femininity. The exposé in the *Revue illustrée* epitomizes La Vaudère's skillful performance of the alluring contradictions of her persona.

The cover image of the *Revue illustrée* hints at the multidimensional iconography presented in the pages that followed. It features a large colored portrait of La Vaudère by artist Charles Atamian (fig. 14), who later provided provocative illustrations for many of her eroticized novels.[84] The depiction of the author in an elegant white ballgown, shoulders and upper chest exposed, suggests that the "documents photographiques" within the issue will explore the disjunction between her graceful refinement and erotic literary penchants. Seated in a medieval cathedra and leaning casually on her elbow in confident command, La Vaudère resembles an empress holding court (or a literary salon) in her home, where readers of the *Revue illustrée* are invited to join her. When compared side by side, La Vaudère's portrait resembles the cover image for her novel *Le harem de Syta*, also illustrated by Atamian and published around the same time (fig. 15). The work's cover depicts the Reine Syta before her harem of men, her arms and legs positioned exactly like La Vaudère's in her portrait for the *Revue illustrée*. Both women are also seated regally in an elevated chair with a stiff wooden frame, their heads slightly tilted. Except for her bare chest, Syta could be a stand-in for La Vaudère, and vice versa. These two images appeared within months of each other, and it is difficult to conclude which one, if any, served as an original template. Did La Vaudère inspire the depiction of Syta, or did Syta inspire the depiction of La Vaudère? The uncertain timeline of these images exemplifies the fluidity of La Vaudère's image and its blend of European and Orientalist tropes of womanhood. The visual parallels between the elegant La Vaudère and the half-naked ruler of a harem also expose the fragility of European bourgeois codes of femininity.

Like its cover, the images featured inside the *Revue illustrée* were representative of the multiple narratives of La Vaudère's celebrity. Many of the photographs in Cahu's article were likely reprinted from other contexts or supplied by La Vaudère herself. These included advertisements for her Orientalist works of fiction in which she appeared in exotic costume

REVUE ILLUSTRÉE

Publication bimensuelle fondée en 1885 à la librairie d'Art L. BASCHET

ABONNEMENTS
Trois Mois. FRANCE 9fr. ETRANGER 10fr.
Six Mois. — 18fr. — 20
Un An — 36fr — 40

Paul-Franz NAMUR directeur
Administration & Rédaction
29 rue Bonaparte
PARIS

16068

Dix-neuvième Année
n° 13 — 15 Juin 1904

SOMMAIRE

THÉODORE CAHU
Jane de la Vaudère
Documents photographiques

Dr ANDRÉ ROBLOT
La Lutte anti-tuberculeuse en France et l'œuvre de la tuberculose humaine
Photos : Bouyer et Marius

DAN-LÉON
La fête des humoristes
Le Bal « Henri Monnier » au Casino de Paris
Photos : du Guy, Mathieu-Deroche, Sescau

HIPPOLYTE BUFFENOIR
Les Beaux jours de Weimar
Documents photographiques

GEORGES CASELLA
Chronique littéraire

LOUIS SCHNEIDER
Echos de Théâtres

La Vie Mondaine

ÉDOUARD DUPONT
Les Grands Sports

ALBERT DE ROCHETAL
Chronique graphologique

Échos Mondains

1 fr. 50 le N°

Mme Jane de la Vaudère

intended to represent, through cultural appropriation, the respective novel's setting (figs. 7–8). The article integrated a second and more conventional portrait of La Vaudère (fig. 16) that stood in contrast to her Orientalist iconography. In some photos, readers encountered a meeker version of the European La Vaudère "en toilette de soirée" and in a lacy white gown adorned with a neck and wrist corsage. The painting's dark background

FIG. 14 (OPPOSITE)
The cover of the *Revue illustrée*. Charles Atamian, June 15, 1904.

FIG. 15
The cover of *Le harem de Syta*. Charles Atamian, 1904.

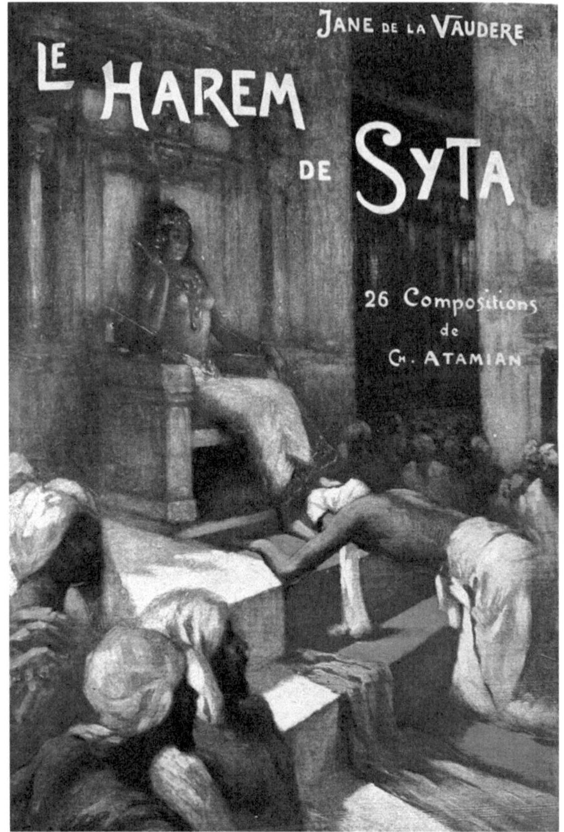

accentuates her halo of blond hair—not unlike Marguerite Durand's—and a closed fan rests passively at her waist as she gazes expectantly into the distance. In addition to these representations, two other photographs provide access to La Vaudère's domestic sphere. In these images, La Vaudère appears in her home, presumably at the Place des Ternes, seated among Orientalist furnishings. Because they were taken in her home, readers would have likely assumed that these two photographs—as opposed to a painted portrait—offered an authentic and unaltered view of La Vaudère's intimate space.

The *Revue illustrée*'s domestic depictions of La Vaudère reaffirmed preestablished ideas about the author. This tended to be the cyclical effect of the "at-home" press exposé, where, as Emery observes, the "author becomes a reflection of his fiction and the descriptions of the home confirm the public's preconceived ideas about both author and work."[85] As her persona became increasingly associated with the exotic cultures that she described

FIG. 16 A meeker La Vaudère. *Revue illustrée*, June 15, 1904.

in her novels, so did her home. For some readers, her home seemed a sanctuary where she could explore and perform orientalized otherness. André de Fouquières, for example, envisioned her as a recluse in her Place des Ternes apartment, "où elle se plaisait à se vêtir comme une geisha."[86] Her domestic space was seen as both an extension of her person and a formidable influence on her character. In turn, descriptions and visuals of her home life provided an opportunity to decipher her eclecticism, to "read dwelling as an indicator of character."[87] For example, in a piece appearing in the journal *L'écho du merveilleux*, Madame Louis Maurecy visited La Vaudère's home to learn about the writer's expertise in the science of the occult, a recurrent theme in her fiction. In her description, Maurecy focuses primarily on the décor of La Vaudère's home as both an expression of her writing and extension of her person. She writes, "Le salon où me reçoit Mme de la Vaudère est en harmonie avec le sujet qui m'a conduit vers elle: des vitraux l'éclairent de lueurs fantastiques et autour de nous les grands bouddahs d'or semblent nous écouter gravement."[88] The unusual structure of Maurecy's article is itself a reflection of the interplay of home, work, and character in La Vaudère's public image. After describing the intrigue of La Vaudère's salon, the journalist moves to direct discourse for the remainder of the piece, and La Vaudère narrates firsthand her experience with the supernatural world. However, what recounts is a nearly verbatim reproduction of the preface to her recent novel, *La sorcière d'Ecbatane*, whose content had supposedly been dictated to her by a transient spirit.[89] Maurecy's textual collage "interview" blurs the boundaries of La Vaudère's work, personal voice, and eccentric home design and reflects the fluidity of her persona. Indeed, uninformed witnesses of this tangled exchange "semblent croire que [La Vaudère] vient de rêver là une page nouvelle d'un roman fantastique."[90]

Cahu emphasized the Orientalist décor of La Vaudère's residencies and described the collection of artifacts that she had supposedly acquired while traveling. In contrasting the demure La Vaudère with the Orientalist embellishment of her apartment, Cahu positioned the author's conventional femininity against the nonconformity of her intimate space. He notes that La Vaudère "s'entoure d'œuvres d'art et de bibelots charmants. Mince et droite dans sa cathèdre moyenâgeuse à haut dossier, nimbée de la lueur changeante des vitraux, elle semble, au milieu des grands bouddahs d'or qui inspirèrent sans doute beaucoup de ses romans, une frêle idole de grâce et de douceur sous la garde des dieux terribles. Un vaste divan, sous un dais fleuragé de vieille soie nipponne, invite aux longues rêveries. Près d'un harmonium aux nombreux registres, une étrange Salomé joue du psaltérion."[91] Among the "meubles aux fines ciselures hindoues" and the "dragons aux écailles flamboyantes," La Vaudère gives off an aura of enchantment as a delicate fairy weaving together storylines: "Une fée habite ce logis de fée et y tisse, de ses doigts fragiles, la toile d'or de ses prestigieux romans."[92] The accompanying photo illuminates the contrast between the looming exotic backdrop and La Vaudère's Western feminine clothing (fig. 17). Captioned "Jane de la Vaudère dans son salon," the photo features an unsmiling La Vaudère, dressed in an elaborate white dress, against a dark backdrop of Orientalist artwork and furniture towering over her. Like the cover portrait of the *Revue illustrée*, La Vaudère is seated in a high-back chair with her head pensively resting on her hand, and a white fur shawl draped over her shoulders. In her "grâce" and "douceur," she nonetheless commands a self-assured authority.

One particular photo of La Vaudère working at her desk strongly communicated this image of discovery and conquest (fig. 18).[93] La Vaudère is seated and writing, her feet positioned upon a female lion's skin—a type

FIG. 17 La Vaudère at home. *Revue illustrée*, June 15, 1904.

of colonial trophy—that lies on the floor under her desk, its legs spilling over the frame of the photograph onto the text of the page. The dead lion, fangs visible, is gazing directly into the camera as La Vaudère's eyes focus on the page under her pen. A sculpture of a partially nude woman likely representing Venus—an emblem of feminine desire—overlooks La Vaudère as she writes. The underlying message is unequivocal: La Vaudère as creative master of the exotic and erotic content of her fiction. The portrait of the

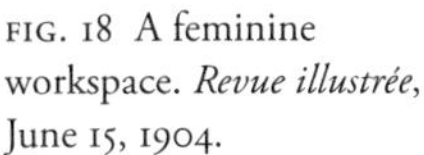

FIG. 18 A feminine workspace. *Revue illustrée*, June 15, 1904.

pensive, laborious (male) writer at his desk was a common trope in the nineteenth century. Nearing the turn of the twentieth century, the corresponding image of the woman writer at her desk grew more common in women's magazines *Femina* and *La vie heureuse*. This symbolic staging situated the woman writer within reach of the intellectual authority associated with the *grand homme*. However, as Rachel Mesch points out, the magazines offset potentially troubling connotations with peripheral reminders of the writer's conventional femininity, such as background floral patterns or embroidered fabrics draped nearby.[94] In particular, visual references to domesticity and motherhood assured readers of a woman writer's inherent bourgeois values. At times, children even made appearances alongside their working mothers.

La Vaudère's pose at her writing desk, diligently at work, provides no hints of her domestic responsibilities, unlike analogous portraits discussed by Mesch. There are no floral silhouettes to offset the harsh angles of her desk or quill pen, and no lingering ornaments that recall traditional womanhood. The pleated opening toward the bottom of her gown suggests that it was designed for the intimate space of her home. In choosing to pose in such attire, La Vaudère refuses to mask or beautify the intimacy of her writing routine.[95] Instead, the image brings into relief the eccentricity of her workspace through two central objects that frame her from head to toe: the female lion's head and the bare-breasted sculpture. Both spill over the margins of the photo into the text of the page, suggesting an unruliness that cannot be contained within the limits of the image, nor the larger montage. These figures combine to create an exclusively feminine space for artistic creativity, and the absence of males—human or animal—hints at female self-sufficiency and desire. The central placing of the sculpture's breasts adds an erotic charge to the image, and the white folds of her clothing mimic those of La Vaudère. The geometrical symmetry between the two figures conflates La Vaudère with female desire, and the statue's elevation in the frame suggests that La Vaudère conjured her through her pen. Furthermore, the Buddha collectibles referenced by Cahu are reminiscent of lesbian poet Renée Vivien (1877–1909), whose obsession with Buddha figurines—she purchased one daily—was later portrayed by Colette in her work *Le pur et l'impur* (1932). Though the seemingly heterosexual La Vaudère did not move in the same Parisian lesbian circles as Vivien, their mutual Buddha collections likely linked La Vaudère, through association, with transgressive female sexuality. The plethora of Asian art, antiques, and religious figures captured in these photos and Cahu's text carries sexual undertones: in evoking what Elizabeth Emery calls "longstanding European associations between the acquisition of Asian art and female sexual appetites," La Vaudère's domestic space is suggestive of unbridled sexual expressions and desires.[96] Certainly, other visuals of Cahu's larger piece offset the erotic ambivalence of these photos, such as the painting (fig. 16) depicting La Vaudère as a model of conventional womanhood. But these signs of conservative feminine values do not infiltrate her workspace, and even the plain white gown in the painting lacks the charm and seductive pull of other images.

The lion's skin at La Vaudère's feet recalls the iconography of Belle Époque actress Sarah Bernhardt, who was photographed by Paul Marsan (alias Dornac) and Paul Nadar in her home and surrounded by various animal-skin rugs. Early in her stage career, Colette also posed with a lion's skin, wearing only a negligée and positioned seductively atop the dead feline. This imagery follows erotic tropes from the nineteenth century, when animal skins were used frequently as props in pornography.[97] By the turn of the century, lions and large cats appeared alongside a series of women challenging the status quo. These felines stood in as metaphors for female emancipation and the strength of unbridled femininity. For example, Marguerite Durand was often seen strolling the city streets with her lion, Tigre. In 1910, Durand appeared on the cover of *Femina* with Tigre resting dutifully at her feet. The photo's caption, however, anticipated Tigre's eventual disobedience: "Mais la petite lionne deviendra une grande lionne, et Mme Durand n'envisage pas sans inquiétude cette inévitable éventualité."[98] Charlotte Foucher Zarmanian highlights the performative subversion inherent in the woman-and-lion duo: "Une façon de 'faire leur cirque!,' pour reprendre l'expression convenue, c'est-à-dire se donner en spectacle, se mettre en scène, afin de provoquer le dérèglement des principes établis."[99] A favorite trope in the popular nineteenth-century imagination portrayed lions at the mercy of the woman trainer, a figure of power and domination. In the second half of the nineteenth century, the "dompteuse" was a thrilling source of entertainment for circus-goers but also a symbol of female authority. The "dompteuse" appeared in artistic renderings, advertisements, and works of fiction, while inspiring real-life copycats. For example, in a declaration of defiance, novelist and socialite Madeleine Deslandes entered a cage at a fair in Neuilly and tamed a lion by reading a poem by Jean Richepin.[100] La Vaudère was surely inspired by this trope, and one of her last novels, *Sapho, dompteuse* (1908), featured a lion tamer with a name that unsubtly rejects conventional heterosexual femininity. In appearing at her writing desk with a lifeless lion skin under her feet, teeth exposed in futile aggression, La Vaudère taps into a visual cult of transgressive womanhood.

LA VAUDÈRE'S ENDURING LEGACY

In tracing La Vaudère's writing career from her early traditionalist poetry to the eroticized fiction of her final years, we can locate the gradual transformation of her public image. Over time, La Vaudère's persona evolved in response to shifting narratives in the press, which themselves were inspired by more daring literary choices on her part. Her relationship with the media was characterized by a cyclical causality: her subversive texts drew increased critical attention, and she fueled this notoriety with new provocative novels, each one more shocking than the last. Through a succession of appropriations, performances, and imitations, La Vaudère marketed a public image that concurrently exposed the arbitrariness and instability of conventional codes of womanhood. Today, though many of La Vaudère's works have been omitted from French literary history, the eccentricities of her persona have survived into the twenty-first century. Recent historical novels by enthusiasts of the Belle Époque attest to this. Tiphaine Mora's *Belles à lier* (2018, Num) and Brian Stableford's *The Quiet Dead* and *The Painter of Spirits* (2019, Black Coat Press) reimagine La Vaudère in the cultural context of the fin de siècle. She appears in *Belles à lier* as a feminist mentor to a young writer, smoking cigarillos and parading through Paris in a kimono. *The Painter of Spirits* envisions her fervent participation in occult séances and hypnosis experiments that reconnect her with her late mother. In our modern cultural imagination, there are few remaining traces of the soft-spoken and sentimental poetess. The influence of La Vaudère's marketing savvy appears to have endured into the twenty-first century.

CHAPTER 3

La Vaudère's Plagiarism

Subversion Through Copy

With the use of modern plagiarism software, I have yet to find a novel by La Vaudère that does not contain passages from other published works. During her career, some critics had already identified her trend for copying and denounced her as a plagiarist. Shortly following the publication of her novel *Le sang* in 1898, a revolted Han Ryner wrote, "J'ai sous la main *le* [*sic*] *Sang*, nouveau recueil de phrases de Barbey d'Aurevilly et de Guy de Maupassant, mises en désordre, rendues incorrectes et salies par les soins de Jane de La Vaudère."[1] As Patrick Chadoqueau has brought to our attention, an 1897 issue of the literary periodical *La province nouvelle* noted the "curieuses *coïncidences*" between Maupassant's novel *Notre cœur* (1890) and La Vaudère's *Les demi-sexes* (1897).[2] Georges Maurevert's *Le livre des plagiats* (1922), a registry of literary forgers, includes a reference to the "aimable bas-bleu" whose serial novel *La belle Émilienne* (1901) bears undeniable traces of Gustave Flaubert's *Madame Bovary*.[3] In a piece on Joris-Karl Huysmans, scholar Jean de Palacio cites La Vaudère's plagiarism to demonstrate the far-reaching impact of her Decadent peer.[4] La Vaudère's rampant copying has not entirely escaped critics from her lifetime or ours. Yet many have been quick to dismiss her as a plagiarist without considering the larger literary, theoretical, or aesthetic implications of her copying in the context of her persona and *œuvre*. This chapter takes an alternative view of her plagiarism as a medium for reappropriation and transgression and lays the groundwork for more comprehensive readings in the future.

There is no question that La Vaudère liberally copied from other works and reproduced countless passages in her writing. In her historical and Orientalist fiction, it was not uncommon for La Vaudère to digress from the plotline to provide lengthy descriptions of the cultures, traditions, or landscapes of Asia or the Middle East. These digressions read as jarring ruptures or stylistic shifts that distract from the progression of the story and conveniently signal the presence of authors like Éliphas Lévi, Ernest Bosc, Gustave Le Bon, Léon Denis, or Gaston Maspero, to name just a few.[5] La Vaudère's Decadent and Naturalist novels drew from major nineteenth-century fiction writers and literary critics, including Émile Zola, Honoré de Balzac, Alfred de Musset, Adolphe Belot, Théophile Gautier, Paul Bourget, and Pierre Loti, among others. She depicted fin-de-siècle nervous conditions (hysteria, madness, degeneration) through the language of medical texts by Henry Maudsley and Théodule-Armand Ribot.[6] The work and influence of Maupassant, in particular, show up frequently in her novels.[7] Whereas *La province nouvelle* (mentioned above) links only four excerpts from *Les demi-sexes* to Maupassant's *Notre cœur*, a more thorough reading shows that this is a gross underestimation of his impact on her novel.[8] In reality, *Les demi-sexes* reproduced a multitude of passages from *Notre cœur* and Maupassant's travel memoirs, "La Sicile" (1886) and "La côte italienne" (1890).[9] This chapter addresses these works in two parts. The first section examines the Mediterranean landscape in *Les demi-sexes*, a novel about clandestine ovariectomies, as an allegorical site of rebirth and female fertility inspired by Maupassant's construction of femininity and Sicily. In copying detailed descriptions from Maupassant's travel memoirs, La Vaudère destabilizes essentialist and medical discourses on female sexuality and invites a more nuanced reading of her novel's conservative conclusion. The second section considers how *Les demi-sexes* subversively reappropriates *Notre cœur*'s underlying warnings against the malevolence of modern femininity to privilege female subjectivity. Despite the traditionalist narratives about womanhood that frame all three works, my reading brings to light the transgressive possibilities of La Vaudère's plagiarism and its disruption of essentialist discourses on gender difference. Comparative readings of passages from *Les demi-sexes* and Maupassant's texts can inform our understanding of how a *femme de lettres* engaged with male-authored works of her time and their preoccupation with malevolent femininity and essentialist conceptions of womanhood. As we have seen in the previous chapter, La Vaudère constructed her public image through a series of imitations and appropriations of popular tropes (like the *bas-bleu*, New Woman, or

Orientalist dancer, for example). Plagiarism is another manifestation of her mimicry. With the collage of voices that makes up her corpus, we may also consider her plagiarism as a metaphor for the fluidity of her persona and a pastiche of identities that she continually reworked and maintained.

Plagiarism is a sticky subject, tied to perpetually evolving legal, cultural, and aesthetic understandings of authorship and intellectual property.[10] In her compelling study on the literary and cultural implications of plagiarism, Hélène Maurel-Indart underscores the inevitable interconnectedness of literary production. "Le livre ne vient jamais seul," she notes. "Le langage littéraire est dialogue de langages. [. . .] Écrire, c'est réécrire."[11] Inspired by the postmodern notions of *bricolage* and intertextuality, Maurel-Indart's emphasis on an infinite network of textual and discursive interchange provides a framework that values literary exchange and reciprocity over ethical questions and criteria for authorship. For the purpose of this study, postmodernist approaches to plagiarism offer the possibility of considering so-called stolen texts as distinct products of literary creation that are in active and continuous relation to their predecessors. Such positions view contemporary notions of originality, ownership, and plagiarism as fluid and in constant negotiation with aesthetic and cultural influences. Recognizing plagiarism as a cultural construct challenges the notion of solitary and exclusive authorship, thereby leaving room for an interrogation of the relationship between texts.[12] A relational approach to La Vaudère's plagiarism is a useful strategy for feminist scholarship seeking to contextualize her contributions to Decadent and Naturalist portrayals of malevolent femininity. As Debora Halbert argues, a postmodern feminist framework for understanding plagiarism is valuable in that it may consider the "copying" of a male-authored text as a subversive act of appropriation.[13] This methodology exposes the ways in which the new, often disputed work actually calls for an interrogation of the original. More specifically, such conceptualizations of authorship enlighten our understanding of La Vaudère's contributions to nineteenth-century literature and reveal how La Vaudère's plagiarism is, paradoxically, a creative tool for reimagining a fin-de-siècle model of femininity.

PART I: *EN SICILE* AND *LES DEMI-SEXES*

Les demi-sexes is representative of La Vaudère's recurrent depiction of nonnormative sexuality. However, its initial resistance to essentialist discourses on female procreative duty—a seemingly feminist position—is ultimately complicated by an eventual restoration of moral and gender codes in the novel's depraved Parisian society. The novel documents the aftermath of Camille de Luzac's *ovariotomie*, a secret procedure that allows her to embark upon a quest for sexual fulfillment that would otherwise be hindered by risks of pregnancy. Despite the novel's assertion of sexual freedom and rejection of normative, procreative gender roles, Camille falls madly in love, marries, embarks on a Mediterranean honeymoon, and ultimately regrets her inability to procreate. She and her coterie of "demi-sexes" are eventually punished by death or imprisonment, and the novel concludes with an emphatic and contradictory return to sexual order.[14] The narrative vacillates between the initial declaration of female sexual agency and a promotion of conservative doctrines advocating marriage and maternity. The shift in moral tone occurs not in Paris but in a Sicilian setting. La Vaudère's sixty-page depiction of Camille's honeymoon draws heavily from Maupassant's travel memoir "La Sicile" and his impressions of the island's scenery and sculptures.[15] Sicily plays a pivotal role in establishing the novel's conservative dénouement: the replicated portrayals of the island's bountiful harvests, untamed coastline, and unruly volcano bring to light the novel's underlying interrogation of sexual (and textual) authenticity. While this natural landscape—a symbol for untainted femininity and hopeful antidote to Camille's loss of womanhood—appears in stark contrast to the artifice of Paris and its sterilized "demi-sexes," Maupassant's passages underscore the novel's preoccupation with "natural" femininity. The copied passages, artificial in their own way, highlight, through a paradoxical *mise-en-abyme*, the artifice and precariousness of the essentialist model of womanhood that they represent.

Ovariectomies in *Les demi-sexes*

As Michael Finn has demonstrated, the *ovariotomie*, first practiced in France in 1882 to combat hysterical symptoms, developed into a controversial method of birth control that pitted feminist and pronatalist groups against one another.[16] At the time of its development, France was still recovering from the devastating Franco-Prussian War, and the threat of depopulation continued to occupy medical and literary texts. By 1895, two years before the publication of *Les demi-sexes*, deaths outnumbered births in the Hexagon (852,000 to 834,000, according to historian Karen Offen).[17] The contentious medical procedure tapped into scientific anxieties about the country's declining birth rate and female sexual autonomy. Female sterilization was a literary plot device in the late nineteenth century used to corroborate the correlation between depopulation and female procreative duties. In the "novel of problematized reproduction," women who opt for sterilization are depicted as oversexed, defeminized beings who irresponsibly swap the joys of motherhood for the pleasures of the flesh.[18] These works often feature Paris as the vice-ridden epicenter for sterilization of the debauched. In addition to La Vaudère's *Les demi-sexes*, other examples in the genre include Camille Pert's *Les florifères* (1898); Armand Dubarry's *Les femmes eunuques* (1899); and Émile Zola's *Fécondité* (1899).

Typical of the contemporary "novel of problematized reproduction," La Vaudère's Paris epitomizes the sexual and moral vice associated with female sterilization. The first section of the novel presents the depraved capital city as its backdrop. In these initial chapters, feminist discourses denouncing the marital and reproductive plights of women abound. At the forefront of these arguments is Nina Saurel, whose championing of gender egalitarianism provides a persuasive defense of Camille's controversial operation. Convinced by her friend's assertions, Camille claims control over her reproductive capacities through the "souverain remède" of surgery.[19] In an act of great irony, Camille's decision to have her ovaries—and conventional womanhood—removed seems the only *natural* option for this modern woman: "Camille nourrissait des idées absolument contraires aux idées reçues; elle avait déjà souffert, seule au milieu du plus affreux désert [. . .]. Dans ces conditions, la résolution qu'elle avait prise était *naturelle* quoique folle."[20] La Vaudère's syntax suggests that Camille's operation allows her to reclaim and redefine femininity as it corresponds to her personal needs and experiences. In other words, the surgical removal of her procreative capacities makes her more of a woman ("plus, peut-être," confirms Nina).[21] However, Camille's forthcoming travels to the fertile Mediterranean coastline expose, through glaring juxtaposition, the moral and physical deficiencies of this mutated womanhood.

As a tribute to this newly defined femininity, Nina holds monthly "soupers des 'demi-sexes,'" exclusive gatherings for this community of women who have each gone under Dr. Richard's scalpel. The women, nearly all Parisian, form their own community in a common declaration of sexual autonomy and refusal of normative gender roles. In a celebration of the artificial, Nina equates sterilization with a rejection of the cruel intentions of *natural* femininity: "Je ne me révolte pas seulement contre l'humanité, mais contre la nature qui nous a donné toutes les souffrances, toutes les peines, tous les châtiments, sans nulle compensation, sans nulle joie réelle."[22] The evenings, which often deteriorate into drunken scenes of sexual debauchery, are affirmations of the unflinching, unforgiving sexual prowess of their attendees. In a call for malevolent dominance over their male partners, the circle of "les demi-sexes" rebuffs the conventions of the heterosexual, procreative union in a celebration of a new kind of womanhood. While the decadent gatherings mark Camille's initiation into a Parisian world of vice and degeneracy, she soon begins to resist this lifestyle choice. Despite the apparent feminist ideals advocated by Nina and her entourage, Camille, unfulfilled by the social and sexual promises of sterilization, profoundly regrets her decision, signaling a tension within the novel's celebration of reproductive emancipation. Camille's trip to Sicily substantiates this conflict.

Copy and *Mise-en-Abyme*: "La Vénus de Syracuse"

From *Les demi-sexes*'s initial pages, La Vaudère associates Sicily with fertility. The novel opens with a sonnet commemorating "La Vénus de Syracuse." A tribute to her "flancs puissants" and her "blanches mamelles," the reproductive model of femininity seems a far cry from the sterilized Parisian "demi-sexes" that occupy the first section of the novel.[23] La Vaudère's epigraph-poem is in fact an homage to the Venus Landolina, a second-century-AD Roman statue discovered in a Syracuse nymphaeum in 1804. The marble statue, on display today at the Syracusan Regional Archaeological Museum, is believed to be a copy of an original Greek statue dating from the second century BC. A great archaeological find of the nineteenth century, the Venus Landolina held significant aesthetic and symbolic value at the time of La Vaudère's sonnet. In fact, Maupassant's highly anticipated travel to the Mediterranean island was largely inspired by the possibility of viewing this piece. In his elaborate tribute in "La Sicile," Maupassant extols the statue's embodiment of authentic, unadorned femininity: "Ce n'est point la femme poétisée, la femme idéalisée, [. . .] c'est la femme telle qu'elle est, telle qu'on l'aime, telle qu'on la désire, telle qu'on la veut étreindre."[24] For Maupassant, this femininity, a sculpted replica that he ironically perceives as pure in form, is also a celebration of procreation, of "l'amour impétueux d'où sort notre race" and "l'affolant mystère de la vie."[25] The statue, a copy of an original, is a re-presentation of normative (i.e., reproductive) femininity for Maupassant.

La Vaudère's sonnet, published roughly ten years later, also reads like a copy. Her Venus Landolina "dort, tout debout, forte, impudique, grasse" and bears unequivocal traces of Maupassant's ("elle est *grasse*, avec la poitrine *forte*, [. . .] qu'on rêve *couchée* en la voyant *debout*").[26] Like Maupassant, La Vaudère recognizes the headless statue as creator of "une virile race" and an embodiment for female reproduction.[27] The conflation of the Italian island with female procreation and fertility, common to both La Vaudère and Maupassant, prefigures the symbolism of the protagonist's honeymoon travels to Sicily. "La Vénus de Syracuse" provides a framework for the novel's underlying tensions concerning the authenticity of womanhood and authorship, or if I may, of sexual and textual reproduction. Because Maupassant's celebration of genuine, untainted femininity here is in fact a celebration of replicated, fabricated femininity, La Vaudère's plagiarism signals a fabrication on multiple levels, a copy of many copies.[28] La Vaudère's "La Vénus de Syracuse" celebrates the "natural" essence of womanhood by lifting Maupassant's description of the Venus de Landolina statue, which is itself a reproduction of an ancient Greek statue of Aphrodite, the goddess of idealized femininity. This sequence of reproductions recalls La Vaudère's mimicry of Cléo Mérode and her Javanese dance, which was also one copy in a series (see chapter 2). As with Mérode's case, the successive (re)constructions of womanhood ironically reflect the artifice of this vision of femininity. In the context of the controversial ovariectomy, La Vaudère's plagiarism has the effect of undermining, through copy, essentialist models of gender difference.

Upon the couple's arrival in Italy, Camille exhibits signs of the profound moral transformation that is underway. In a break from the debauchery and remorse that characterized her Parisian lifestyle, the sterile urbanite assumes a newfound normative femininity that is born out of her seaside travels with her husband. "Camille était devenue une autre femme," writes La Vaudère, "toute de tendresse et de grâce. Elle plaisait, elle ravissait par l'imprévu de sa féminité."[29] Her moral rebirth within a heterosexual marriage also has sexual implications, for it is with her husband, while in Italy, that she experiences erotic fulfillment for the first time: "Camille trouvait son *premier amant* dans son mari!"[30] La Vaudère establishes a causality between the restoration of Camille's womanhood and the lush Mediterranean landscape that surrounds her. In stark juxtaposition to the decadence and depravity embodied by the Parisian circle of "les demi-sexes," Italy's unsullied coastline initially invigorates the newlyweds. The Mediterranean scenery, in its purest, most natural state, is a metaphor for the regeneration promised by Camille's union with Georges. However, as a comparison between the two texts reveals, it is also nearly a direct copy of Maupassant's reflections in "La côte italienne."

> *Les demi-sexes*: "Jamais ils n'avaient senti une impression de béatitude comparable à celle du repos qu'ils goûtèrent dans cette crique verte solitaire et silencieuse. [. . .] Ils trouvèrent des grottes mystérieuses et fraîches, des écueils à fleur d'eau qui portaient des crinières d'herbes marines. Ils voyaient flotter, sous eux, dans les ondulations de la vague, des plantes roses et bleuâtres où glissaient d'immenses familles à peine écloses de jeunes poissons."[31]
>
> *En Sicile*: "Jamais peut-être, je n'ai senti une impression de béatitude comparable à celle de l'entrée dans cette crique verte [. . .]. [E]t moi je vais rôder dans mon canot, le long des côtes, dans les grottes où grogne la mer au fond des trous invisibles [. . .], et sur les écueils à fleur d'eau qui portent des crinières d'herbes marines. J'aime voir flotter sous moi, dans les ondulations de la vague insensible, ces longues plantes rouges ou vertes où se mêlent, où se cachent, où glissent les immenses familles à pleine closes de jeunes poissons."[32]

This supposed natural landscape, copied from Maupassant's text, exhibits its own signs of artificiality on a textual level. This textual artificiality parallels an artificiality associated with Camille's sexuality and womanhood, or more specifically, her inability to procreate. In duplicating Maupassant's passages that conflate the Sicilian terrain with untamed, fertile femininity, La Vaudère problematizes male-authored constructions of womanhood in the literary and medical realms alike.

Camille's next destination—Sicily—marks a stylistic rupture in the text and brings the reader back full circle to the novel's epigraph, "La Vénus de Syracuse." As we have seen, La Vaudère's partially plagiarized sonnet frames the text and establishes an association between female fertility and the Italian island. Camille's arrival, the culmination of a desperate attempt to escape the realities of her sterilization, signals a pivotal moment in a novel riddled with ideological tensions. La Vaudère confirms the symbolic significance of this phase of the journey through a narrative shift that strays from the storyline to laud the natural and artistic attractions of the region. Now in the present tense, this jarring section reads like a French tourism guide and provides a detailed portrait of the island as a metaphor for femininity. La Vaudère brings into relief the seductive and impetuous nature of a landscape that has yet to be sufficiently tamed by French travelers.

> *Les demi-sexes*: "On est convaincu, en France, que la Sicile est d'un accès difficile, et si quelques voyageurs courageux s'aventurent parfois jusqu'à Palerme, ils s'en reviennent satisfaits, sans pousser plus loin leur visite. [. . .] Pourtant, les beautés naturelles et artistiques de la Sicile sont particulièrement remarquables et méritent bien de retenir l'attention. Tous les peuples désirèrent et possédèrent cette contrée charmante, ardemment convoitée comme une jeune et belle maîtresse . . . Autant que l'Espagne, elle est le paradis des fruits d'or, le sol fleuri dont l'air, au printemps, n'est qu'un parfum, et elle allume, chaque nuit, au-dessus de la mer, le fanal mystérieux d'Etna, le plus grand volcan d'Europe!"[33]
>
> *En Sicile*: "On est convaincu, en France, que la Sicile est un pays sauvage, difficile et même dangereux à visiter. De temps en temps, un voyageur, qui passe pour un audacieux, s'aventure jusqu'à Palerme, et il revient en déclarant que c'est une ville très intéressante. [. . .] A deux points de vue cependant, la Sicile devrait attirer les voyageurs, car ses beautés naturelles et ses beautés artistiques sont aussi particulières que remarquables. On sait combien est fertile et mouvementée cette terre, qui fut appelée le grenier de l'Italie, que tous les peuples envahirent et possédèrent l'un après l'autre, tant fut violente leur envie de la posséder, qui fit se battre et mourir tant d'hommes, comme une belle fille ardemment désirée. C'est, autant que l'Espagne, le pays des oranges, le sol fleuri dont l'air, au printemps, n'est qu'un parfum; et elle allume, chaque soir, au-dessus des mers, le fanal monstrueux de l'Etna, le plus grand volcan d'Europe."[34]

At first glance, La Vaudère's feral and unpredictable Sicilian landscape seems an obvious contrast to the sterilized women of the capital, whose reproductive capacities are conquered through the removal of their ovaries. Her comparison of the island with a seductive and wild mistress yet to be possessed is reminiscent of medical anxieties about "untamed" sterilized women and their nonreproductive, unbridled—volcanic—sexuality. As Finn remarks, discussions of ovariectomies in nineteenth-century medical texts expressed increasing concern that the removal of a woman's reproductive capacities would unleash insatiable and pathological sexual desire.[35] In this context, La Vaudère's metaphoric depiction of unconquerable femininity hints at an impending narrative shift that condemns the protagonist's nonreproductive sexuality. Given that the text's discursive change occurs at this critical moment in Camille's travels, La Vaudère's depiction here deserves a second look. This crucial moment is marked by Maupassant's presence in the text, for this description is a near-verbatim reproduction of his portrayal of the island's scenic and artistic appeal. While this explains the stylistic rupture, it also suggests a pivotal symbolic intrusion of male-authored constructions of female sexuality. It is therefore no coincidence that while in Sicily, amid such charged portrayals of untamed femininity and conventional discourses on womanhood, Camille expresses both a moral drive for motherhood and remorse for her sterilization. Camille tragically realizes—while in a landscape of inauthentic, fabricated femininity—that the only remedy for her sullied life is also the impossible: a child.

In spite of an ostensible promotion of normative womanhood, La Vaudère's copying provides us with a new vision of these conventional perceptions of femininity. Instead of merely replicating Maupassant's depiction of an essentialized femininity, her plagiaristic act hints at the very discursive vulnerability and instability of such constructions. As a result, these duplicated passages bring attention to a larger structural and thematic interrogation at the core of the novel: the legitimacy of literary and medical discourses on womanhood. Despite the novel's endorsement of procreative womanhood, La Vaudère's plagiarism in fact interrogates the validity of male-authored constructions of conventional femininity. In this context, the novel's shift in tone paradoxically underscores the mutability of normative, one-dimensional models of sexual difference.

PART 2: *NOTRE CŒUR* AND *LES DEMI-SEXES*

Like *Les demi-sexes*, Maupassant's *Notre cœur* privileges conventional discourses on femininity and gender. The novel centers on André Mariolle's unrequited relationship with Mme de Burne, an enigmatic and seductive widow whose character draws upon the clichéd figures of the narcissistic *femme fatale* and frigid lesbian. Like many contemporary works of fiction, the novel traces the male protagonist's emotional and psychological devastation at the hands of a merciless mistress.[36] There are many thematic similarities between the two novels, and both Maupassant and La Vaudère perpetuate discourses that vilify nonprocreative femininity. However, La

Vaudère's plagiarism and her novel's conflicting messages complicate those parallels. Many of her pivotal passages on feminine subjectivity and sexuality are taken from Maupassant's most vehement portrayals of malevolent womanhood. At first glance, these male-authored, misogynist conceptions of femininity appear to shape La Vaudère's novel about female sexual emancipation and its consequences. However, a dialogic reading reveals a far more nuanced understanding of Maupassant's discursive contributions to La Vaudère's work and vice versa. La Vaudère reappropriates and revises Maupassant's clichéd depiction of the *femme fatale*—itself a reproduced trope—to privilege female subjectivity and challenge reductive portrayals of womanhood.

Malevolent Female Sexuality

At the core of Maupassant's novel is a lamentation about the modern woman. Among the many stock characters that form Mme de Burne's loyal entourage of suitors, writer Gaston de Lamarthe best embodies the deep nostalgia for conventional femininity of earlier times. A "romancier psychologue," Lamarthe is particularly interested in "les détraquées contemporaines" of "cette race nouvelle de femmes agitées par des nerfs d'hystériques raisonnables."[37] As a *porte-parole* for Maupassant, Lamarthe classifies Mme de Burne within this new category of women. He warns protagonist Mariolle of her break from traditional femininity and from "les femmes d'autrefois, les femmes à âme, les femmes à cœur, les femmes à sensibilité, les femmes des romans passés."[38] Lamarthe's meditation on evolving ideals of womanhood extends to the realm of literature. In evoking a shift in contemporary fictional representations of femininity, he draws attention to Mme de Burne, whose very name (slang for "testicle") confirms the trend. For what Lamarthe and Maupassant bemoan most about the modern woman is her rejection of conventional doctrines of marriage and procreation. Mme de Burne recalls the figure of the New Woman, or *femme nouvelle*, a popular trope at the turn of the century. Ubiquitous in the Belle Époque imagination, the masculinized New Woman was ridiculed for her rejection of conventional gender norms and rebellion against the duties of marriage and motherhood. Gesturing toward Mme de Burne and her female peers, Lamarthe explains to Mariolle, "Non, ce ne sont pas des femmes. [. . .] Voyez-vous, mon cher, la femme n'est créée et venue en ce monde que pour deux choses [. . .]: l'amour et l'enfant. [. . .] Or celles-ci sont incapables d'amour, et elles ne veulent pas d'enfants. En vérité, ce sont des monstres."[39] The conflation of modern womanhood with the refusal of procreation provides a provocative backdrop for La Vaudère's novel about sterilized women. In that regard, her barren "demi-sexes" are the end result of a regressive form of femininity and are symbolic descendants of Mme de Burne. Though La Vaudère plagiarized numerous texts throughout her career, the fact that she borrowed from a work that overtly condemns nonreproductive femininity to write about *ovariotomies* must not be dismissed as arbitrary. Instead, those thematic parallels suggest the possibility of an active exchange between the two novels, in which La Vaudère privileges the complexities of female subjectivity and revises the trope of the New Woman.

In the early pages of his novel, Maupassant introduces Mme de Burne's character with an emphasis on her predatory drive. Nearly verbatim, La Vaudère draws upon this clichéd portrayal of feminine malevolence in *Les demi-sexes*. Nina, the unscrupulous lesbian figure and scheming ringleader of the "demi-sexes," appears to have been modeled from Mme de Burne when she describes herself to Camille:[40]

> *Les demi-sexes*: "Je suis née méchante; j'aime à poursuivre et à dompter des êtres humains, comme le chasseur poursuit des bêtes, rien que pour les voir tomber! Mon âme est violente et point avide d'émotions comme celle des femmes tendres et sentimentales. Je dédaigne l'amour unique d'un homme et la satisfaction dans une passion. Je veux l'admiration de tous, les hommages, les agenouillements, les soumissions et les prières devant l'autel de ma beauté. [. . .] Je gouverne avec une adresse savante, suivant les défauts, les qualités, la nature des jalousies, et je reste, au moral, indifférente et glacée."[41]

> *Notre cœur*: "Mais surtout [Mme de Burne] était née coquette; et, dès qu'elle se sentit libre dans l'existence, elle se mit à poursuivre et à dompter les amoureux, comme le chasseur poursuit le gibier, rien que pour les voir tomber. Son cœur cependant n'était point avide d'émotions comme celui des femmes tendres et sentimentales; elle ne recherchait point l'amour unique d'un homme ni le bonheur dans une passion. Il lui fallait seulement autour d'elle l'admiration de tous, des hommages, des agenouillements, un encensement de tendresse. [. . .] Elle les gouvernait avec une adresse savante, suivant leurs défauts et leurs qualités et la nature de leur jalousie."[42]

Like Maupassant's character, Nina possesses the typical qualities of the *femme fatale*. Her dangerous influence extends to many of the women in her entourage whom she repeatedly convinces to be sterilized. La Vaudère's reproduction of these passages, however, does not perpetuate masculine discourses about malicious femininity, but instead allows her to subtly modify those demonizing representations. For example, as a closer look at this amorous *tête-à-tête* reveals, Nina encourages the newly sterilized Camille to take full advantage of her seductive powers over her vulnerable suitors:

> *Les demi-sexes*: "Tu sais faire naître, avec une adresse féline et une curiosité inépuisable, le mal secret et torturant dans les yeux de tous ceux que tu veux séduire; tu ne crains rien et tu méprises les plus redoutables! . . . Si tu savais comme cela m'amuse de sentir tous ces beaux messieurs envahis, conquis, dominés par ma puissance invincible; de devenir pour eux l'unique idole capricieuse et souveraine! . . . Et puis, est-ce que nous n'avons pas toutes cet instinct secret qui pousse en nous doucement et se développe: l'instinct de la guerre et de la conquête?"[43]
>
> *Notre cœur*: "Elle avait fait naître si souvent, avec une adresse féline et une curiosité inépuisable, ce mal secret et torturant dans les yeux de tous les hommes qu'elle avait pu séduire! Cela l'amusait tant de les sentir envahis peu à peu, conquis, dominés par sa puissance invincible de femme, de devenir pour eux l'Unique, l'Idole capricieuse et souveraine! Cela avait poussé en elle tout doucement, comme un instinct caché qui se développe, l'instinct de la guerre et de la conquête."[44]

Whereas Maupassant's description focuses solely on Mme de Burne's one-dimensional cruelty and vanity, Nina's monologue takes a feminist turn, and La Vaudère amends her predecessor's text with a rallying cry for sexual equality. "Seulement, nous sommes désarmées par la nature et le mâle brutal a sur nous le droit du plus fort," Nina pontificates. "N'est-ce donc rien, ma chérie, de pouvoir traiter, enfin, d'égal à égal et d'en avoir fini avec toutes les misères de notre sexe?"[45] For Nina, voluntary sterilization is a gesture toward sexual autonomy and a refusal of what she sees as the tragic destiny of motherhood: "Je ne me révolte pas seulement contre l'humanité, mais contre la nature qui nous a donné toutes les souffrances, toutes les peines, tous les châtiments, sans nulle compensation, sans nulle joie réelle."[46] Maupassant's modern (predatory) woman refuses motherhood because she is a "monstre"; La Vaudère's does so because she suffers a tragic inequality. Though clearly inspired by Mme de Burne, Nina articulates in her own voice what Maupassant's enigmatic character cannot: the principles and motivations behind her lifestyle.

But Nina is far from blameless. At the novel's conclusion, readers learn of her suspicious financial arrangement with the surgeon, and her self-interest and manipulation quickly eclipse her feminist ideals. Certainly, in this context, Nina's predatory character is a familiar cliché of both Decadent and Naturalist fiction, and her death in the final pages reads as fitting punishment for her moral and sexual corruption of her female peers. However, when considered against Maupassant's original descriptions of Mme de Burne, Nina's character demonstrates an added dimension that complicates her demonization. La Vaudère transforms the enigmatic and indifferent Mme de Burne into Nina, a champion of sexual emancipation who, though eliminated at the novel's conclusion, provides a noteworthy feminist element to the novel that comes to light through textual comparison.

Female Romantic Subjectivity

A comparison of the two novels reveals the many ways in which La Vaudère deviates from her predecessor to value female sexual subjectivity. While *Les demi-sexes* addresses the possibilities of female sexual pleasure and autonomy, much of Mme de Burne's mystification in *Notre cœur* lies in her disinterest in her sexual encounters with Mariolle. Perplexed and disheartened, the protagonist ponders her unresponsiveness against his own understanding of the stages of female sexual experience. "Comment n'avait-elle pas eu au moins cette période d'entraînement qui succède chez presque toutes les femmes à l'abandon volontaire et désintéressé de leur corps? Elle est courte souvent, suivie par la fatigue et puis par le dégoût. Mais il est si rare qu'elle n'existe pas du tout, pas une heure, pas un jour!"[47] Mme de Burne's break from formulaic notions of women's sexuality is the veritable source of her perceived cruelty. Her inability to conform to Mariolle's perception of feminine desire and emotion is the foundation of her enigma and the driving force of the novel's plot. La Vaudère's text, by contrast, begins as a celebration of sexual independence from similar discourses that aim to define—and confine—female sexual experiences. Though the novel eventually concludes with a condemnation of these nonprocreative women, La

Vaudère's preoccupation with sexual emancipation and her unique appropriation of corresponding passages from *Notre cœur* betray an engagement with masculine discourses on female sexuality. Instead of reducing the novel's final message to a contradictory promotion of normative gender roles, La Vaudère's plagiarism reveals a complicated rewriting of conservative male-authored discourses on femininity, sexual difference, and sexual fulfillment. In one particular passage in *Les demi-sexes*, La Vaudère borrows from Maupassant to describe the intense sexual connection between Camille and Nina. Maupassant's original passage, however, concerns Mariolle's heterosexual attachment to Mme de Burne, not lesbianism:

> *Les demi-sexes*: "Elle s'attachait à elle par la caresse, lien redoutable, le plus fort de tous, le seul dont on ne se délivre jamais quand il a bien enlacé et quand il serre jusqu'au sang la chair d'une femme. Camille allait chez Nina régulièrement, sans résistance, attirée, semblait-il, autant par l'amusement de ces rendez-vous, par le charme du petit rez-de-chaussée discret devenu une serre de fleurs rares que par l'habitude de cette vie coupable, à peine dangereuse, puisque chacun avait intérêt à se taire. C'était encore auprès de madame Saurel qu'elle avait goûté les joies les plus vives, et, de toutes ses folies, aucune ne lui avait laissé une impression aussi durable."[48]
>
> *Notre cœur*: "Il s'attachait à elle par la caresse, lien redoutable, le plus fort de tous, le seul dont on ne se délivre jamais quand il a bien enlacé et quand il serre jusqu'au sang la chair d'un homme. [. . .] Elle venait de trois jours en trois jours, sans résistances, attirée, semblait-il autant par l'amusement de ce rendez-vous, par le charme de la petite maison devenue une serre de fleurs rares, et par la nouveauté de cette vie d'amour, à peine dangereuse, puisque personne n'avait le droit de la suivre, mais pleine de mystère cependant, que séduite par la tendresse prosternée et grandissante de son amant."[49]

The most notable difference between these two passages is *Les demi-sexes*'s privileging of the female perspective. While Maupassant's passage opens with a discussion of the powers that the feminine touch ("lien redoutable") hold on a man, La Vaudère subversively reappropriates those details by shifting the focus to female subjectivity ("quand il [le lien redoutable] serre jusqu'au sang la chair *d'une femme*"). Though Maupassant offers a rare glimpse into Mme de Burne's motives for continuing her visits with Mariolle, La Vaudère takes this one step further to include details about Camille's momentous sexual awakening with Nina. La Vaudère thus rewrites masculine discourses on female sexuality to value a subjective experience that excludes men: lesbianism.

In Maupassant's text, Mariolle's suffering and desperation revolves around Mme de Burne's emotional and physical frigidity. As Lamarthe laments, modern women such as Mme de Burne are "incapables d'amour" and abandon conventional romantic doctrines of marriage and family for a lifestyle of autonomy and sentimental impenetrability.[50] Mariolle is the victim of this new form of femininity, and in a moment of great anguish, he reflects on the physical and emotional transformation that he has undergone since meeting Mme de Burne. The corresponding passage in *Les demi-sexes*, however, does not adhere to typical fin-de-siècle discourses on feminine malevolence. In La Vaudère's episode, Camille contemplates her physical and emotional transformation upon meeting her husband, artist Georges Darvy. However, unlike with Mariolle, the looming menace to this love is not malicious femininity. Instead, Camille's adversary is the jealous Philippe de Talberg and his unrelenting threats to reveal her sterilization to the unknowing Georges. La Vaudère underscores Camille's profound love for her husband and her emotional vulnerability in the face of Philippe's blackmail:

> *Les demi-sexes*: "Son âme tressaillait de colère impuissante, ses jambes ne la soutenaient plus, son cœur battait follement, tout son corps semblait meurtri par une inconcevable courbature. [. . .] Elle se disait: '[. . .] Avant de connaître Georges, je n'avais subi aucun entraînement; je n'avais que des instincts, des curiosités et des appétits [. . .]. Mes sens savouraient sans se griser jamais; je comprenais trop pour perdre la tête, je raisonnais et j'analysais trop bien mes goûts pour les subir aveuglément. Et voilà que cet homme [Philippe] qui me menace aujourd'hui s'est imposé à moi; malgré moi, malgré ma répulsion et ma résistance, il m'a dicté sa volonté et me soumet encore par sa seule présence!'"[51]
>
> *Notre cœur*: "Ses jambes ne le soutenaient plus, défaillantes de faiblesse; son cœur battait; tout son corps semblait meurtri par une inconcevable courbature. [. . .] Il se disait: 'Je n'avais jamais subi d'entraînement. [. . .] [J]'ai plus de jugement que d'instinct, de curiosités que d'appétits, de fantaisie que de persévérance. [. . .] J'ai aimé les choses de la vie sans m'y attacher jamais beaucoup, avec des sens d'expert qui savoure et ne se grise point, qui comprend trop pour

> perdre la tête. Je raisonne tout, et j'analyse d'ordinaire trop bien mes goûts pour les subir aveuglément. [. . .] Et voilà que cette femme s'est imposée à moi, malgré moi, malgré ma peur et ma connaissance d'elle; et elle me possède comme si elle avait cueilli une à une toutes les aspirations diverses qui étaient en moi.'"[52]

Though an obvious reproduction of Maupassant's text, this passage differentiates Camille from the enigmatic and indifferent Mme de Burne, whose cruelty depends on her inability to reciprocate Mariolle's devotion. Instead, readers witness Camille's transformation from an emotionally detached seductress to a sensitive and compassionate wife. While Mariolle's anxiety lies with Mme de Burne's amorous incapacities, Camille is unsettled here by the intensity of her emotional development with Georges and the threat that Philippe poses to their marriage, which, given her secret, is doomed to fail. In other words, this copied passage draws parallels between Camille's victimhood and that of the amiable and sympathetic Mariolle. Through plagiarism, La Vaudère rewrites masculine discourses that portray the modern woman as cruel and unfeeling and instead focuses on female romantic subjectivity.

It is here that La Vaudère's text diverges most significantly from Maupassant's. Unlike the cold-hearted Mme de Burne, Camille's intense attachment to Georges provides a crucial glimpse into her humanity. Although both characters have similar points of departure and have never experienced unconstrained love for any man, their trajectories differ. Reflecting on her relationship with Mariolle, Mme de Burne admits, "Oui, je l'aime, mais je manque d'élan: c'est la faute de ma nature."[53] Camille, however, is genuinely capable of love. As Rachel Mesch notes, her emotional vulnerability allows for a narrative shift in the last chapters that centers on her tragic love with Georges.[54] Longing in vain to have a child with her husband, Camille's ultimate suicide signals her inability to reconcile modern feminist values with a deeper, ultimately stronger, drive for love. This modern woman thus deviates from her cold-hearted, self-sufficient predecessor to embody a poignant sentimentality that remains faithful to conventional notions of femininity. La Vaudère's version of modern femininity is not centered on male victimhood, but on female experience. In that specific case, focusing on Camille's failed marriage and ensuing death elicits sympathy from readers. The protagonist's love story breathes new life into the plotline and serves as a response to Maupassant's Lamarthe, who disparages contemporary literature's influence on feminine sensibilities. "Au temps où les romanciers et les poètes les exaltaient et les faisaient rêver," he preaches to Mariolle in an ironic *mise-en-abyme*, "elles cherchaient et croyaient trouver dans la vie l'équivalent de ce que leur cœur avait pressenti dans leurs lectures. Aujourd'hui, vous vous obstinez à supprimer toutes les apparences poétiques et séduisantes, pour ne montrer que les réalités désillusionnantes. Or, mon cher, plus d'amour dans les livres, plus d'amour dans la vie."[55] The elevation of feminine subjectivity in the final chapters of *Les demi-sexes* becomes the space in which to negotiate the terms of the modern romantic storyline, bemoaned by Maupassant's *porte-parole*.

A NEW UNDERSTANDING OF LA VAUDÈRE'S PLAGIARISM

While contemplating his troubled relationship with Mme de Burne, Mariolle lauds the transparencies of an epistolary correspondence to conclude that "les mots noirs sur le papier blanc, c'est l'âme toute nue."[56] Mariolle is especially interested in Mme de Burne's letters because he believes that women, unlike men, are incapable of concealing their true emotional state when they pick up a pen:

> L'homme, par des artifices de rhétorique, par des habilités professionnelles, par l'habitude d'employer la plume pour traiter toutes les affaires de la vie, parvient souvent à déguiser sa nature propre dans sa prose impersonnelle, utilitaire ou littéraire. Mais la femme n'écrit guère que pour parler d'elle, et elle met un peu d'elle en chaque mot. Elle ne sait point les ruses du style, et elle se livre tout entière dans l'innocence des expressions. Il se rappela les correspondances et les mémoires des femmes célèbres qu'il avait lus. Comme elles apparaissaient nettement, les précieuses, les spirituelles, et les sensibles! [. . .] La femme ne travaille point ses termes: c'est l'émotion directe qui les jette à son esprit; elle ne fouille pas les dictionnaires. Quand elle sent très fort, elle exprime très juste, sans peine et sans recherche, dans la sincérité mobile de sa nature.[57]

His reflections on his personal correspondence with Mme de Burne lead Mariolle to reduce women writers to overly sentimental dilettantes who lack sufficient intellect for critical and creative literary production. These vitriolic comments reflect contemporary discourses on gender and women writers that targeted La Vaudère herself (see chapter 2). Ironically, rather than confirming Mariolle's views, La Vaudère's novel challenges those ideologies through the so-called plagiaristic act. In copying various passages, she creates a space in which to further explore and rework the discursive tensions inherent in both novels.

In her work on plagiarism and pragmatics, Marilyn Randall has argued that acts such as these are examples of "guerrilla plagiarism," or ways in which plagiarism serves as an "oppositional stance with respect to prevailing aesthetics, as well as to the political ideologies that support those aesthetics."[58] As we have seen, La Vaudère challenges male-authored, one-dimensional notions of femininity by rewriting and amending various passages in order to center a woman's subjectivity. In addition, this comparative study has demonstrated how La Vaudère has contributed to literary discourses on womanhood and why she deserves continued scholarly attention. By appropriating male-authored portrayals of femininity and reimagining them with her own creative and aesthetic twists, La Vaudère reminds us of the precariousness and instability of such discourses as they evolved within fin-de-siècle fiction.

CHAPTER 4

The Plagiarized Plagiarist

Missy de Morny, Colette, and the Scandal of "Rêve d'Égypte"

> Non, rien ne meurt! . . . Tout change simplement et se transforme comme la chrysalide qui devient papillon, et la fleur immaculée, fruit vermeil et délicieux.
>
> —Jane de La Vaudère, *Le rêve de Mysès*

In January 1907, just days after the opening of Colette's and Missy de Morny's notorious pantomime *Rêve d'Égypte*, Jane de La Vaudère sought legal action against the Moulin Rouge for theft of creative property. Though the production at the Moulin Rouge was cloaked in scandal—a kiss between lovers Colette and Missy led to uproars and a suspension of future performances—La Vaudère was quick to declare artistic ownership of the lesbian pantomime. Months earlier, La Vaudère had supposedly circulated a similarly titled Egyptian pantomime, *Le rêve de Mysès*, in various Parisian music halls, including the Moulin Rouge. Though traces of this manuscript have since disappeared, La Vaudère published a revised novella version of the work in June 1907, five months after the Moulin Rouge production that Missy claimed to have written. There are undeniable similarities between the novella *Le rêve de Mysès* and Missy's *Rêve d'Égypte*, which both feature the resuscitation of a female mummy by an amorous onlooker and a titillating backdrop of Sapphic liaisons. However, ever the savvy marketer, La Vaudère seems to have reworked elements of the published edition of *Le rêve de Mysès* in response to Missy's legendary production. Though she claimed to be a victim of artistic fraud, La Vaudère co-opted the scandal of the Moulin Rouge for her own promotion. When she published the novella version of *Le rêve de Mysès* a few months later with the Librairie d'art technique, the work featured numerous erotic photos "d'après nature" that seem to recall the provocative and infamous performance at the Moulin Rouge.

The unearthing of the alleged plagiarism of *Rêve d'Égypte*, absent from biographies and scholarly work on Missy and Colette, sheds light on the intersections of authorship, performance, and artistic notoriety within the context of La Vaudère's larger *œuvre*. As we saw in the previous chapter, La Vaudère frequently "borrowed" from her contemporaries and committed her own acts of plagiarism in a significant number of works. One only has to look so far as the *Le rêve de Mysès* itself to find reproductions of passages from historical works on ancient Egyptian customs and the mummification process. To complicate matters, La Vaudère also inserted selected passages from her own previously published fictional works, creating an intertextual patchwork from a piece that Missy and the Moulin Rouge had supposedly appropriated. The complex collage of the *Le rêve de Mysès* thus deserves to be read as both a prelude and epilogue to the *Rêve d'Égypte* and part of a larger dialogue on the artistic marketing and public reception of nonnormative female sexuality in the early twentieth century. Mummies, in their literal and metaphorical forms, are central to this exchange, and as they blur the boundaries between life and death, between mortality and immortality, they may inform our understanding of La Vaudère's pursuit for recognition and preservation.

SELLING SAPPHISM: THE MARKETING OF *RÊVE D'ÉGYPTE* AND *LE RÊVE DE MYSÈS*

Le rêve de Mysès and *Rêve d'Égypte* are products of a larger literary trend of mummy fiction that was popular throughout nineteenth-century Europe. As literary, historical, and anthropological scholars have shown, Napoléon's Egyptian Campaign (1798–1801) sparked a cultural fixation with ancient Egypt.[1] Popular culture became saturated with stereotypical representations, and mummies recovered on expeditions were fetishized in museum display cases or unwrapping viewings. By midcentury, Théophile Gautier's works "Le pied de momie" (1840) and *Le roman de la momie* (1857) announced a growing presence of the mythical Egyptian mummy in French and European fiction. Fueled by Orientalist models of Egypt as a land of fantasy and magic, popular fiction depicted exaggerated visions of exoticized—and eroticized—otherness. Female mummies were admired, yet feared, capable of seducing a Western male protagonist or causing his ruin. Accordingly, the mummy possessed ancient secrets and magical powers that allowed her to transgress the laws of death and time, and dream sequences often made this more plausible.[2]

La Vaudère's *Le rêve de Mysès* and Missy's *Rêve d'Égypte* both belong to this heritage of fantastical (female) mummy fiction. Their titles aside, how similar are the two works? Unfortunately, our only knowledge of the actual content of *Rêve d'Égypte* comes from contemporary accounts of the Moulin Rouge incident that appeared in the press in the days following the premiere. Colette scholars and archivists are unable to verify that a transcript with the pantomime stage directions or musical score ever existed; if it did, it was not conserved.[3] In addition, while we now have access to a published and revised version of *Le rêve de Mysès*, the original manuscript that La Vaudère distributed to theatres has been lost. We are forced to rely on secondary sources, La Vaudère's accounts in her correspondence, and a selection of fictional works to reconstruct the content of the two pantomimes. While media reports of the *Rêve d'Égypte* debut consist mostly of sensationalized descriptions of the performance and the commotion that ensued, a compilation of these reviews allows us to reconstruct the work's plotline, setting, and general content. In late 1906, as rumors of the upcoming performance hinted at moral depravity, newspapers began reporting on the *Rêve d'Égypte*'s content, whetting the public's appetite for the impending scandal and arousing La Vaudère's suspicions. On December 30, *Le Figaro* provided previously unreleased information about the work's subject matter: "Donnons quelques renseignements inédits sur cette originale tentative qui sera une évocation très exacte des mœurs de l'Egypte [*sic*] d'autrefois. L'action se passe dans le bureau d'un vieux savant qui étudie dans des bouquins poussiéreux les sciences occultes. Soudain, des visions fantasmagoriques se dressent devant lui. Il lui semble que les tableaux, les livres, les statuettes qui sont dans son bureau s'animent. La momie même qui se trouve dans son sarcophage s'avance vers lui et le charme par ses chants et ses danses. On finit heureusement par persuader au pauvre homme qu'il a rêvé."[4] In an interview on December 30 in *Gil Blas*, Missy supplemented plot summaries with logistical details: "Ce que l'on va représenter de moi est une pantomime intitulée *Rêve d'Égypte*. J'ai deux interprètes: Colette Willy, que tout le monde connaît, et une débutante, Mlle Dusson. Je joue, moi, le rôle d'un vieux savant, qui, par ses incantations, fait ressusciter une momie qu'il possède. La momie, c'est Colette. Elle exécutera des danses de style que nous avons reconstituée [*sic*] avec Georges Wague, le mime."[5] Based on these descriptions, we can begin to reconstruct the major elements of Missy's plotline: a male scholar played by Missy draws on the sciences of the occult to resuscitate an ancient Egyptian mummy. The mummy emerges from her sarcophagus and performs an ancient sensual dance, and the savant finally awakens to discover that it was all a dream (as the title of the piece suggests). There was one glaring detail that Missy curiously omitted: the kiss shared with Colette. This enactment of lesbian eroticism would draw fervent reactions from the crowd at the show's opening. *Le Figaro* journalist Alfred Delilia, who attended the debut on January 3, recounted the audience's response to their embrace. "Le tapage redouble lorsque Colette Willy, s'animant dans son sarcophage, vient mimer une scène d'amour avec sa partenaire Mme de Belbeuf [Missy]," he wrote the following day.[6] Class difference played a significant role in the controversy: many consider the staged kiss between a cross-dressing woman of nobility and her real-life female lover to be the central catalyst for the uproar and ultimate ban.[7] Of course, as rumors of the future event gained momentum among the artistic elite, Missy's (perhaps strategic) neglect of this erotic detail further tempted the public's voyeuristic curiosity about the premiere.

Many of the press reports lauded *Rêve d'Égypte*'s historical accuracy and emphasized the extensive research that Colette conducted on ancient Egyptian customs in preparation for the performance. For example, Delilia praised the pantomime's faithful representation of these traditions and recounted Colette's thorough investigation of materials from the period. He noted, "La mise en scène de *Rêve d'Egypte* est d'une exactitude rigoureuse et Mme Colette Willy a passé plusieurs journées entières au musée du Louvre à étudier les mosaïques de l'époque."[8] Delilia claimed that ancient artifacts also informed the mummy's dance sequence that was in exotic contrast to the contemporary fads best known to its audience: "Ajoutons qu'elle doit danser un pas, qui ne ressemble en rien à nos mattchiches et à nos kraquettes modernes, qui a été reconstitué grâce à des textes anciens, d'une façon très précise."[9] While insisting on the pantomime's historical authenticity, these narratives also exploited the exotic otherness of its content, a promotional strategy that La Vaudère would adopt in the months that followed.

La Vaudère's novella *Le rêve de Mysès* can be summarized as follows: Mysès, an ancient Egyptian embalmer, steals the corpse of the recently deceased queen Ahmosis and applies his secret formula to skillfully preserve the body. His expertise in the science of mummification brings his beloved queen back to life and she declares her reciprocated love. However, Mysès eventually awakens to discover he had been dreaming and finds the corpse of the queen, now decomposed, at his side.[10] Like Colette, La Vaudère also valued historical authenticity and supplemented her depiction of ancient Egypt with detailed descriptions of rituals and conventions. Based simply on their respective titles and storylines, the parallels between *Rêve d'Égypte* and *Le rêve de Mysès* are flagrant: both are set in ancient Egypt and feature dreamt romantic encounters between a female mummy and the expert who brought her back to life. With these elements in mind, La Vaudère's accusations appear plausible. As we dig further and examine her own account of the Moulin Rouge incident in correspondence and fiction alike, we uncover a series of revisions and intertextual exchanges that allowed La Vaudère to reclaim ownership of the pantomime.

LA VAUDÈRE'S LEGAL AND CREATIVE ACTIONS

As the press began reporting in late 1906 on the forthcoming production at the Moulin Rouge, La Vaudère grew suspicious of the parallels between her *Le rêve de Mysès* and Missy's *Rêve d'Égypte*. Certain she was the victim of plagiarism even before the show premiered, La Vaudère considered her authorial rights over the impending performance of *Rêve d'Égypte*. On January 1, in a letter addressed to the Société des auteurs et compositeurs dramatiques (SACD), she inquired about the legal protection afforded to association members like herself: "Je vois, dans les journaux, l'annonce d'une pantomime en un acte de Mme la Marquise de Morny: *Le Rêve d'Egypte* [*sic*]—qui sera représentée prochainement au Moulin Rouge. Or, j'ai écrit, il y a un an, une pantomime égyptienne, en un acte, intitulée *le Rêve de Mysès*. Cette œuvre fut étudiée aux Bouffes, il y a sept mois, puis abandonnée et remise à l'Olympia. Je vous envoie, par la poste et recommandé, le manuscrit de ma pantomime, afin d'établir mes droits, s'il y a bien."[11] Unfortunately, the SACD contains no traces of the pantomime manuscript that La Vaudère submitted with her letter.[12] Though there is no record of the legal advice provided by the SACD in response to her inquiry, the association conserved the *procès-verbal* that took place on January 11 between La Vaudère and Rip, a writer from the Moulin Rouge. Rip denied having any involvement with the *Rêve d'Égypte* script but identified Missy as a possible culprit. However, because Missy was not a member of the SACD, the association was not able to further pursue the incident: "Mme de la Vaudère sollicite l'appui de la commission pour obtenir réparation du préjudice qui lui est causé. M. Rip déclare qu'il n'est pas l'auteur de cet ouvrage et que c'est par un abus que son nom a été indiqué; il croit que cet auteur serait Mme de Morny portée sur le programme. La commission ne pouvant arbitrer vis-à-vis d'un tiers étranger à la société engage Mme Jane de la Vaudère à se pourvoir devant les tribunaux si elle le juge à propos."[13] Despite the SACD's suggestion, it appears that La Vaudère had already exhausted her prospects in the French courts. In the days following the premiere and scandal, the press reported on La Vaudère's legal actions against the Moulin Rouge. On January 8, *Le temps* noted that La Vaudère opened a case against the Moulin Rouge for theft of her pantomime, listing it among the theatres to which she submitted her manuscript: "Mme Jane de la Vaudère a été autorisée par le président du tribunal civil de la Seine à faire dresser un constat par huissier au Moulin-Rouge au sujet de la ressemblance du *Rêve d'Egypte* [*sic*], signé marquise de Morny, avec *le Rêve de Mysès*, sa pantomime égyptienne que doivent créer, cet hiver, Mlles Christine Booss et Blanche Mante de l'Opéra. Cette œuvre de Mme Jane de la Vaudère avait été déposée aux Bouffes-Parisiens, à l'Olympia et au Moulin Rouge."[14] Unfortunately, despite a comprehensive search of multiple archives, there appear to be no records of the "constat par huissier" or any contractual agreements between La Vaudère, the Opéra, or the actresses mentioned.[15] Furthermore, in her letter, La Vaudère makes no mention of any plans for the Opéra to produce her pantomime. Equally puzzling is the reference to the "constat par huissier," which, in the French judicial system, is only a preliminary step to gather evidence to open an investigation. Accordingly, because no traces of the "constat par huissier" exist in the related court documents housed at the Archives de Paris, it may be safe to conclude that the legal element of this case was resolved before it could further advance in the courts. Perhaps La Vaudère received a financial settlement, or the third party investigating her claim found no evidence of wrongdoing. Regardless, with her hands tied judicially, she chose to pursue retribution through another medium in which she had more agency: her writing.

By the late spring of 1907, La Vaudère had published two works that can be read as direct responses to the controversy of the *Rêve d'Éygpte* production: the novella *Le rêve de Mysès* and the novel *Le peintre des frissons*. *Le peintre des frissons* came out in April 1907 in near conjunction with *Le rêve de Mysès*, which appeared two months later. It was not unusual for La Vaudère to publish multiple novels per year, and *Le peintre des frissons* and *Le rêve de Mysès* were each representative of two distinct genres in La Vaudère's corpus: the Parisian "roman de mœurs" and the erotic Orientalist novel, respectively. The proximity of their publication dates and the overlapping themes compel us to read them as dual responses to the *Rêve d'Égypte* performance and Missy's alleged theft from earlier in the year. The main storyline of *Le peintre des frissons* revolves around an opportunist Parisian painter named Lucius and the female models whom he exploits. However, it contains a parodic subplot about a scandalous Parisian production of an Egyptian pantomime, an overt reference to the Moulin Rouge affair. Through this satirical depiction, La Vaudère rewrites public perceptions of the origins of *Rêve d'Égypte* and provides her own account of the legendary evening at the Moulin Rouge. Of particular interest are the lines of verse that La Vaudère incorporates into this section, which she claims in a footnote originated with *Le rêve de Mysès* pantomime. While Belle Époque pantomimes were generally free of dialogue, some featured narration sung in verse, and the sixty-five lines that appear in *Le peintre des frissons* suggest that her original (stolen) manuscript may have taken this form. They also represent what may be the only remnants of La Vaudère's earliest vision for the pantomime. Both *Le peintre des frissons* and *Le rêve de Mysès* provide clues about La Vaudère's accusations and illuminate her creative revisions in the aftermath of the performance.

The backdrop of *Le peintre des frissons* (subtitled "roman parisien") is not the Egyptian sarcophagi of ancient times but rather Parisian art studios and music halls of the Belle Époque. Among the novel's principal themes is the shameless opportunism running rampant in the artistic circles of the capital city. Through a peripheral storyline featuring a lesbian couple named Faunette Hassim and Princesse Minny, La Vaudère invented an effective way to tell her version of creative fraud and the Moulin Rouge incident. While their names are already blatant allusions to Colette and Missy, the Egyptian pantomime that they perform at the Fantaisies-Perverses music hall leaves no doubt about their identities. Throughout the novel, La Vaudère parodies them as being devoid of talent as they ineptly prepare for the pantomime performance that occupies two entire chapters. La Vaudère further scrutinizes Missy and Colette through her rather homophobic portraits of Minny and Faunette. Minny, whose short hair and man's suit strikes a certain resemblance to her real-life inspiration, is also a drug addict: "À ses yeux troubles, d'une expression souffrante et lasse, l'on devine que l'éther ou la morphine ont dû charmer bien des heures d'ennui et de solitude."[16] Her companion Faunette is loud, arrogant, and oblivious to her surroundings at the studio: "[Faunette] parle haut, dérange quatre élèves pour atteindre sa place, renverse une toile, fraîchement peinte, dont les couleurs se brouillent sur le parquet, et rit bruyamment de sa maladresse."[17] They frequent Lucius's studio, but Minny and Faunette are not seriously interested in art. While others paint and work to master their craft, the two women devise schemes to seduce the female models at the studio. In this derisive portrayal, the dilettante couple's cunning plots to seduce women eclipse any artistic talent, for "leur souci d'art est d'un esthétisme plus complet."[18] Like the devious arriviste Lucius, Faunette and Minny are social climbers who intentionally provoke scandal for media attention. "Ce qu'il y a de certain," writes La Vaudère, "c'est que Faunette et Minny s'exhibent dans tous les endroits où l'on s'amuse, ne craignent pas d'intéresser les journaux à leurs tentatives artistiques et littéraires."[19] La Vaudère's denigration of the couple's real-life counterparts is brazen. Under La Vaudère's pen, Colette and Missy are fame-seeking, talentless charlatans, and their prominent presence in artistic circles and press exposés alike is attributed to their taste for scandal. This initial representation serves La Vaudère's claims of theft on two accounts. First, it delegitimizes Colette's and Missy's artistry as writers or stage performers. Second, it establishes Colette and Missy as unscrupulous status seekers who pursue stardom at any cost.

The tenth and eleventh chapters of the novel's second section are devoted entirely to the night of January 3, 1907. This noticeable digression from the main storyline reads as an unrelated and independent episode, suggesting that La Vaudère may have inserted these chapters to a work in progress and in reaction to the January performance. There is one notable difference in La Vaudère's account of the events at the Moulin Rouge: in a jab to Colette and Missy and a declaration of ownership over *Rêve d'Égypte*, she renames the pantomime in question *Le rêve de Mysès*. To prepare for the performance, Faunette, like Colette, consults the Egyptian collection at the Louvre ("Quelle science!" mocks Lucius), while Minny relies on a morphine-induced vision to transport her to the pantomime's ancient setting.[20] However, La Vaudère indicates that the couple's ultimate knowledge of ancient Egyptian customs comes not from thorough background research but rather ruthless creative theft. "En réalité," she writes, "Faunette et Minny avaient adopté la version d'un auteur imprudent qui avait oublié son manuscrit dans les bureaux des Fantaisies-Perverses. Mais l'on ne saurait trop ménager ses méninges."[21] La Vaudère supplements this intriguing remark with the following footnote, intended to elucidate her claims while also strategically providing publicity for her forthcoming novella: "*Le Rêve de Mysès*, 1 vol. illustré par le nu photographique, du même auteur. Roman et pantomime."[22] The published version referenced here of *Le rêve de Mysès* is the prose novella, not the original (verse) pantomime that she circulated. La Vaudère's note thus links the published novella *Le rêve de Mysès* to its original unpublished pantomime that she "imprudently" left behind at the Théâtre des Bouffes-Parisiens and Moulin Rouge. Most interesting here, perhaps, is her mention of the nude photographs that complement the edition throughout. As noted above, *Le rêve de Mysès* was published through the Librairie d'art technique, a Parisian press known for works featuring erotic photography. The nude photography is yet another ingenious marketing tactic of La Vaudère's that visually connects the titillation of the Moulin Rouge scandal with her published novella. In addition, the inclusion of this detail in her footnote is a strategic form of publicity in which she reclaims the rights over the work and entices readers with promises of feminine flesh, not unlike those provided by Colette at the premiere of *Rêve d'Égypte*. Ironically, La Vaudère seeks to capitalize on the publicity generated by the scandal while, just pages prior, she overtly condemns Colette's and Missy's opportunistic tactics to arouse media attention.

La Vaudère's portrayal of the events of January 3 in *Le Peintre des frissons* illustrates her deep familiarity with the fickle appetites of a Parisian public. In the chapters dedicated to the pantomime's premiere, La Vaudère observes audience members' reactions to the events as they unfold. Press accounts of the night claim that "tout-Paris" was present, and it would not be a far stretch to assume that La Vaudère was also in attendance.[23] Her depiction of Faunette's and Minny's performance, as well as her commentary on its reception, provide a glimpse into her personal perspective on a scandal that dominated the pages of the press in the days to come. In setting the scene, La Vaudère points to the public's capricious moral makeup and their expectations as spectators. In what reads as a brief analytical exposé that breaks from the novel's storyline, La Vaudère belittles Faunette and Minny for their lack of awareness of the spectators' moral complexities:

> Faunette et Minny, dans leur inconscience, ne se doutaient pas qu'il est une corde qu'il ne faut point exaspérer chez le spectateur

> bénévole, celle du respect humain. L'on peut tout dire à mots couverts, tout laisser deviner, mais il est dangereux de heurter de front l'opinion publique.
>
> Celui qui cherche, dans ses lectures solitaires, les pires dépravations, demande dans une salle de théâtre une tenue relative. Un spectateur peut être libertin, deux spectateurs sont vertueux. L'on rougit devant les autres de paraître admettre certaines esquisses renouvelées de l'antiquité, et les plus pervers, en pareil cas, deviennent les plus réservés.[24]

Unlike Faunette and Minny, La Vaudère demonstrates an artistic sensitivity to the desires of the modern theatregoer, in all of his or her hypocrisy. In deriding both the performers and the audience, La Vaudère asserts her own mastery over the stage and public reception. By extension, she also speculates on her own capacity for success, had her version of *Le rêve de Mysès* been performed under her guidance as intended.

The remaining passages of this section feature direct citations from what we may assume was the original *Le rêve de Mysès* pantomime. In her account of Faunette's and Minny's performance, she inserts sixty-five lines of verse narration, thus reclaiming the infamous night of January 3 at the Moulin Rouge with her own script. Curiously, her footnote here once again cites the novella *Le rêve de Mysès* as the source, labeled as both "pantomime et roman" published by the Librairie d'art technique. As we know, this work appeared in prose just two months later, and the verse cited here is likely the only printed version that remains of her original pantomime. It is certainly conceivable that La Vaudère revised the manuscript before incorporating it into this section of the novel, but because her manuscripts were lost, changes are impossible to verify. Nonetheless, *Le peintre des frissons* does provide unique access to one iteration of a work that was apparently evolving. To complicate matters, the content of the *Le rêve de Mysès* novella differs notably from the verse printed here in *Le peintre des frissons*. As we examine more closely later, these discrepancies bring to light La Vaudère's revision process, a valuable resource when archival documents are lacking. More specifically, they also point to an effort on her end to adapt her work according to the public's reaction.

Readers of *Le peintre des frissons* may note that the pantomime that she cites here, likely the original, contains no hints of same-sex desire. If Colette and Missy did steal La Vaudère's manuscript, it appears that the shared kiss that attracted so much media attention was their own initiative.

Through this lens, Colette and Missy put their own scandalous spin on La Vaudère's *Le rêve de Mysès*: in casting Missy in the role of male scholar, they amended the original to give emphasis to gender nonconformity and lesbian desire. The power of this logistical choice was not lost on La Vaudère, who describes this scene in *Le peintre des frissons* as the spectacle's climactic moment: "Toute la salle était debout, criant et protestant, car cet insolent baiser était l'outrage suprême, l'impardonnable insulte que deux faibles femmes osaient adresser à de vertueux spectateurs, à d'incorruptibles critiques."[25] In fact, Colette also hoped to turn the titillating performance of the Moulin Rouge to her advantage. In a letter to Georges Wague on January 5, upon learning that *Rêve d'Égypte* was shut down indefinitely, Colette eagerly awaited future opportunities generated by the scandal. She called on the famous mime, who trained her for *Rêve d'Égypte*'s dance sequence, to consider other performance prospects: "Nouvelle interdiction, radicale cette fois. Je le regrette—pour beaucoup de raisons. Mais je crois qu'il y a d'autres affaires à emmancher de cette pantomime, vous et moi."[26]

Like Colette, La Vaudère sought to rebound from the Moulin Rouge scandal and assert her own artistic agency. In what can be considered the next installment in a creative back and forth with Missy and Colette and the larger genre of mummy fiction, La Vaudère published the prose edition of *Le rêve de Mysès* with the provocative Librairie d'art technique. As part of the publisher Albert Méricant's catalog, the Librarie d'art technique collection featured erotically charged works that were illustrated with nude photography. These publications ranged from academic studies for painters and sculptors to provocative works of fiction with sexually evocative subplots. In addition, Méricant published the *L'étude académique* (1904–13), a periodical of nude models that happened to run advertisements for La Vaudère's suggestively titled novels *Le harem de Syta* (1904) and *La vierge d'Israël* (1906).[27] As Geneviève de Viveiros has noted of his fiction catalog, Méricant frequently chose a work's most sensationalist scenes to be represented through illustration.[28]

La Vaudère published numerous novels with Méricant, many of which were illustrated by painter Charles Atamian. Her works *Le rêve de Mysès*, *Les prêtresses de Mylitta* (1907), and *Sapho, dompteuse* (1908) contained suggestive photos of nude women that were intended to illustrate plotlines. As we recall from chapter 2, with their provocative images and themes, these editions allowed La Vaudère to capitalize on the growing popularity of the photo-literary genre. *Le rêve de Mysès* was the first of the three to be published, and its slightly disorderly layout reflects the early stages of this new marketing approach. The photos are coded numerically and only vaguely represent the novella's plot, leading scholar Paul Edwards to speculate that they were selected from a preexisting catalog and not originally created with La Vaudère's work in mind.[29] Conversely, La Vaudère's other two novels in this genre were each published shortly after *Le rêve de Mysès* and contain erotic photos that were clearly created to be included in her respective works. This development suggests that *Le rêve de Mysès* was one of the first of its kind, an experimental marketing strategy that also, uncoincidentally, appeared on the heels of the Moulin Rouge scandal.[30]

Méricant's edition of *Le rêve de Mysès* features photographs of women posing naked in natural and domestic scenes, and at times with each other or animals. What's more, the novella's storyline is more provocative than that of the verse version that was printed in *Le peintre des frissons*. La Vaudère thus likely modified and revised her prose version of *Le rêve de Mysès* in light of Colette's and Missy's performance. As though taking a cue from her rivals, *Le rêve de Mysès* incorporates a peripheral lesbian character who was otherwise absent from the verse form. In adding an exclusively female subplot, La Vaudère inscribes her work in a Western cultural imagination that, as Michael Lucey argues, associates ancient Egypt with lesbian eroticism.[31] In this variation, Mahdoura, the female villain, entices the savant Mysès with voyeuristic promises of Sapphic love. In an attempt to distract him from his beloved embalmed queen, she evokes the sexual expertise of her friend and lover Aracknis. The figures of Mahdoura and Aracknis were absent from the verse printed in *Le peintre des frissons* and Colette's and Missy's pantomime; La Vaudère likely added this lesbian storyline as an amendment to her original vision for the work. This edition of *Le rêve de Mysès* also features accompanying photographs of two nude women dancing closely, with captions referencing encounters between Mahdoura and Aracknis (fig. 19). In supplementing these references with photographic representations, La Vaudère adds a visual dimension to her work that appeals to the voyeurism of her audience, as Colette and Missy did months earlier at the Moulin Rouge. In fact, such photographs complement the storyline throughout and create a visual representation that unfolds before the reader's eyes. Given the polemic surrounding the manuscript of *Le rêve de Mysès* and the sensationalized production of *Rêve d'Égypte*, this can hardly be an accidental choice by La Vaudère. Through these explicit auxiliary images, she proposes a modified *Le rêve de Mysès* novella that can compete with the titillating scenes of Colette's and Missy's interpretation of *Rêve d'Égypte*.

P - 889
— Aracknis, par mille jeux charmants, a déjà tenté de me détacher de toi, car elle ne croit pas aux promesses des hommes!...

FIG. 19 Sapphism in *Le rêve de Mysès*. Source: gallica.bnf.fr / BnF.

INTERTEXTUALITY AND *L'AMANTE DU PHARAON*

Mummies appeared in La Vaudère's fiction prior to *Le rêve de Mysès*. Two years earlier, in 1905, La Vaudère published *L'amante du pharaon*, a story of an ancient Egyptian who preserves his dead lover through embalmment. When read side by side with the novella *Le rêve de Mysès*, this novel appears to be its thematic and stylistic precursor. Archival documents suggest that La Vaudère had been writing *L'amante du pharaon* as early as the spring of 1904, and many passages from the novel appear verbatim in *Le rêve de Mysès*.[32] Though the storyline is rather complicated, the overarching themes are familiar to readers of La Vaudère: protagonist Hary-Thé mourns his deceased lover Zélinis and has her body preserved through mummification. Unbeknownst to him, Zélinis is still alive, and what he believes to be her mummified body has really been swapped with that of a courtesan. At the end of the novel, Zélinis reappears disguised as a revived mummy and reunites with her beloved Hary-Thé. Based on their respective plots and themes, there are numerous parallels between *L'amante du pharaon* and *Le rêve de Mysès*. To begin, both showcase ancient Egyptian traditions and reanimated female mummies.[33] Both also blur the liminal space between life and death: the practice of embalming interrupts decomposition and conserves the mortal beauty of a female lover. Finally, both depict mummification as a means for dissimulation in which bodies are reworked, transformed, and disguised.

The parallel themes and storylines of the two works suggest that Hary-Thé and Mysès are analogous character types. Indeed, for her profile of Mysès, La Vaudère reuses (with slight modifications) passages depicting Hary-Thé's spiritual reflections on death:

> Pourtant, la mort ne se présentait pas à son esprit avec son cortège de douleur et d'épouvante. Comme tous les hommes de sa caste, [*Hary-Thé*] méprisait la vie. L'inerte momie, toute raidie sous ses bandelettes, avec la fixité de son regard d'émail dans son masque d'or, n'éveillait en lui aucune répulsion. Il aimait la solennité des sarcophages, le mystère des chambres de pierre où dormait l'âme des morts.
>
> Toute l'architecture égyptienne, à l'image des pensées de l'homme, ne s'inspirait, d'ailleurs, que d'un rêve funèbre. Les pyramides, les obélisques, les pylônes, les colonnes immenses représentaient une vague forme humaine: celle du mort enlinceulé dans ses bandelettes. L'Égyptien ne pensait qu'à la résurrection et ne travaillait que pour l'éternité![34]

Hary-Thé's—and Mysès's—ruminations on mummification and immortality gesture toward larger questions of artistic creativity and preservation. Mummification in these works is itself a fitting metaphor for the origins and transformations of *Le rêve de Mysès*. La Vaudère describes the Egyptian technique in *L'amante du pharaon* and *Le rêve de Mysès* and emphasizes the subsequent risk of body swapping:

> La substitution d'un corps était chose grave que l'on punissait sévèrement dans la classe sacerdotale. Cette fraude, cependant, s'accomplissait assez fréquemment, grâce au mystère qui entourait les pratiques de l'embaumement. Le défunt n'étant montré aux familles que recouvert de son masque et enveloppé de ses bandelettes, il était aisé de le faire disparaître, et des morts obscurs occupaient parfois des sarcophages princiers. [. . .]

> Nul ne les soupçonnait [les prêtres], nul n'était tenté de défaire les masques d'or ou d'ivoire, de dérouler les bandelettes des corps confiés à leurs soins; aussi, arrivait-il parfois qu'un grand personnage, enveloppé de toile grossière cousue à grands points, vînt, après un séjour plus ou moins prolongé dans le natron, prendre sa place anonyme dans les caveaux publics. Les jeunes mortes, violées par les embaumeurs, étaient livrées aux crocodiles sacrés.[35]

The pilfering of mummies—artistic products themselves—is analogous to Missy's creative theft, which threatened the preservation of La Vaudère's name and work. However, La Vaudère reclaimed ownership of her pantomime through revisions (the inclusion of a lesbian character or the accompanying erotic photography, for example) and the publication of *Le rêve de Mysès*. Like one would mummify a body, La Vaudère altered and reworked *Le rêve de Mysès* so that it would live on in some other immortal form. In this context, despite their similarities, I do not wish to reduce *Le rêve de Mysès* to a mere offshoot of *L'amante du pharaon*. Instead, I choose to consider it in dialogue with other texts (and performances) that allowed La Vaudère to revise and recover it as her own original concept.

LA VAUDÈRE'S PLAGIARISM

In a great twist of irony, many passages that are common to both *L'amante du pharaon* and *Le rêve de Mysès* did not originate with La Vaudère. Instead, like Missy and Colette, she also appropriated others' works, as she frequently did in her fiction (see chapter 3). In *L'amante du pharaon* and *Le rêve de Mysès*, many of the extensive details on Egyptian customs were copied word for word from nineteenth-century Egyptology texts and provide yet another layer of intertextuality to La Vaudère's mummy fiction. For example, in her depiction of mummy burial rites in both works, La Vaudère recycles a passage that originated in Gustave Le Bon's *Les premières civilisations* (1889), an eight-hundred-page historical study of ancient civilizations:

> *L'amante du pharaon*: "Parfois, la sépulture consistait uniquement en une petite chapelle recouvrant un puits. La momie, souvent, était simplement placée au centre d'un édifice, de forme pyramidale, dans lequel on avait ménagé une cavité murée. Dans les sépultures les plus simples on se bornait à creuser un trou de quelques mètres

de profondeur au fond duquel on descendait le cercueil et qu'on recouvrait avec de la terre et des pierres."[36]

Le rêve de Mysès: "Parfois, la sépulture consistait uniquement en une petite chapelle recouvrant un puits. La momie était simplement placée au centre d'un édifice de forme pyramidale, dans lequel on avait ménagé une cavité murée.

Dans les sépultures les plus simples, on se bornait à creuser un trou de quelques mètres de profondeur au fond duquel reposait le cercueil et que l'on recouvrait avec de la terre et des pierres."[37]

Les premières civilisations: "Parfois la sépulture consiste uniquement en une petite chapelle recouvrant un puits au fond duquel est le caveau renfermant la momie. D'autres fois la momie est simplement placée au centre d'un édifice de forme quelconque, généralement pyramidal dans lequel a été ménagée une cavité murée et précédée d'une chambre, où se trouve la momie. Dans les sépultures les plus simples, on se bornait à creuser un trou de quelques mètres de profondeur au fond duquel on descendait le cercueil et qu'on comblait ensuite avec des pierres."[38]

In fact, Le Bon's exhaustive work inspires multiple passages appearing in these two works. In a detailed digression, La Vaudère inserts another lengthy description of Egyptian mummification and burial customs from *Les premières civilisations*, a sample of which I cite here:

L'amante du pharaon: "L'embaumement ne s'employait pas seulement pour la dépouille des êtres humains, on l'appliquait aussi aux cadavres des animaux sacrés, tels que le chat, le crocodile. Au-dessous de l'Égypte qu'arrose le Nil, il y a une Égypte souterraine composée des innombrables momies qu'y a entassées la piété singulière d'un peuple."[39]

Le rêve de Mysès: "L'embaumement ne s'employait pas seulement pour la dépouille des êtres humains; on l'appliquait aussi aux chats, aux crocodiles, aux serpents, etc . . .

Au-dessous de l'Egypte [*sic*] qu'arrose le Nil, il y a une Egypte [*sic*] souterraine, composée des innombrables momies qu'y a entassées la piété singulière d'un peuple."[40]

Les premières civilisations: "L'embaumement ne s'employait pas seulement pour conserver les cadavres humains; il s'appliquait aussi aux cadavres d'animaux considérés comme sacrés, tels que le chat, le crocodile, par exemple. En fait, au-dessous de l'Égypte qu'arrose le Nil, il y a une autre Égypte souterraine habitée par les millions et les millions de momies que la piété d'un peuple y a entassées pendant 5,000 années."[41]

Both *L'amante du pharaon* and *Le rêve de Mysès* also contain passages from Ernest Bosc's *Isis dévoilée ou l'égyptologie sacrée* (1891), a study of ancient Egyptian religion and mythology. Bosc outlines the mummification techniques of Egyptian *taricheutes* or *paraschites*, whose responsibilities included removing the organs and viscera of the deceased. La Vaudère incorporates these details in a depiction of the embalming procedure:

L'amante du pharaon: "Le prêtre, chargé de ce soin, avait revêtu le costume symbolique de l'emploi; sa tête, coiffée par celle du chacal, emblême [*sic*] d'Anubis gardien de l'hémisphère inférieur, était complètement rasée et il portait le *schenti* écarlate, fixé sur la hanche par une ceinture d'or."[42]

Le rêve de Mysès: "Pour toucher à ces restes sacrés, il avait revêtu le costume symbolique des 'Paraschites.' Sa tête, coiffée par celle du chacal, emblème d'Anubis, gardien de l'hémisphère inférieur, était complètement rasée, et il portait le 'schenti' écarlate, fixé sur la hanche par une ceinture d'or."[43]

Isis dévoilée ou l'égyptologie sacrée: "Le Taricheute qui était chargé de retirer les entrailles et les intestins du cadavre était revêtu du costume symbolique; il avait la tête coiffée par celle du chacal, emblême [*sic*] d'Anubis gardien de l'hémisphère inférieur."[44]

Ironically, to render her portrayal of ancient Egypt more authentic, La Vaudère liberally copied from authors such as Le Bon and Bosc. There are other digressions on ancient Egyptian civilization that appear throughout *Le rêve de Mysès* and *L'amante du pharaon*. Given La Vaudère's penchant for plagiarism and the curious shifts in tone, subject matter, or style of these passages, it is not a stretch to assume that they also originated elsewhere. La Vaudère's copying adds yet another intertextual element to *Le rêve de Mysès* and draws further attention to the series of revisions, variations, and adaptations that are central to both the pantomime and novella.[45] With their emphasis on ancient Egyptian customs, the stolen passages—likely from sources in Egyptology—also reaffirm La Vaudère's thematic and aesthetic contributions to the mummy fiction genre. Indeed, in an act analogous to embalming, plagiarism allows La Vaudère to revitalize an earlier text and transform it into a unique and enduring artistic product of her own.

NINETEENTH-CENTURY MUMMIES AND PRESERVATION

During her most productive writing years, Jane de La Vaudère lived among "mummies." On the property of the Château de La Vaudère in Parigné-l'Évêque (Sarthe), there is a small burial chapel that houses the remains of her relatives. Of the six cadavers buried here, three have been discernibly embalmed: those of Sophie Debonte, her grandmother; Estelle Huet, her mother-in-law; and a family member who has yet to be identified. While the current states of the bodies show significant signs of decomposition, certain visible clues confirm that these three family members were embalmed upon their deaths. All three bodies were laid to rest under a partial viewing glass, a typical practice of embalming that provided visual access to the preserved head and face of the deceased. The corpse of Sophie Debonte appears to be the most effectively preserved of the family, and we can still see traces of soft tissue on her face (figs. 20 and 21). The remains of Estelle Huet (fig. 22) and the unidentified corpse both bear the signs of a craniotomy, a technique used to remove the brain in earlier methods of embalming.[46]

The nineteenth century witnessed major transformations in embalming practices that were the result of groundbreaking developments in the sciences (and chemistry in particular). As Anne Carol contends, the surge in the embalming industry at this time coincided with the establishment of the modern cemetery.[47] New cemeteries required durable burial plots and markers, and an ensuing cultural shift gave emphasis to body conservation. Initially, embalming required three crucial steps: evisceration of organs, drying out the corpse, and then injecting it with antiseptic solutions to prevent decay. The cranial cavity was opened to remove the brain, was carefully washed, and then filled with chemical compounds, balms, and powders. Finally, the body was tightly wrapped in strips of cloth and placed in a lead coffin with powders and herbs that was then sealed.[48] Inevitably, embalming methods recalled the mummification practices of ancient Egypt, already pervasive in the popular imagination. Terminology reflected these associations, and the older, traditional procedure that required cotton wraps—eventually deemed unnecessary—was often referred to as the "méthode égyptienne" or "méthode à l'ancienne." During

FIG. 20
Embalmed remains of Sophie Debonte, with window.

FIG. 21
Embalmed remains of Sophie Debonte, without window.

FIG. 22
Embalmed remains of Estelle Huet, with window.

La Vaudère's lifetime, it was not unusual for wealthy families to turn to these modes of preservation when they laid their loved ones to rest. In his 1904 piece on La Vaudère, Théodore Cahu captured the serenity of the burial chapel on the château property and the remarkable preservation of the writer's family members: "C'est une construction très simple surmontée d'une croix de pierre où dorment, côte à côte, dans des cercueils à couvercle de verre, les parents aimés, embaumés depuis des longues années déjà. Rien de lugubre dans cette exposition des personnes chères, à peine défigurées par la mort, et qui demeurent, ainsi, toujours près du souvenir."[49]

La Vaudère only had to take a short stroll on the château grounds to come into contact with contemporary "mummies." Though impossible to verify, it is plausible that living—and writing—among embalmed corpses inspired her fiction on ancient Egyptian mummies. In her mummy fiction, La Vaudère's meticulous descriptions of ancient embalming techniques occupy a dominant place in her storylines. Mummification is both a science and an artform, and its practice, successful or not, drives the narrative and plot development. Characters seek to perfect methods of body conservation, with magical results. In *Le rêve de Mysès*, Mysès insists that his special concoction of balms, herbs, and flowers has the unprecedented power to preserve the queen's beauty and lifelike appearance: "J'ai découvert un procédé merveilleux qui conserve aux morts l'apparence de la vie, supprime toute l'affreuse cuisine des préparations ordinaires, ne nécessite point de masque ni de bandelettes."[50] In fact, his techniques are so advanced that they appear to provoke the ultimate miracle: resuscitation and immortality.

The transcendent powers accorded to embalming unquestionably reflect nineteenth-century discourses that associated the Orient with the supernatural. However, La Vaudère's nuanced depictions are not simply a product of clichéd visions but rather a complex allegorical reflection on artistic ownership. Upon awakening from visions of a resuscitated Ahmosis, Mysès finds the rot and decay of the queen's body, described in graphic detail: "Un cadavre noirci, aux membres tordus et calcinés, s'y dressait sinistrement. D'Ahmosis, de la grande fleur voluptueuse, conservée dans les baumes, il ne restait plus rien. Une nuit avait suffi pour parfaire l'œuvre du tombeau. Les restes de la reine, rongés, hideux, étaient semblables à ceux qui, longuement, ont séjourné dans la terre, oubliés des humains."[51] Within just a day, Ahmosis's body shows years of decay, and instead of reviving the embalmed corpse, Mysès's formula has accelerated its decomposition. What remains of the mummy reflects a powerful statement about artistic creation and lasting recognition. Given the contentious backdrop of *Le rêve de Mysès*'s theft and the Moulin Rouge performance, this becomes even clearer with the novella's final line, which justifies Mysès's tragic destiny as his punishment for seeking eternal preservation: "Tout le bonheur était perdu pour lui, car il avait outragé les dieux en se targuant d'une vaine science."[52] Ultimately, Mysès's efforts to immortalize are both useless and (self-) destructive, provoking the wrath of the gods to hasten the decay of his artform: mummification. Could this be read as a warning to Missy and Colette, whose desire for fame might lead to an analogous fate in the artistic world? Was La Vaudère's *Le rêve de Mysès* also a condemnation of "le rêve de Missy"?[53]

Or perhaps this is a self-conscious and cynical commentary on La Vaudère's own demands, however futile, for proper name recognition for her work from years past and in those to come. Like Mysès, an artist who dreamt of impossible formulas for eternal preservation, La Vaudère's visions of resuscitation and immortality were seemingly unrealistic. For in one final symbolic blow to La Vaudère's quest for artistic eminence, her grave in Paris's Montparnasse Cemetery remains unmarked. Likely due to tensions with surviving relatives who disapproved of her transgressive writing and lifestyle (see chapter 1), her emblematic erasure is indicative of the legacy that she was unable to realize beyond the grave. According to archival documents, La Vaudère's unsuccessful efforts for preservation in artistic circles also extended to her family life. As we recall, her sister Marie, otherwise absent from her estate planning, rebuffed La Vaudère's modest bequest of a portrait from her deathbed. This symbolic rejection seems to have foreshadowed La Vaudère's exclusion from the family grave. In 1918, Marie was the next and final family member to be buried in the Scrive family sepulture, and her name occupies the plaque that would have been attributed to her late sister. With its emphasis on preservation and immortality, La Vaudère's mummy fiction seems to have anticipated such symbolic gestures of repudiation and neglect. However, there is recent evidence of her literary revival and the staying power of her works. Snuggly Books, which specializes in Decadent literature, has published a selection of her novels and short stories translated into English. It seems appropriate that *Le rêve de Mysès* and *L'amante du pharaon* are among them.[54]

CHAPTER 5

Deciphering La Vaudère's "Fierce" Feminism

La Vaudère's shifting and contradictory depictions of womanhood and feminist causes made her a dual target for misogynistic critics and feminist journalists alike. At different points in her career, the literary press vilified her as a militant feminist, while journalists at *La fronde* denounced her as an antifeminist.[1] La Vaudère never aligned herself with one political stance or movement, but her recurrent allusions to "féminisme" indicate that she was closely following debates about gender and women's rights as they unfolded and took various shapes around her. If, by 1905, she had come to declare herself a "féministe farouche," she had never fully embraced—or been embraced by—any feminist movement or faction.[2] Her fluctuating positions on gender roles and gender expression over the course of her career was complicated. In novels, for example, she advocated for women's emancipation from the conventions of the heterosexual union or promoted modern visions of female desire. In short stories and press editorials, La Vaudère repeatedly illustrated the inherent disparities of heterosexual courtship, sexual expression, fidelity, and divorce that she claimed benefited men and left women emotionally and physically unfulfilled. At times, however, while critiquing gender inequality, she mocked prominent women's rights activists through caricature or rebuked organized feminism as impractical and unrealistic. She also reverted to essentialist notions of womanhood that celebrated a woman's "natural" role as a dutiful and chaste wife.

Nonetheless, La Vaudère was consistently interested in women's issues and promoted initiatives intended to empower them emotionally, intellectually, and sexually. As we will see, La Vaudère expressed a critical consciousness about gender inequalities in the private (marital, familial) and public (educational, artistic) spheres. Through the 1890s and until her death, she condemned the gendered double standards within two specific realms: the literary profession and the institution of marriage. As a woman writer having gone through her own bitter divorce, La Vaudère could speak from her own experience, and for her, the personal was political. The works in La Vaudère's *œuvre* that consider questions of sexual difference are vast and varied, spanning a range of years and genres that go beyond her more commonly referenced novel *Les demi-sexes*.[3] This chapter focuses on a selection of lesser-known editorials, short stories, and novels and tracks the nuances of her positions and their evolution throughout her career.

I have organized the pages that follow into three specific yet overlapping categories. First, I examine La Vaudère's engagement with feminist campaigns and activists in their historical and social context. While allusions to organized feminism are profuse in her writing, they are also inconsistent, a reflection of feminism's own diverging branches and ongoing development. Her frequent use of the terms "féminisme" and "féministe" placed her in dialogue with activists of the period and created a space to explore her own developing feminist consciousness. La Vaudère most often applied this consciousness to critiquing the institution of marriage, which constitutes my second category of analysis. Many of her works addressed the obstacles that marriage posed to female autonomy, and her reflections on divorce betray an awareness about ongoing debates about its legal frameworks. Echoing an important polemic at the turn of the century, she pushed for the emotional *and* sexual fulfillment of the female spouse through a transparent approach to educating young girls about sex. The third category concerns La Vaudère's spiritist texts, where she filtered her viewpoints on inequality through male spirit voices. The popular genre of spiritist fiction allowed La Vaudère to highlight the arbitrariness of gender codes through multilayered narratives. She channeled male voices that denounced gender essentialism and, in a *mise-en-abyme*, incarnated a fluidity that resisted the gender binary. Her spiritist pieces contained plagiarized passages, once again allowing La Vaudère to deftly move between positions without fully binding herself to one particular or controversial stance. By examining La Vaudère's recurrent intertextual references, we can trace how she scrutinized and revised a heritage of canonical works and their representations of sexual and gender difference. As these three areas of interest will show, La Vaudère's contradictory positions reflect an engagement with organized feminist agendas as well as an evolving critique of gender essentialism.

A CHRONOLOGY OF LA VAUDÈRE'S TERMINOLOGY

The terms "féministe" and "féminisme" appear repeatedly—and ambivalently—throughout La Vaudère's corpus, and most notably in her editorials. Despite the multiplicity of feminist factions and divergent ideologies at the time, La Vaudère employs the term "féminisme" more broadly to denote an organized movement of political activists. Whether the object of reverence or the target of parody, her recurrent references suggest an attentiveness to the progress and limitations of contemporary feminist agendas. La Vaudère's first reference to "féminisme" appeared in 1896 and signaled a timely response to the feminist momentum around her. By the 1890s, feminist rhetoric was omnipresent in sociopolitical debates about education, divorce reform, and parity in the workplace.[4] Periodicals circulated that were devoted entirely to women's causes, and *La citoyenne*, *La revue féministe*, and *La fronde* disseminated feminist ideals to a broad audience.[5] Newspapers unaffiliated with the movement printed columns penned by leading feminist figures and reported on a new surge of feminist conferences.[6] These meetings allowed activists of different factions to convene and debate and were instrumental for articulating agendas and implementing plans of action. Clearly in tune with the current climate, La Vaudère was skeptical of organized feminism's efficacy in eliciting change. In her 1896 editorial condemning misogyny in the literary and medical fields, she acknowledges the efforts of contemporary feminist advocates but regrets the futility of their message: "Malgré la croisade que l'on mène en faveur du féminisme, les choses demeureront en l'état. L'*Eve* [*sic*] *nouvelle* de M. Jules Bois et l'*Humanisme intégrale*, de M. Léopold Lacour, sont de jolies tentatives littéraires qui resteront dans le domaine de la littérature. Si l'homme a besoin de lutter pour se prouver sa force, il a aussi besoin de 'mépriser' pour croire à sa supériorité. L'*Avant-courrière*, de Mme Schmahl, n'y pourra rien!"[7] The three figures that she cites were well known beyond feminist circles. Bois and Lacour, who had published their respective feminist treatises earlier that year, had collaborated on a series of well-attended feminist lectures at the Paris Bodinière theatre. Jeanne Schmahl had founded the woman's group "Avant-courrière," which targeted laws preventing women from serving as legal witnesses and wives from controlling their own incomes. La Vaudère was supportive of the activists' causes, and her cynicism lies with the theoretical framework of their works, not the content. La Vaudère would repeat this claim in the next few years, targeting organized feminism's elitist and exclusionary rhetoric as a hindrance to change.

A few months later, La Vaudère made a call to action to counter what she perceived as French feminism's limitations. In 1897, inspired by Nashville's Tennessee Centennial Exposition, she wrote an editorial whose headline placed feminism under the spotlight. Entitled "Une exposition pour le féminisme," the piece highlighted the opportunities for international recognition that the Woman's Building offered female artists like herself.[8] As indicated by the title of the article, La Vaudère views the Exposition through a feminist lens and considers opportunities for women outside of France. She implores French women artists to take advantage of what she calls a "feminist cause" that is not readily available to them in their home country: "À une époque où la cause du féminisme est si bien défendue à l'étranger, il est pénible de voir l'indifférence ou la mauvaise volonté qui accueillent, chez nous, toutes les tentatives faites en faveur du relèvement de la femme."[9] She once again alludes to Bois, Lacour, and Schmahl and regrets that their important feminist work has been ignored in her country. La Vaudère is, however, skeptical of Schmahl's ambitious agenda, which she believes "risque fort de ne jamais atteindre le but qu'elle se propose."[10]

Instead, she proposes a more practical, realistic, and immediate approach to women's advancement. She argues that the Tennessee Centennial Exposition is an alternative occasion for French women to gain international exposure in a more welcoming setting. "La femme française," she writes, "si dédaignée dans son beau pays, trouverait là un appui sympathique et sérieux; elle pourrait être assurée d'obtenir, à Nashville, comme à Chicago, tout le succès que méritent son goût si délicat et son talent si puissamment original."[11] Though the term for "feminism" originated in France, the United States was regarded internationally for its revolutionary progress in women's issues.[12] Around this time, American women enjoyed a reputation as fully autonomous beings and were frequently portrayed by contemporaries as more emancipated than their French counterparts.[13] La Vaudère's enthusiasm for American feminism in general and the Tennessee Exposition in particular was likely linked to women's notable participation in the World's Columbian Exposition in Chicago in 1893. Like its Tennessee successor, the Chicago Exposition included a Woman's Building that displayed thousands of female-authored books—including six by La Vaudère—from around the world. La Vaudère exploits her media visibility to facilitate networking and provide women readers with the contact information of the Exposition's organizers. As a call to French women to seek out opportunities abroad, the article is both a rallying cry and a critique of the reception of feminism within the Hexagon. La Vaudère takes a pragmatic approach, moving away from theoretical rhetoric to offer something practical and direct to French women: the name and address of the Woman's Building representative in Paris.

At times, La Vaudère incorporated conservative reasoning as justification for a pro-woman, if not feminist, position. In 1897, when the Parisian École des beaux-arts announced that it would begin admitting female students, she wrote an editorial for *La presse* that addressed the perceived threat of women's education. The column's initial assertions are unequivocal: women are continually denied equal access to education because men fear a subsequent loss of control over their wives. She writes, "Les maris craignent peut-être avec raison que le savoir de l'épouse ne se tourne contre eux; un ennemi armé résiste à l'oppresseur et peut être dangereux. Il faut donc le tenir en lieu sûr, le mettre dans l'impossibilité de se révolter."[14] La Vaudère overtly attacks men for restricting their wives and daughters to an "éducation d'esclaves": "Les ignorants sont les ennemis nés de l'élévation de l'intelligence féminine. [. . .] Que deviendrait leur prestige si leurs compagnes s'avisaient d'apprendre quelque chose? . . . En résumé, ce sont les imbéciles qui sont les plus grands ennemis de l'émancipation de la femme."[15] After designating bourgeois men as ignorant imbeciles, La Vaudère recalls the recent momentum of the feminist movement to defend her charges. "Depuis quelque temps, cependant, la mode a tourné," she notes. "Il est de bon ton d'être féministe et de prêcher l'émancipation de la femme."[16] The reference to feminism serves to convince readers of an impending shift in modern thinking, yet in characterizing the movement as socially fashionable, La Vaudère reveals her own skepticism about its staying power and practicality.

Despite her progressive position on women's education, La Vaudère resorts to conventional conceptions of femininity to reassure readers that an educated woman poses no risk to the organization of the domestic sphere. The final passages of the piece take a more conservative turn through an espousal of strict biological difference: "Que les sots se rassurent, les femmes jamais ne deviendront les rivales de l'homme, car rien pour elles ne saurait remplacer l'amour."[17] La Vaudère concludes her editorial with a romanticized portrait of womanhood driven by an instinct for conjugal love. While still endorsing educational opportunities for women, she proposes that feminine intelligence ultimately enhances a woman's ability to be a devoted wife: "Or, l'amour entre deux êtres d'une égale intelligence s'épurera à son tour, deviendra une chose vraiment grande et belle. [. . .] Le désir de plaire met, d'ailleurs, la délicatesse, l'élégance et toutes les séductions féminines hors de l'atteinte de l'éducation. Les femmes, dans leur jeunesse, n'en aimeront pas moins [. . .]. [E]lles mettront leurs connaissances acquises et leur supériorité aimante aux pieds de l'homme choisi entre tous, et la grandeur du sacrifice les enchaînera davantage, parce qu'elles restent toujours et avant tout: sœurs de charité!"[18] This final image—a wife at her husband's feet, chained to him for eternity—restores the conventional structure of the couple in this piece. In privileging a woman's role as dutiful wife, La Vaudère evokes the rhetoric of what historian Karen Offen classifies as nineteenth-century "relational" feminism. As opposed to individualist feminism, which promoted women's full actualization independent of the heterosexual union, relational feminism drew from an essentialist and heteronormative model that considered men and women as complementary. Also referred to as "familial" feminism, relational feminism emphasized women's societal contributions as mothers and wives in order to benefit its cause.[19] La Vaudère celebrates women's uniqueness as wives, but she diverges from relational agendas by advocating for women's intellectual emancipation. She reassures husbands of their authority—but only in matters of the heart, not intellect. This final distinction is an important one: she reproduces essentialist tropes of subservient femininity but stops short of extending this biological determinism to intelligence. In other words, women are naturally good wives to men, *and* equally intelligent.

The following year, in her most conservative editorial to date, La Vaudère doubled down on her essentialist vision of womanhood and targeted contemporary feminism as a threat to marital harmony. In *Le petit bleu de Paris*, she portrays the feminist agenda as a danger to the family and the wife's mental state: "Si les théories des féministes étaient plus répandues, on pourrait les accuser de nous avoir conduits à la désorganisation de la famille par de dangereuses revendications égalitaires. Mais les théories des féministes n'ont pas dépassé un clan minime de jongleurs intellectuels."[20] La Vaudère's condemnation of the "revendications égalitaires" seems to suggest that she is specifically denouncing individualist feminism, which critics tended to view as menacing to the conventional family structure. La Vaudère nearly blames feminism for suicidal tendencies among bourgeois women, citing the attack on marital conventions as a danger to a wife's emotional stability. Fortunately, she notes, feminism has yet to make a significant impact beyond elitist intellectual circles, a belief that she has articulated before. In a final gesture toward essentialist models of womanhood, La Vaudère rejects a feminism that she sees in opposition to a woman's natural instinct: "La vérité," she writes, "c'est que la Femme suit dans l'oubli l'amour, le devoir, le patriotisme, la foi, toutes les belles choses qui ensoleillaient le chemin et consolaient de la douleur de vivre. Au fond, elle se soucie peu d'être *officiellement* l'égale de l'homme, puisqu'elle sait bien qu'elle a bouleversé la terre et qu'elle avait tous les pouvoirs alors qu'on ne lui en accordait aucun! . . . Son émancipation? . . . Des mots! des mots! des mots!"[21] Though she denounces organized feminism in general terms, she draws from elements of relational feminist rhetoric, which celebrates the uniqueness and power ("tous les pouvoirs") of womanhood. Her italicized use of the adverb "officiellement" ("*officiellement* l'égale de l'homme") has legal connotations, and she values the power of biological determinism over formal legislation in shaping gender roles. Once again, La Vaudère rebuffs organized feminism and the activists working to establish rights for women through legal and "official" means.

La Vaudère's criticism did not go unnoticed by prominent activists of the period. This particular editorial elicited a response the following week from *La fronde*, a leading feminist periodical of the time. In her editorial, the renowned journalist Camille Bélilon claims that "Mme de la Vaudère parle en antiféministe."[22] Bélilon argues that La Vaudère's concern for the organization of the family ignores the gendered double standards of marriage under the Civil Code. Accordingly, without the realization of La Vaudère's so-called dangereuses revendications égalitaires, the husband, already benefiting from the social acceptance of male adultery, may freely abuse the household finances: "Le mari prend sans permission la dot de sa femme et la donne à une fille!"[23] Bélilon's retort is curious for a few reasons. First, and as we examine later in this chapter, one of La Vaudère's greatest preoccupations in her writing was the gendered disparity within marriage. In her fiction and newspaper columns, she repeatedly condemned arranged unions that benefited the husband's finances at the wife's emotional and sexual expense. Why had she supported maintaining the conventional structure of the family, given the circumstances of her divorce? The contradiction is not lost on Bélilon, and the specificities of her argument deserve a second look. As readers may recall from chapter 1, La

Vaudère was granted a divorce after her husband had spent the entirety of her dowry on his mistress. Though impossible to verify, these details make one wonder if Bélilon's rebuke was personal, assuming she was aware of the particulars of La Vaudère's divorce just three months earlier. It seems unlikely that the degree of similarities between La Vaudère's personal life and the hypothetical scenarios evoked by Bélilon are merely coincidental. Bélilon's deductions about marital strife seem strangely specific: Was she trying to convince, if not provoke, La Vaudère by alluding to her personal life? La Vaudère's personal circumstances may have changed her views, and to my knowledge, this was the last time that she targeted feminism with such unwavering and unequivocal hostility. Its personal nature notwithstanding, Bélilon's editorial designates La Vaudère as a noteworthy player in feminist debates and exemplifies how prominent activists addressed the complexities of her relationship with feminism.

This was not the only time that La Vaudère's name appeared in *La fronde*. The newspaper regularly promoted and reviewed her fiction between the years 1898 and 1903. Her absence from subsequent issues seems to have coincided with the newspaper's move from a daily to a monthly publication (it closed its doors in 1905). By appearing in *La fronde*, La Vaudère's name was associated with feminist ideals that targeted a readership committed to social and political reforms. To my knowledge, Bélilon's piece was exceptional in its critique of La Vaudère's traditionalist views. Other references to La Vaudère were mostly positive (*Le sang*, for example, was commended as a novel that "ne manque ni de puissance ni de talent").[24] The newspaper's more conservative critics, however, rebuked her erotic works for adopting a masculinist gaze of the female body. One journalist condemned *Le mystère de Kama* as a "livre pornographique [. . .] écrit à l'usage des vieux messieurs libertins" and bemoaned La Vaudère's representation of womanhood in relationship to male desire.[25] La Vaudère's diverse portrayals in the feminist press reflect her continually shifting and evolving engagement with feminism, as well as the divergent views within the movement. For some, she was too conservative, while for others, she was too radical. This wide range of responses from feminists themselves attests to an inability to comfortably position La Vaudère within a single faction or philosophy. And her views continued to evolve.

In 1899, La Vaudère wrote an editorial for *La presse* that addressed sexism in the literary profession, and again emphasized a woman's natural and instinctive duty to her husband. However, this piece marked a significant shift in La Vaudère's views and argued that conventional womanhood—which she had often extolled—was harmful to the woman writer. In "Protestations: la femme," she promotes an ideology that she calls feminist yet distanced herself from its label. The piece opens with a defense of women writers, a response to a recent work of criticism targeting "amazones" through a "jeu de massacre."[26] Her word choice is an obvious reference to *Le massacre des amazones*, Han Ryner's misogynist "study" of two hundred women writers whom he overtly belittles (as readers may recall from chapter 2, he therein labeled La Vaudère a "goose"). La Vaudère refuses to name the work directly, a gesture that both invalidates and silences Ryner's "opuscule." For her, the "apprentis écrivains" who condemn contemporary *femmes de lettres* are symptomatic of a larger anti-feminist response to the increase in women in public roles: "La femme, disent les anti-féministes, empiète sur le domaine masculin, dispute à l'homme ses moyens d'existence, lui fait une concurrence déloyale. La riposte est facile: les empiètements sont égaux."[27] Directed toward an anti-feminist faction, La Vaudère's retort establishes her own position, by extension, as feminist. However, she avoids labeling her perspective outright and quickly distances herself from the term. "Sans parler du *féminisme* qui, trop célèbre par quelques esthètes équivoques, nuit plutôt à la bonne cause," she writes, "il est permis de juger impartialement et de reconnaître le mérite quand, par hasard, il se présente. [. . .] Je pourrais citer des œuvres de tout premier ordre dues à des plumes féminines, de hautes études sociales et philosophiques qui témoignent d'un sens critique et d'une profondeur de vue admirables."[28] As we have seen in previous editorials, La Vaudère's critique of contemporary feminism lies in its impracticality, obscurity, and elitism ("esthètes équivoques"), not its ideology ("la bonne cause"). Paradoxically, her use of italics and the rhetorical device of paralepsis draws more attention to the feminist cause: in declining to explore it in depth, La Vaudère actually invites contemplation of contemporary feminism and makes it central to the discussion.

As she has done before, La Vaudère then incorporates a narrative that draws from essentialist notions of sexual difference. However, what distinguishes this seemingly conservative and familiar position is her critical interrogation of normative femininity. As part of her defense against critics like Ryner and to reassure readers, she emphasizes the innate feminine virtue inherent to all female intellectuals. A woman writer is, after all, a woman nonetheless: "Que de dévouement, de générosité, d'abnégation, de tendresse chez la mère, la sœur, l'amante, l'épouse! Ne nous dit-on pas que certains hommes célèbres ne doivent leurs lauriers qu'à leurs compagnes, qui, discrètement, restent dans l'ombre? Et le plus beau succès dramatique de ces derniers temps n'est-il pas dû, en grande partie, à la femme de l'auteur, qui ne fut même pas nommée?"[29] While Ryner vilifies the woman writer, La Vaudère instead highlights her silent contributions and redirects the criticism to challenge the legitimacy of prominent male authors. The woman writer that she chooses to celebrate is not the one at the forefront, aggressively asserting herself in the artistic realm, but rather the dutiful and self-effacing wife, whose own intellectual pursuits come second to her husband's literary production. La Vaudère undercuts Ryner's amalgam of the woman writer with the clichéd *bas-bleu* (as reflected in his volume's subtitle, "études critiques sur deux cents bas-bleus contemporains"). Instead of hyper-masculinized or neglectful of her domestic duties, La Vaudère's woman writer is deferential to her family life and maintains conventional codes of womanhood. Herein lies the crux of the piece. Unlike previous editorials, in which she celebrated women's natural instinct to dutifully honor their husbands, La Vaudère attributes a woman writer's inferior social status to her own self-effacement and modesty. In a word, "la femme n'a pas de pire ennemie qu'elle-même," and she encourages both men and women to break from normative gender roles that are detrimental to women's intellectual actualization.[30] Feminism does indeed play a role here. Given the article's structure and organization, the woman writer is also implicated in larger evolving feminist concerns of the period. La Vaudère skillfully interweaves references to contemporary feminism alongside a defense of women writers, establishing a link between the two discourses and defusing the threat that they pose to traditional family structure and stability. As she had argued previously, a woman can be both a good wife and an intellectual figure. Her allusions to feminism, although seemingly dismissive, suggest an instinct to reflect on its implications for the modern woman writer. In a powerful self-referential gesture, she suggests that for a woman, writing is, in fact, a feminist act.

"FÉMINISTE FAROUCHE": LA VAUDÈRE'S FEMINIST FICTION

In La Vaudère's fictional works, references to contemporary feminism were often more sardonic and one-dimensional. At times, feminist figures appeared briefly in passing and were reduced to caricatures with radical agendas. For example, in her 1900 novel *L'amuseur*, a group of "féministes névropathes" delights at the chance of attending a male wrestling match, their enthusiasm fueled by the violence inflicted upon men.[31] One short story in particular, however, stands out for depicting militant feminism through parody and, though comical, also encourages a thoughtful interrogation of gendered social norms. "Une révolution" was originally published in *La presse* in 1897 but later appeared in La Vaudère's *Les mousseuses* (1901), a collection of playful short stories centered around the modern Parisian woman. Most stories in the volume are satirical yet message driven, and La Vaudère performs a careful balancing act in exposing gendered double standards in marriage and courtship while comically mocking overzealous feminism. She uses various devices of humor in these stories—satire, parody, caricature, hyperbole, irony—to counterbalance poignant messages about gender inequality with amusing derision. As a result, even the most militant female protagonists are harmless, and their naiveté and clumsy demands for equality allow La Vaudère to downplay through humor their hostility toward the male sex. In his review of the collection, Félicien Champsaur classified these women as simultaneously "compliquées, cruelles et charmantes."[32]

"Une révolution" opens with Crespeline des Orgelets (whose name evokes feminist Hubertine Auclert), "une des plus fougueuses propagatrices de l'émancipation féminine," as she prepares a presentation for an approaching feminist conference.[33] Given the story's original publication date (June 23, 1897), La Vaudère was likely inspired by the Paris Congrès féministe international of 1896, in which participants debated strategies to advance women's rights in the political, professional, and domestic spheres.[34] From the story's initial lines, La Vaudère establishes, with hyperbolic humor, a portrait of her protagonist that recalls familiar stereotypes. From the parodic name of the conference, "L'union des *Vierges mûres*" (original emphasis), La Vaudère draws from the trope of the spinster and virginal feminist, a New Woman, whose physical undesirability ("Orgelet" denotes both a French commune and "stye") is inherently linked to her demands for gender parity. La Vaudère does not provide any information about Crespeline's political or social objectives, but instead details her incompetency and erratic notetaking that literally puts her to sleep. Exhausted by the disorder of her work, Crespeline falls into a deep slumber and a detailed dream unfolds that occupies the central focus of the story. In her dream, the women of the world, "lasses d'avoir été, pendant des siècles, classées au rang des êtres inférieurs," unite, revolt, and eliminate their male counterparts.[35] Men and male children are put to death, with the exception of a select few who are kept alive solely for reproductive purposes. The women rule through a socialist vision: financial assets are pooled and distributed among the people, instead of belonging solely to the most privileged groups, and education in the arts and sciences is available to all citizens. Due to the significant decrease in population and relative abundance of resources, the women eradicate all poverty. They also reorganize social practices that have traditionally benefited men. Marriage, "cette institution baroque et vexatoire, cessa d'enchaîner pour la vie les forçats de l'amour! . . . On s'aima purement et noblement, l'ancienne et unique cause de discorde—l'homme—n'existant plus qu'à l'état d'exception nécessaire."[36] This exclusively feminine utopia, which thrives on a shared interest in the well-being of every citizen, is peaceful and diplomatic: "Cela se fit simplement, naturellement, sans fausses théories anarchiques, sans beaux gestes et sans bombes, la femme étant toujours juste et désintéressée."[37]

Though utopic from her perspective, Crespeline's vision promotes a militant brand of feminism, defined by violence against men, infanticide, and female homosociality. Yet through a *deus ex machina* plot device, La Vaudère restores conventional gender norms: a deadly epidemic strikes and takes the lives of the remaining men that were preserved for procreation. Thus ends Crespeline's dream-turned-nightmare, now a dire warning against an exclusionary feminist agenda. La Vaudère notes, "Alors les femmes, *abandonnées à leurs propres ressources*, moururent sans progéniture, et c'est ainsi que finit le monde!"[38] At first glance, an anti-feminist and pronatalist lesson emerges amid the apocalyptic failure of these leaders: women, when left to their own devices, will destroy the world. It is worth recalling that France was battling its own depopulation crisis at this time, and La Vaudère seems to suggest that feminism posed a direct threat to reversing the worrisome trends.[39]

But La Vaudère's story does not end here, and she resumes her tongue-in-cheek message about masculine violence. Crespeline awakes in a panic and looks anxiously for signs of male life, evidence of a lesson learned about the dangers of extremist feminism. Ironically, upon learning of a recent anarchist bombing that left six dead and twenty-four wounded, Crespeline makes a reassuring deduction: in the wake of such senseless violence, men must still be among us! La Vaudère juxtaposes the bleakness of the massacre with her protagonist's relief, who, drunk with joy concludes, "Il y avait donc encore des hommes sur la terre! . . ."[40] French readers were surely sensitive to the anarchist violence referenced here, having witnessed a series of bombings and attacks in Paris in the 1890s. In this historical context, Crespeline's perverse celebration of the terrorist bombing creates a space for a satirical and hard-hitting message about male brutality. In this final sentence, Crespeline's reasoning eclipses the third-person narration, and the use of free indirect discourses renders the reader complicit in her conflation of manhood and aggression. In ending her story here and with a hanging ellipsis, La Vaudère maintains a denigrating depiction of masculinity without any conclusive commentary. Through this narrative structure, she distances herself from the text's provocative ending, leaving the reader to reconcile the humor of Crespeline's deduction, the reality of male violence, and the philosophies of "militant" feminism. As we have seen elsewhere, "Une révolution" ultimately takes aim at the movement's plan of action. However, the story's embedded narrative leaves La Vaudère space to explore and bring to light her own points of convergence with an otherwise caricatural brand of feminism.

In 1905, La Vaudère came to fully embrace the label of feminist in her fiction, without parody or ambiguity. By then, nearly ten years had passed since she first referenced "féminisme" and miscalculated the ineffectiveness of political activists. Now, La Vaudère embraced the term to advocate more generally for women. Instead of addressing feminist thinkers with reticence and mockery, she employed strategies that bolstered their validity and refuted their stigma as extremist and exclusionary. That year, La Vaudère and Théodore Cahu (Théo-Critt) cowrote *Confessions galantes*, a light-hearted epistolary exchange about love, courtship, and marriage from the "female" and "male" perspectives. The volume is a patchwork of literary and artistic citations, anecdotes (some fictional, others perhaps based on life experience), and philosophical reflections on romance, and is supplemented by a series of erotic illustrations by René Préjelan. Cahu published the work under his recognized pen name, Théo-Critt, which is also the name of the male correspondent. The female correspondent signs her letters "Arlette" and serves as an unequivocal stand-in for La Vaudère for a couple of reasons. Arlette composes her letters from the "Château des Bruyères," an obvious nod to the "Château de La Vaudère" from which La Vaudère derived her own pen name. Additionally, in two self-referential gestures, La Vaudère quotes from her sonnet "La Vénus de Syracuse" and her novel *Les androgynes*, and unabashedly cites herself as the author in a footnote ("un peu de publicité ne nuit pas").[41] However, with the use of her pen name "Arlette," as well as the plethora of literary citations, secondhand stories, and anecdotes, La Vaudère articulates a feminist message through a variety of voices that strengthen her claims and provide her a strategic layer of distance.

What is most interesting about this work is the distinctly gendered viewpoint that Arlette/La Vaudère and Critt/Cahu each embody. In their extended discussions about love and marriage, Arlette comes to the woman's defense—at times in the name of "feminism"—and highlights the double standards pertaining to courtship, adultery, or divorce at the woman's expense. In response, Théo-Critt, though demonstrating empathy for his female peers, provides counterpoints in support of a "male" understanding of gender norms. In this pleasant "battle of the sexes," Arlette's contributions are woman centered and reiterate positions seen elsewhere in La Vaudère's writing. What differs, however, about *Confessions galantes* is that the work is structured around a dialogue about sexual difference that showcases male and female perspectives with equal attention. Such a space elevates Arlette's subjectivity as a woman and allows her to respond thoughtfully to discourses about normative gender roles. As such, this overlooked work deserves recognition as one of La Vaudère's most explicitly feminist pieces, written just three years before her death.

In a discussion about the gender norms of heterosexual relationships, Arlette recognizes the implications for modern feminism and alludes to the general movement on two occasions. In the opening letter of the text, while denouncing the sexual objectification of women and the brutality of male sexuality, she sympathizes with feminist activists who, though marginalized from society, refuse to submit to the outdated laws of the Civil Code. "Ah! cher ami," writes Arlette, "combien elles sont excusables celles qui se vengent et, *même*, les féministes qui cherchent dans la vie un idéal autre que celui que leur ont fait des lois caduques et imbéciles!"[42] Arlette paints feminists as more fanatical than those who seek revenge through adultery or violence, and her use of "même" is reflective of their exceptional classification as social outliers—even they, as women, are relatable. La Vaudère's syntax is significant: through the passive construction and indirect object pronoun "leur" ("leur ont fait des lois"), she emphasizes the powerlessness of all women (feminists or otherwise) in the face of institutional conventions. These feminist figures, victims of a larger system, are strikingly different from the one-dimensional Crespeline des Orgelets, and Arlette defends their quest for a better life, independent of the heterosexual union.

In a subsequent letter, Arlette explicitly identifies with feminism. Though she characterizes herself as a "fierce feminist," she consciously avoids biased overgeneralizations about male and female behavior. In her debates with Théo-Critt, she refuses reductive and denigrating examples in her portrayal of the male sex: "Je suis impartiale. Le bien et le mal se trouvent partout et je ne prétends pas, féministe farouche, garder mon éloquence pour la seule défense du sexe faible. Suivant les caractères et les circonstances la balance penche à gauche ou à droite . . . Je me bornerai à rétablir l'équilibre autant qu'il sera en mon pouvoir."[43] Arlette qualifies her unapologetic declaration as a "féministe farouche" by insisting that feminists can and should maintain objectivity and consider men and women as equal in their virtues and flaws. This commitment to impartiality extends to the larger structure of the work, where Théo-Critt has an opportunity to respond and articulate his perspective. The dialogic organization of *Confessions galantes* is itself an embodiment of the balance that Arlette promises to establish: while La Vaudère had once herself been accused of exclusionary feminism, she now provides men and women with an equal possibility for exchange and reflection.[44] Cahu also values this gendered equilibrium, even expressing admiration for feminist objectives that are focused on equitable alternatives to marriage ("l'union libre [. . .] arrangerait tout," he proposes).[45] As readers may recall, Cahu and La Vaudère had maintained a professional and personal relationship in the latter years of her life: La Vaudère added Cahu to her will from her deathbed and bequeathed the collection of her manuscripts to him. The interchange of ideas with a male friend and established author is a safe space for La Vaudère to explicitly proclaim a feminist position. In this way, *Confessions galantes* differs from prior works, where her use of the term "feminist" was riddled with ambivalence, oversimplification, or parody. By 1905, she had come to terms with the label and her own definition, which privileged an inclusive and productive dialogue with men about sexual difference (the opposite of Crespeline's exclusionary model). Though she did not break from the heteronormative model of her earlier works, she embraced a more developed and multidimensional feminist model. She combined elements of relational and individualist feminist philosophies in emphasizing family structure and female autonomy, respectively.[46] Over a period of roughly ten years, while participating in ongoing debates among diverse feminist voices, La Vaudère had finally reconciled her vision of womanhood with a comprehensive and inclusive label.

"PÈRE, JE VEUX DIVORCER": THE GENDERED PLIGHT OF MARRIAGE AND DIVORCE

Though her use of the term "féministe" fluctuated throughout her career, La Vaudère's most consistent feminist cause concerned the institution of marriage.[47] Many of her novels, short stories, and editorials scrutinize the conditions under which women enter marriage. Depicted as naïve and misinformed, La Vaudère's young bride is unsuspecting of the financial interests that drive most bourgeois marriages. Under this model, she is the victim of both a loveless union and the education that failed to prepare her for the realities of the wedding night. Novels such as *Rien qu'amante!* (1894), *Le droit d'aimer* (1895), *Ambitieuse* (1896), and *L'amuseur* (1900) underscore the gendered double standards of conventional courtship and marriage. In this corpus, female protagonists are used for physical pleasure or duped into unhappy marriages where divorce is not a viable option. It is perhaps no coincidence that these recurring themes coincided with the infidelity of La Vaudère's husband and the consequential collapse of her marriage. But in the 1890s, this series of works also helped cement La Vaudère's persona, built largely on her commitment to female perspectives that challenged bourgeois norms of femininity (as I discuss in chapter 2).

In October 1898, two months after the exchange with Bélilon, La Vaudère described marriage as "une affaire, un vil marchandage devant notaire et maire."[48] To replace this defective institution, she proposed the "union de tendresse," a relationship model that favored sentimental interests over economic interests, "sans espoir de dot ni d'héritages facilement réalisables."[49] Specifically, La Vaudère traced the malfunction of modern marriage to the inadequate education of brides-to-be. She believed that only frank, transparent conversations about sex could ensure the sexual well-being of the future couple. Her position alluded to a polemic of the period, in which doctors, religious figures, and feminists weighed in on the relationship between a woman's procreative role and her sexuality. As Mary Lynn Stewart has shown, girls' sexual education was often inhibited by bourgeois modesty, and though mothers were often responsible for preparing their daughters for their wedding night, many conversations were vague and insufficient. Under strict Catholic moral codes, girls' convents also tended to supress open discussions of sexuality.[50] La Vaudère, who was both orphaned at a young age and attended a convent, likely received little practical information about her body or what to expect as a sexual being. The topic of sex education appeared on programs of feminist lectures and conferences in the 1890s. Jules Bois, whom La Vaudère had cited in her editorials, promoted female sex education in a lecture in 1895, and activists denounced the sexual ignorance of young brides and the double standard of "acceptable" sexual behavior.[51] Nelly Roussel, for example, advocated for a woman's sexual education and right to pleasure, but strategically framed her argument in the context of marriage: a wife's knowledge about her body would allow her to love freely and without fear of an unwanted pregnancy.[52]

La Vaudère adopted a similar line of reasoning that tapped into conservative fears about unbridled female sexuality. She argued that without appropriate knowledge about sex, young women were susceptible to falling victim to their own erotic imaginations. Accordingly, the unknown had the potential to lead young women down paths of debauchery, to transform them into "créatures perverses, troubles, aux étranges curiosités, aux fantaisies inquiétantes."[53] Paradoxically, La Vaudère argued that knowledge about sex, though empowering, would encourage women to behave as chaste bourgeois wives. She made a parallel argument years later in *Confessions galantes* and proposed that young women who had freely explored their erotic desires were more likely to be faithful to their husbands. "Ce qu'il y a de certain," she writes, "c'est que les femmes qui ont connu, dans leur jeunesse tumultueuse, tous les secrets de volupté, ne sont plus friandes, plus tard, que des joies chastes du mariage et demeurent, pour le tardif époux, d'une fidélité parfaite."[54] La Vaudère thus presented a tactfully crafted message about female sexual agency: women who understood and had access to their own pleasure were more likely to lead lives as respectable wives and mothers.[55] Like the more progressive feminists, La Vaudère's advocacy for women's erotic gratification posited that female sexuality was distinct from reproduction. To offset potential outrage, she simultaneously prioritized the stability of the family, as she had done in previous editorials. While arguing that female sexual realization would benefit both women and men, she also criticized the hypocrisy of bourgeois values that risked alienating women from their own physical desires: "Tout innocentes encore, elles apprennent à mépriser la grande et noble loi de nature que la société a rabaissée au rang des choses honteuses, des tares physiques et morales dont on ne parle qu'en rougissant à mots couverts."[56]

La Vaudère's advocacy for female sexual autonomy in marriage marked a sharp divergence from mainstream medical figures of the time. As Rachel Mesch has demonstrated, France's depopulation crisis led many doctors to focus their attention on the social structure of marriage, which they viewed as essential to the nation's well-being.[57] Medical literature grew increasingly preoccupied with the intimate dynamics of marital life, and in particular, procreation and sexual desire. According to Peter Cryle, doctors and social hygienists at the turn of the century held husbands responsible for women's sexual satisfaction, and by extension, their fidelity. The sexual initiation of the wedding night was particularly decisive of a wife's conduct thereafter, and a clumsy or unskilled man risked driving her to seek erotic fulfillment elsewhere. Medical literature linked wedding-night trauma to a wide range of female pathologies, including vaginismus (painful contraction of the vagina), sterility, or nymphomania.[58] It was first and foremost the groom's performance that would forever shape the psychosexual health of his spouse. Through this lens, doctors dismissed the woman's agency in her own sexual experience. As one summarized, "The role of the wife is completely passive and straightforward; the active role of the husband is very difficult."[59] La Vaudère, on the other hand, linked marital fidelity to a woman's self-knowledge and extricated female sexual subjectivity from the dominion of her male partner.

Laure Adler examines the nineteenth-century trope of the bourgeois wedding as "la victoire ignoble de l'homme, comparé bien souvent à une bête en rut, à un monstre," and the subsequent wedding night as the "premier viol légal de la conjugalité."[60] La Vaudère contributed to this familiar literary trend. In many of her works, she depicts the "nuit de noces" as a brutal rape between an unknowing bride and a violent husband, insensitive to the physical and emotional needs of his partner.[61] La Vaudère argues that these violent encounters could be avoided if marriage were not treated as a mere financial transaction between families. Instead, she suggests that couples grow well acquainted before the wedding night, a particularly distressing moment for the new bride. She writes, "Les fiancés ne sont pas garantis au marché comme les chevaux que l'on peut encore essayer préalablement. Les erreurs sont donc fréquentes, surtout en France, où les questions d'intérêt, seules, déterminent presque toujours le choix des parents. Deux époux, le soir de leur noce, se connaissent à peine; ils ont dissimulé leurs tares morales commes [*sic*] leurs tares physiques, et les surprises sont parfois lamentables au lendemain du viol légal."[62] Without additional commentary, the editorial thus concludes, leaving the reader with the shocking characterization of the wedding night as a "legal rape."

La Vaudère knew from personal experience that divorce allowed some women to escape unbearable conditions, but the legislation was far from perfect. Though divorce had been reestablished in France in 1884 under the Loi Naquet, La Vaudère regularly underscored its shortfalls—especially for women—and called for continued modifications of divorce and separation laws. Revisions in 1893 accorded divorced women legal majority status and complete control over their property. However, La Vaudère argued that the circumstances under which divorce was granted remained favorable to the husband. In her novels *Le droit d'aimer* (1895); *Ambitieuse* (1896);

L'amuseur (1900); and *Confessions galantes* (1905), she drew attention to the social and financial restraints that women endured when seeking divorce. In 1897, one year before her own case, La Vaudère published an editorial on divorce for *La presse*. Subtitled "Réformes nécessaires," the piece advocated for two significant changes to the current divorce law: that adulterers be able to marry their accomplices and that couples be free to divorce by mutual consent. La Vaudère's concerns echoed a dominant theme of the Congrès féministe international (held in Paris the previous year), where participating activists collectively agreed that women would benefit from expanded grounds for divorce, especially by mutual consent.[63] La Vaudère's editorial was timely. On a more personal note, it also signaled a cynicism about the institution of marriage itself, perhaps due in part to the progressive unraveling of her own union. For example, she claims that prohibiting adulterers from marrying their accomplices unjustly benefits the male lover. According to her logic, the male accomplice may break up a marriage yet escape any legal repercussions.[64] She underscores these double standards with a playful tongue-in-cheek suggestion: "Si l'amant perturbateur du ménage était toujours tenu d'épouser sa maîtresse après sa condamnation, il réfléchirait probablement davantage avant de la détourner de ses devoirs. Cette réparation obligatoire serait excellente à tous les points de vue: on ne rirait plus du mari trompé, mais du séducteur pris au piège!"[65] With humor as a buffer, La Vaudère highlights the gendered disparities of conventional marriage and need for legal and social reform, messages that she disseminates in varied literary forms for the remainder of her career. Though she does not refer to feminism by name, her editorials are timely contributions to debates about women's conditions in the domestic sphere.

LA VAUDÈRE'S FEMINIST SPIRITISM AND GENDER

In the second part of the nineteenth century, Europe witnessed an expanding interest in spiritist philosophies and communication with spirit phenomena. As French popular culture became increasingly drawn to questions of the supernatural, artistic figures incorporated practices like mesmerism, magnetism, hypnotism, and table-turning into their writing. La Vaudère's contemporary Rachilde, for example, famously derived her pen name in the 1870s from a male spirit who, she claimed, inhabited her body during a séance. Given Rachilde's gender nonconformity, Rachel Mesch argues that spiritism operated as a liberating medium for the writer to explore identity and gender variance.[66] As for Rachilde, mediumism offered La Vaudère a pretext to reappropriate male voices and defy the rigid boundaries of gender. However, La Vaudère's spiritist works and their interrogation of the gender binary were instead framed around her advocacy for women and constitute an important part of her feminist writing. For La Vaudère's texts, the use of spiritist philosophy and the practice of mediumism served to subvert male-authored tropes, often through parody and intertextuality. In her spiritist fiction and editorials, La Vaudère often transcribed feminist narratives from male spirits that she said to have channeled through mediumism. In a strategic act resembling ventriloquism, she transmitted her own pro-woman ideologies through the authoritative voices of supernatural phenomena. La Vaudère's penchant for plagiarism complicated these embedded narratives and created an additional possibility for transgression. Many of the messages that she claimed to communicate through mediumism were actually excerpts from well-established male authors of spiritism and occultism. Via mediumism, La Vaudère integrated these texts into her work and recontextualized them from a feminist perspective.

La Vaudère's spiritist works were inspired by the philosophies of Allan Kardec, a founding father of the spiritism movement in nineteenth-century France.[67] In his seminal book *Le livre des esprits* (1857), Kardec famously transcribed a conversation with spirits that he claimed was channeled through female mediums in his circle. By today's standards, the spirits' views on sexual difference were quite progressive. They reported, for example, that souls were sexless and only temporarily occupied male and female bodies, a concept that La Vaudère would also transmit in her spiritist texts. Spirits viewed gender hierarchy as a social construction and called for the emancipation of the modern woman through appropriate legislation: "La loi humaine, pour être équitable, doit consacrer l'égalité des droits entre l'homme et la femme; tout privilége [*sic*] accordé à l'un ou à l'autre est contraire à la justice. *L'émancipation de la femme suit le progrès de la civilisation*; son asservissement marche avec la barbarie."[68] As the foundational text of French spiritism, it is not difficult to imagine why manuals like *Le livre des esprits* may have appealed to women. These texts opened the door to reconceptualize restrictive gender norms and offered new possibilities for self-expression.

Indeed, scholars have emphasized the agency that Kardec's doctrine afforded to female spiritists in the late nineteenth century. Charlotte Foucher Zarmanian brings to light a "feminist" spiritism that valued the conventional feminine traits of intuition and sensitivity. Correspondingly, various circles designated women as central and authoritative figures in communicating with spirits.[69] La Vaudère, for example, was first introduced to spiritist practices by an important female guardian—her grandmother—and claimed to have first witnessed occult phenomena in the exclusively feminine space of her home.[70] Marlene Tromp argues that séances were queer spaces where women could transgress gender norms and engage in homoerotic touching, kissing, and flirting. She also notes that in channeling (or impersonating) male spirits, female mediums disrupted and transgressed gender codes and muddled the boundaries between men and women.[71] Mediumism offered women opportunities to serve as intermediaries between the living and dead, between private and public spaces. Through this role, female mediums occupied exclusive positions for transmitting select information or knowledge, otherwise inaccessible.[72] With this new visibility, some women also disseminated progressive social messages.[73] However, given its numerous layers of narration, mediumism risked blurring the boundaries between source, medium, and transcriber. This narrative fluidity and ambiguity provided ample opportunities to plagiarists. In an ironic twist, some have speculated that sections of Kardec's otherwise feminist *Le livre des esprits* were stolen from the notebooks of Celina Bequet (known sometimes as Japhet), a renowned female medium of the period who had collaborated with Kardec.[74] Kardec had likely committed acts of plagiarism under the guise of mediumism, masquerading intellectual theft as automatic writing. La Vaudère's plagiarism realized a more subversive objective. Unlike Kardec, who co-opted female occultist experiences and silenced female mediums, La Vaudère reappropriated authoritative male voices of spiritist and occultist communities to advocate for women's equality. For both Kardec and La Vaudère, mediumism and plagiarism exposed the unstable and precarious boundaries of masculine and feminine.

La Vaudère's first collection of short stories, *L'anarchiste* (1893), explored the themes of spiritual apparitions, hypnotism, and reincarnation, laying the groundwork for forthcoming depictions of the supernatural. In 1897, she published *Les sataniques*, a collection of short stories that recalled Barbey d'Aurevilly's celebrated 1874 work *Les diaboliques* (as the title suggests). Novels such as *Le mystère de Kama* (1901) further immersed readers in spiritism, and as we shall see, the contents of *La sorcière d'Ecbatane* (1906) were supposedly dictated to La Vaudère by a Persian mage. She also contributed to debates about the supernatural in fiction and theatre. In an editorial for *La presse* in 1897, she maintained that the surging interest in spiritism and occultism in art and popular culture marked a regrettable divergence from their original doctrines.[75] La Vaudère was well versed in related theoretical works and cited a lineage of male writers whom she respected: Edgar Allan Poe, E. T. A. Hoffmann, Éliphas Lévi, Stanislas de Guaita, Papus, and Joseph Alexandre Saint-Yves, among others.[76] Through intertextual references, La Vaudère engaged with influential writers and practitioners of associated philosophies, many of whom were men, whose works she had studied thoroughly. Her own writing drew heavily from an established corpus of spiritist and occultist texts, such as Éliphas Lévi's *Histoire de la magie* (1860); Stanislas de Guaita's *Essais de sciences maudites* (1890); and Léon Denis's *Après la mort* (1891). In a *mise-en-abyme* of the mediumistic premise of some of her novels, she often reproduced passages from these seminal works and passed them off as her own.

Often through irony or intertextual parody, La Vaudère adopted theories of the afterlife to condemn fin-de-siècle gender norms that were detrimental to women. For example, *La sorcière d'Ecbatane* (subtitled "roman fantastique") begins with a "Préface par un esprit" that immediately blurs the lines between author, narrator, and spokesperson for the supernatural world. The preface does not open, however, with the voice of the Persian mage in question, but rather with a first-person female narrator (presumably La Vaudère herself) who recounts her encounter with the spirit during a séance with the famous "Docteur X." Within a few pages, La Vaudère cedes her narration to the mage, whose voice occupies a significant section of the preface. He provides a general overview of spiritist practices and the afterlife to prepare readers for the novel's plot. However, one particular comment reads like a jarring digression from his larger narrative about the spirit world. "La différence des sexes n'est que momentanée," he explains, echoing Kardec. "Dans leur retour à la vie les êtres sont alternativement hommes ou femmes, et souffrent les uns par les autres pour expier d'antérieures injustices, jusqu'au moment où ils redeviennent androgynes, leur incarnation parfaite."[77] The rather random placement of this commentary calls attention to the gender dynamics of the novel's setting, an ancient civilization where men subjugate their female companions to sexual tyranny. The mage resituates the misogyny of the storyline in a larger, more equitable context in current day where men and women come together as equals after death to form one ideal entity. Through his voice, La Vaudère denounces violence against women and claims that biological sex is momentary and arbitrary. Her own channeling of his spirit is itself an example of the transience and fluidity of sexual difference that she describes. This novel, written two years before her death, marks a noteworthy departure from La Vaudère's earlier rhetoric, which was based on essentialist models of femininity and biological determinism.

Like the novel itself, which weaves passages from occult writings into its narrative, the spirit's channeled speech is multilayered. For example, while La Vaudère relays his address, the spirit cites directly from a presumed dialogue that he held with Krishna. Furthermore, large sections of his address are verbatim (and uncredited) reproductions of the writings of Léon Denis's *Après la mort* and Stanislas de Guaita's *Essais de sciences maudites*. Through these acts of plagiarism (not the novel's last), La Vaudère bolsters the theoretical framework of the novel by seamlessly integrating expert male perspectives.[78] However, her concurrent role as a medium (she transmits the mage's voice) and the transcription process also position her within a sequence of voices. In these enactments of masculinity, spiritism and plagiarism allow La Vaudère to suspend the rigid codes of gender and expose their instability.

Elsewhere, La Vaudère combined mediumism with satire to filter and mitigate her evolving interrogation of biological determinism. In 1899, she claimed to have been visited by Napoléon's ghost. In response to a scathing editorial by Paul Adam that lamented the physical disgrace of the modern woman, La Vaudère provided her own take on sexual difference that drew from her "conversation" with Napoléon. In his piece for *Le journal*, Adam evokes the charmlessness of the female body, with its rolls of fat, yellowing teeth, and heavy hindquarters, and implores readers to rethink the gendered categories of "beau sexe" and "sexe laid." Men, he suggests, are perhaps more suited to the former term, as their svelte silhouettes and balanced musculature reflect an aesthetic appeal that women—especially mothers—lack.[79] One week later, La Vaudère published an editorial in *La presse* that addressed Adam's claims. In her piece, she recalls her "dialogue" with Napoléon, who, during a recent séance, enlightened her on the arbitrary mechanisms of sexual difference: "Les humains, après leur mort, ne sont plus ni hommes ni femmes . . . Les âmes n'ont pas de sexe."[80] La Vaudère's syntax recalls an essay published in 1866 in Kardec's *Revue spirite* that postulated that "les âmes ou Esprits n'ont point de sexe."[81] Napoléon explains that the dead transform into "astral balls" and are reincarnated through a random system similar to the lottery. The most sinful of souls are punished appropriately, and the emperor reveals the fateful role that gender plays in the process. Napoléon emerges as a spokesman for La Vaudère (who, until now, has been transmitting his voice), and offers a witticism on gender: "'Ces boules astrales, chargées de tous les péchés d'Israël, sont introduites dans des corps féminins, en dernière expiation. Ce sont toujours des numéros mâles!'"[82] In an amusing dénouement, Napoléon claims that men are punished for their exceptional sinfulness through reincarnation in the female body. For Napoléon and La Vaudère, the randomness—and instability—of gender roles is poetic justice. La Vaudère provides the final punchline in her retort to Adam: "Et voilà comme quoi les hommes deviennent femmes au jeu du loto terrestre . . . Dame, chacun son tour!"[83]

La Vaudère's editorial provides a sharp-witted response to Adam's misogynist attacks on womanhood. Through the authoritative voice of Napoléon, she offers an alternative to Adam's vision of sexual difference and casts guilt upon men for modern woman's fall from grace. Reincarnation allows for a less rigid system of gender roles in which men and women may occupy differently sexed bodies ("les hommes deviennent femmes"). Adam, in his disgust for the female body, should therefore heed her warning, for he, too, may one day be susceptible to "becoming a woman." Despite La Vaudère's lifelong interest in spiritism, its use here to counterattack Adam was particularly well designed. Like La Vaudère, Adam was active in numerous occultist circles and claimed to find writing inspiration in mythic practices like Tarot and automatic writing.[84] Also in 1899, Adam published *La force*, the first of a series of historical novels about Napoléon's empire and legacy.[85] Napoléon's "appearance" during an occult séance was a parodic nod to Adam's public image, familiar to contemporary readers, and now redirected against him to undercut his position. As La Vaudère's ally, Napoléon also served a second purpose. In transmitting this message of gender parity, Napoléon undermines his own Civil Code of 1804, which stripped women of legal autonomy and organized the family around the authority of fathers and husbands. Feminist campaigns targeted principal components of these laws that stipulated that married women could not control their own property, serve as court witnesses, or work without their husband's permission. Now all-knowing about the intricacies of sexual difference, Napoléon returns from the afterlife with a revised vision that renders the gendered organization of his laws obsolete.

It is unlikely that La Vaudère conversed with the emperor's spirit. However, evoking Napoléon's ghost allowed her to propose a less restrictive and more fluid vision of gender while maintaining some distance through satire. Shielded by an act of mediumism, La Vaudère brought to light the arbitrary conventions of gender roles and, by extension, inequality, ideas that she continued to explore as she developed her feminist philosophy.

La Vaudère's "passive" transmission of male voices—through mediumism, intertextuality, or plagiarism—momentarily obscured an active dissemination of a pro-woman ideology. More generally, La Vaudère's response to Adam exemplified a combination of strategic techniques that she implemented repeatedly throughout her feminist works. Through parody, she revealed the disruptive power of spiritism. As Tromp demonstrates, the séance by definition was a liminal and murky space that dissolved the boundaries of self and other, of body and spirit. Mediumism was conducive to a "slippage of identity" and gender play, and the landscape of the séance thus lends itself to a queer reading.[86] Though I do not believe that La Vaudère was a "queer" figure as we understand it today, her use of spiritism to channel male voices contested—and parodied—the boundaries between male/female and masculine/feminine. She thus undermined the perceived "natural" order of the gender hierarchy to promote women's equality. What the works in her corpus have shown, however, is that she was continuously engaged with contemporary women's issues. The content of her editorials, short stories, and novels exemplifies her active participation in dialogues about organized feminism, the institution of marriage, female sexual education, and the social and biological factors of sexual difference. While her contradictory views are symptomatic of an evolving feminist consciousness, they also reflect her mutability and strategic refusal to be restricted by a single position.

CHAPTER 6

Driving into the Future

The Château de La Vaudère and Continued Legacies

In 1906, *Le carnet de la femme* printed a photograph of La Vaudère seated behind the steering wheel of a car (fig. 23). Captioned "Madame Jane de la Vaudère en Auto," the image appeared without context as part of a literary review for one of her recent novels. Though La Vaudère is alone in the car and her hand rests comfortably on the wheel, it is impossible to confirm that she was driving. Nonetheless, her pose exemplified her repeated challenges to the codes of normative femininity. At the turn of the century, the expansion of the automobile industry generated new concerns about women's mobility outside of the home. In simulating driving in the absence of a male companion, La Vaudère embodied concurrent anxieties about female independence. Though there is no archival evidence that La Vaudère could or did drive, her captivation with cars surfaced in her writing, where she frequently discussed the social impacts of the emergent automobile industry or the mechanical and engineering potential for future vehicles. For La Vaudère, the motor vehicle offered endless technological possibilities, and she embraced its promises of new freedom for the bourgeois woman. Given the charged iconography of women and cars, the automobile's allure allowed La Vaudère to explore modern and rapidly evolving models of femininity in her writing and self-representation. In a poetic coincidence, her instinct about the power of women with automobiles anticipated future generations at the Château de La Vaudère, which is currently occupied by rally racer Anne-Charlotte Rousseau and her collection of antique cars.

FIG. 23 In the driver's seat. *Le carnet de la femme*, October 15, 1906.

WRITING THE *CHAUFFEUSE* AND HER AUTOMOBILE

In her fiction and nonfiction, La Vaudère underscored the social progress and engineering breakthroughs that the developing automobile embodied. With light humor, her portrayals also parodied the modern car's precariousness and unpredictability. Beginning in 1896 and continuing throughout the remainder of her career, references to cars appeared consistently in her editorials, short stories, and novels. These respective works reflect La Vaudère's preoccupation with the cultural and technological implications of a rapidly expanding automobile industry. In 1896, under the prophetic title "Les automobiles de l'avenir," La Vaudère speculated on the leisurely prospects afforded by automobiles. She opens her column with a revealing commentary about the social influence of the modern car: "Les automobiles, après avoir effrayé et déconcerté, d'abord, les gens paisibles à opinions routinières et surannées, ont fini par s'imposer sérieusement."[1] She predicts that cars are here to stay, and as horses are retired to the stables, refined engineering will allow for a new focus on the aesthetics of the automobile. She writes, "Quand les derniers perfectionnements auront été apportés dans la construction des machines et qu'on aura enfin découvert le moteur idéal, on s'occupera de l'embellissement des voitures, en cherchera des types confortables et élégants."[2] She was not wrong: within just a few years, in an effort to increase comfort, car manufacturers started to revisit the rear placement of doors and the open body design.

In the same piece, La Vaudère considers other possibilities for the automobile that privilege pleasure over functionality. Inspired by the sight of a disassembled fairground trailer, she contemplates a lifestyle of wandering and immersion in the natural world. To realize the romanticized vision of the nomad, she proposes the "roulotte d'agrément," a recreational version of the fairground trailer. In what reads as a patent proposal, she persuasively lays out the benefits of this apartment on wheels, which would facilitate countryside vacationing without the hassle of hotels or rail travel. For that "at home" feel, La Vaudère suggests decorating the interior of these "demeures de poupées" with fine fabrics and works of art. This leisure vehicle could also appeal to newlyweds embarking on their honeymoon and might even serve as a remedy for France's worrisome depopulation rates! Behind La Vaudère's humor lies an astute attentiveness to the evolving presence of automobiles in French bourgeois society, as well as an innovative viewpoint on their diverse capacities. She closes her piece by inviting readers to embrace both the promising future of the industry and the novelty and modernity that it announces: "Saluons la voiture de l'avenir qui portera en tout lieu nos rêves, nos ambitions et nos tendresses, et où nous trouverons tous les doux souvenirs du passé dans un cadre éternellement jeune."[3]

Intuitively, La Vaudère continued to contemplate the automobile's potential and soon considered it as a metaphor for women's emancipation. In the short 1898 story "Chauffeuse," the act of driving protects Maud, the adulterous female protagonist, from her husband's jealous rage.[4] The structure of the story consists of two embedded narratives: Maud's nightmare, which occupies most of the piece, and her reaction upon waking. In her nightmare, Maud's husband discovers his wife's infidelity and kills her lover in a brutal car chase. As he recklessly accelerates his car and unleashes his fury, Maud, who is in the passenger's seat, is powerless, and begs her husband to spare her lover. The dream ends with a deadly crash and Maud awakens, relieved and determined to protect her lover from a similar fate: she decides she will learn to drive. She then turns over to her husband and kisses him affectionately, cajoling, "Les chauffeurs ont vécu! . . . C'est le tour des chauffeuses! . . . Tu me montreras, dis?"[5] Wielding her feminine charm, Maud appeals to her husband's authority and driving expertise for her own gains. Paradoxically, seducing her husband guarantees her greater freedom outside of marriage. In learning to drive, Maud removes her husband from both the literal and metaphorical driver's seat and keeps her lover out of harm's way. Additionally, driving affords Maud access to sexual gratification and physical mobility, two symbols of women's increasing autonomy at the turn of the century. The two narrative frames—the dream sequence and the conversation with her husband—are distinguishable by one notable element: Maud's capacity to drive. When Maud awakens from her nightmare, she also awakens to a new cultural reality where women are learning to drive, both cars and their own storyline. It is no coincidence that this story was originally published in 1898, the same year that the Duchesse d'Uzès became the first French woman to be granted her driving certificate. Through an emphasis on the gendered terms of "chauffeur" and "chauffeuse," the story brings to light new possibilities for women's equality that are associated with the automobile. Additionally, the modern automobile itself is an uncontainable and powerful beast and a double symbol for the progress of the industry and women's sexual liberation. La Vaudère's zoomorphic description of the husband's car highlights its wild abandon: "Tout à coup, dans le calme de la campagne, une forte respiration se fait entendre. Le souffle grandit, s'élargit, semble emplir l'espace de son rauque halètement, et la bête fantastique, terrifiante, indomptable, passe dans un nuage de poussière."[6] As the accompanying illustration of a languorous and satisfied Maud suggests, the sexuality of the modern woman has been unleashed into the new century.

Unbridled and unpredictable, La Vaudère's automobile often takes on animal characteristics in the urban landscape. The short story "Soleil d'hiver" depicts an unruly and wild machinery plummeting down the Champs-Élysées. In a description that recalls that of "Chauffeuse," La Vaudère highlights the unruliness of a pack of automobiles, with their "rauque halètement de bêtes roulantes, fantastiques, indomptables" that evoke an "invasion de fauves."[7] Though La Vaudère emphasized the freedom of movement that the car provided, animalistic depictions like those in "Chauffeuse" and "Soleil d'hiver" highlight its capricious and erratic nature. Given the car's novelty, it was, after all, a work in progress. As Alexandre Buisseret notes, it was not uncommon for the fin-de-siècle press to stress the loud and offensive nature of these imperfect machines. "Moche, sale, puant," he writes, "l'appellation de monstre n'est pas si injuste pour une automobile qui avance en pétaradant, dans un nuage de poussière et d'huile, qui perd eau et graisse à l'arrêt, salissant ainsi les rues de Paris."[8] In her play

La panne, subtitled a "tragi-comédie automobiliste," La Vaudère satirizes similar inconveniences of the modern car. The play's cleverly nicknamed "Brisetout," a capricious and erratic vehicle, exemplifies the deficiencies of automobile design. As one character summarizes, "Sur ces satanées machines, on n'a pas le temps de voir la belle nature. On évolue dans un nuage de poussière, un encens de pétrole, et l'on a l'air, en descendant de voiture, d'avoir traversé le Sahara, par un temps de simoun!"[9] In defense of his beloved "Brisetout," the owner flaunts its superb engine, cylinders, carburetor, and brakes, and his jargon betrays La Vaudère's knowledge of basic car mechanics, typically viewed as overly intricate for the female mind.[10] He also boasts of his puncture-proof tires, acquired at the "grande maison Patelin et Cie," a clear allusion to the popular tire manufacture, Michelin et Cie.[11] As we see from these examples, La Vaudère did not always supplement her depiction of automobiles with a commentary on gender or the new freedoms available to women. However, as a woman writing about the technological and social implications of the bourgeoning automobile industry, La Vaudère had inscribed herself in the developing iconography of women and cars. Like the boundless and boisterous vehicles of her fiction, she made clear that women drivers, like women writers, were barreling into the modern age.

WOMANHOOD AND THE *CHAUFFEUSE* OF THE BELLE ÉPOQUE

In 1893, the "certificat de capacité"—the equivalent of the driver's license—was available exclusively to men in the Paris region. Beginning in 1897, women were permitted to take the test, and the Duchesse d'Uzès became the first certified female driver in 1898 (and also the first to be fined for speeding). Born into an aristocratic family, the Duchesse was a sculptor and published author, as well as a sports enthusiast and avid supporter of women's causes.[12] She paved the way for pioneering female drivers at the turn of the century, including Camille du Gast and Hélène van Zuylen, who were the first women to compete in international races. In the early 1900s, the figure of the *chauffeuse* was especially fraught. The mobility and independence that a car provided threatened to remove women, physically and figuratively, from their domestic duties. A woman who drove was active in public spaces and no longer confined to the home or her familial obligations. A more acceptable place for the woman was in the passenger's seat next to her driving husband. There, she was forced to submit to the expertise of her husband, who maneuvered the car and controlled her displacement in outdoor spaces.

Female motorists directly challenged conservative ideologies about gender difference and elicited commentary on their innate inferiority as drivers. In her research on women and automobiles in America at the turn of the century, Virginia Scharff identifies three arguments that were used to explain a woman's poor driving skills: emotional instability, physical weakness, and intellectual deficiency.[13] Though her research focuses on discourses that circulated across the Atlantic, the same trends could be found in the French press. In 1906, in an editorial entitled "Pourqoui les femmes ne savent pas conduire les automobiles," G. Labadie-Lagrave reminds readers of the dangers of the distracted female mind: "Une femme qui, dans un salon, interviendra tout à coup dans une conversation pour poser une question sur un événement qui, trois minutes auparavant, a été expliqué tout au long, ou qui lira deux fois de suite la même page du livre qu'elle a sous les yeux parce qu'elle a l'esprit trop distrait pour chercher à comprendre la pensée de l'auteur, mènera tout droit une machine à quelque effroyable catastrophe."[14] Though women's access to driving increased after 1897, these narratives reflect the ongoing resistance to their legal certification. In the early 1900s, very few women were equipped with the official "certificat de capacité." Driving records from this period are scarce if nonexistent, but partial statistics confirm the rarity of the *chauffeuse*. Based on limited archival data, Buisseret reports that between 1911 and 1914, of the 1.5 million women living in Paris, only three hundred received driving certificates.[15] The majority of these women lived in the wealthiest neighborhoods in the city.

In 1906, the year that La Vaudère was photographed in a car, the number of licensed female drivers was likely substantially lower. My quest for documented proof of La Vaudère's driving practices has been unsuccessful. In Paris, archivists at the Préfecture de Police believe that related records were likely lost or destroyed over time, but in Le Mans, the collection is more complete. As we recall, La Vaudère regularly returned to her ex-husband's property in Parigné-l'Évêque following their 1898 divorce. Records in Le Mans would therefore indicate if she had pursued a certificate in the region. Remarkably, the archives contain a rare registry of certificates that were administered from 1899 to 1913 and indicate that her son, Fernand, obtained his in 1903 while living in Parigné-l'Évêque. La Vaudère's name, however, is absent, eliminating any likelihood that she obtained certification while staying at the château. Fernand's name confirms that La Vaudère's immediate family owned at least one automobile and kept current with the developing industry. Indeed, on La Vaudère's father's side, the Scrives in Lille were involved in car manufacturing and were active members of the Automobile Club du Nord. In 1901, Albert Scrive, a distant cousin, co-organized Lille's Exposition Internationale de l'Automobile et du Cycle, which featured the "Auto-démarreur progressif Scrive."[16] In 1906, Albert registered the Scrive model car—"une nouvelle marque française"—for the "Circuit Européen."[17] This five-thousand-kilometer event inaugurated the Scrive brand into long-distance competitions. A few months later, Albert entered a Scrive model car (with a four-cylinder, two-stroke engine) in the "Coupe du 'Matin,'" a six-thousand-kilometer race.[18] La Vaudère was certainly aware of her extended family's role in car manufacturing. Though this does not guarantee her own involvement in the industry, it may explain her access to automobiles and the interest in social and mechanical trends that manifested in her writing.

Though it is impossible to draw reliable conclusions about La Vaudère's driving capacities, the photo printed in *Le carnet de la femme* inscribes her in the popular iconography of women and cars in the early twentieth century. In his discussion of Belle Époque poster advertisements, Buisseret identifies the omnipresence of the "femme/automobile" duo.[19] As the industry evolved and cars became more prolific among the wealthy classes, women, often associated with fashion, luxury, and modernity, were incorporated into automobile advertisements.[20] However, in contrast to La Vaudère's photo, very few images actually depicted women driving, and the presence of male drivers reinforced markers of conventional femininity and masculinity. Clothing was also an essential reminder of gender differentiation, especially given the design of the modern automobile. Until the early 1900s, most cars were devoid of a roof and bumper, and natural elements like rain, dust, and insects posed a threat to clothing and hairstyle. While men easily adapted their attire for these occasions, women were expected to maintain their femininity and had fewer options. Those who chose to entirely cover themselves with bulky full-body cloaks risked sacrificing their elegance and erasing their markers of womanhood.[21] Other driving accessories included goggles, hoods, veils, and capes, and the mere necessity for this protective, unflattering gear stoked anxieties about women's shifting social role. As Scharff notes, "The idea of wearing clothing for practical rather than decorative purposes flew in the face of standards of femininity, particularly for middle- and upper-class women."[22]

Despite the absence of a male companion, La Vaudère maintains distinct feminine markers in her photo (fig. 23), particularly through her choice of clothing. For example, instead of a heavy dark cloak, she wears a white embroidered dress, certainly not ideal for the dust and dirt of the roadways. Her floral hat, which seems to lack a veil, offers little protection against the gusts of wind of the countryside where the photo appears to have been taken. We may make several deductions from these sartorial clues. First, given the impracticality of her clothing and lack of protective gear, it is not likely that La Vaudère was actually driving when she was photographed. Assuming this setting was staged, we may then consider what such a "performance" of driving evokes about La Vaudère in the larger context of the article. The car's positioning suggests that it has just been removed from a storage shed, and the *mise-en-scène* emphasizes La Vaudère's departure. With just one hand on the wheel and her gaze directed at the camera, La Vaudère embodies confidence and autonomy. However, the image rehearses a careful balancing act between independence and femininity, and her white dress and the flowers upon her head are a conscious reminder of her womanhood. As she has repeatedly done in her visual self-construction, La Vaudère underscores the precariousness of normative femininity through its own careful staging. With the addition of the car, she performs two iterations of womanhood simultaneously, both conventional and modern. This single photo thus embodies the friction between two opposing narratives, and La Vaudère—as both writer and creator of her own image—represents women's inevitable transition into modernity.

The accompanying book review in *Le carnet de la femme* contextualizes these conflicting discourses while also considering La Vaudère's transgressions as a woman writer. In a discussion of La Vaudère's recent novel *La vierge d'Israël*, the journalist promotes a conservative distinction of gender roles and celebrates the conventional gender expression of the female protagonist. The article applauds La Vaudère's heroine for her "attirance pudique et chaste conservée jusque dans la chute, la candeur, le charme, auxquels les ouvrages de l'auteur ne nous ont pas habitués."[23] For the conservative critic, the novel signals a refreshing break from the excessive immorality and debauchery portrayed in La Vaudère's previous erotic Orientalist works. The reviewer's praise for feminine modesty and virtue extends to La Vaudère: as a woman writer, her perceived threats to the social order appear to be no longer relevant. However, the text's traditionalist tone is complicated by an underlying recognition of the modern woman. Nearing the conclusion, the reviewer recommends, "Ce n'est certes pas un livre d'enfant, mais toute femme cultivée devra le lire."[24] Like the car photo, the article captures the tensions between normative femininity and the evolving activity of women in the public sphere, whether through writing, driving, or education (as the adjective "cultivée" partly suggests). The contradictions inherent in La Vaudère's photo thus signal the convergence of two troubling figures: the woman who writes and the woman who drives.

THEN AND NOW: THE CHÂTEAU DE LA VAUDÈRE

In 1904, Théodore Cahu depicted La Vaudère perched at a window and writing, finding creative inspiration from the idyllic view. "Dans sa propriété de la Vaudère," he wrote, "elle s'isole pour travailler plus à son aise, la fenêtre ouverte sur l'étang aux reflets glauques, sur le parc aux arbres touffus" (fig. 24).[25] This romanticized portrait of La Vaudère, published six years after her divorce, emphasizes the importance of her ex-husband's property to her writing career. As though its name were not indication enough, the Château de La Vaudère was instrumental in launching La Vaudère's professional trajectory. As La Vaudère tended to draw from her personal experiences, the château also informed the content of her fiction, appearing in various forms in novels and short stories.[26] It is forever indissociable from her persona, works, and personal life, as Cahu's article—replete with château pictures—exemplifies. He stressed La Vaudère's continued use of the property to work and his article helped perpetuate the association between the château and her persona. Today, the Château de La Vaudère is a symbolic site for recovery and legacy, where the lives of La Vaudère and its current owner, Anne-Charlotte Rousseau, share some striking parallels.

In her study on literary tourism, Anne Trubek reflects on the powerful draw of the writer's house. "There is something curious and ultimately insatiable about visiting a dead writer's house," she writes. "It has something to do with pilgrimage, the hushed aura of sacredness; it has something to do with loss, and objects as compensation for loss. And it has something to do with the way literature works, with the longing created by the fact that words separate writers from readers yet create an ineluctable intimacy between the two, structured by marks on paper."[27] Given my efforts to recover lost elements of La Vaudère's life and works, a pilgrimage to her home, the birthplace of her persona, seemed essential (fig. 25). Enticed by

FIG. 24 The Château de La Vaudère in 1904. *Revue illustrée*, June 15, 1904.

the romance of the deceased writer's home, I anticipated that a visit would bridge the past and present and flesh out my contemplations on loss and legacy. When I first contacted Anne-Charlotte about viewing La Vaudère's home, she graciously offered to host me when I was in France for research. It was shortly upon my arrival that I learned about her childhood in the château, her success in saving it from foreclosure, and her passion for automobiles and rally racing.

When Anne-Charlotte speaks of her childhood at the Château de La Vaudère, she evokes the "culte de la maison."[28] Contemplating the house like a place of enchantment, she marvels at it as a continued source of comfort, nostalgia, and wonder. Anne-Charlotte became the owner of the château through a series of events that were set into motion by the death of La Vaudère's son, Fernand Crapez. In 1951, Fernand, La Vaudère's sole inheritor and ex-mayor of Parigné-l'Évêque, drafted his will. Because he had lost his two children (Alain died in 1934 and Jean in 1940), his principal beneficiary was the commune of Parigné-l'Évêque. The terms of the will stipulated that in exchange for 112 hectares of land—which included the château—the commune was to build a retirement home in honor of

FIG. 25 The Château de La Vaudère today.

his two sons. Fernand and his wife, Léopoldine Simonot, died in 1953 and 1966, respectively, and in 1967 the commune took the first steps to realize his wishes. The château was soon put up for sale and funds were used to plan the construction of the Maison de Retraite Alain et Jean Crapez, which opened in 1973. The burial chapel on the château property—home to La Vaudère's embalmed relatives—was placed under the care of the retirement home and remains so today.

In 1968, Anne-Charlotte's parents purchased the Château de La Vaudère from the commune of Parigné-l'Évêque. Anne-Charlotte became the sole proprietor in 2002 and spent the next decade renovating the property for room rentals and events. She preserved the "maison de famille" atmosphere of the château, and unlike the impersonal feel of a traditional hotel, common spaces like the living room are accessible to guests for socializing. Today the château and the neighboring *orangerie* contain a total of twenty-eight rooms, as well as a reception hall that can hold over two hundred people. What used to be the property's stables now houses Anne-Charlotte's collection of classic and rally cars. She has been racing in international rally competitions since 2015. Because of the significant parallels we can see between her life and that of La Vaudère, she has come to be known affectionately by her friends as "Anne-Charlotte de La Vaudère." Against the backdrop of the château, automobiles exemplify Anne-Charlotte's and La Vaudère's respective presence in male spaces, from the rallying competitions of the present day to the literary circles of the Belle Époque.

VILLAGE LEGACIES

Like most transgressive or legendary figures, La Vaudère has been the subject of gossip. Anne-Charlotte and her sister Isabelle have relayed a selection of these stories to me and have contributed in transmitting and conserving La Vaudère's legacy. Though the veracity of these anecdotes remains suspect, their content is revealing of La Vaudère's lasting impressions in the region and may relay information for additional exploration. In her work on Gisèle d'Estoc, Melanie Hawthorne has equated writing a biography to charting geographic space. As she explains, early mapmaking relied heavily on anecdotal details and personal impressions that are now considered less precise than the purely scientific and evidence-based methods today. However, Hawthorne regrets the omission of such approximate and subjective details and values their potential to inform on a more minute level: "The role of rumor in biography, then, is to preserve those traces of information that may be 'unmappable' at one time but may later be verified by higher standards of scholarship."[29] Rumors, many sensationalist, had inspired Anne-Charlotte's and Isabelle's mother to pursue research on La Vaudère and share her archival and anecdotal findings with her family. She had heard, for example, that La Vaudère was the shame of the Crapez family and that her mother-in-law, in a symbolic act of retaliation, burned the contents of her library. This rumor, though a poignant metaphor for La Vaudère's erasure from literary and familial history, remains unsubstantiated. Yet it reinforces her reputation as a contentious female figure whose greatest threat to the status quo was her intellect.

The village of Parigné-l'Évêque has also been a steady source of rumors about La Vaudère. An elder in the community once told Isabelle that La Vaudère always arrived from Paris by car—and that she was often driving. My efforts to confirm La Vaudère's official driving capacities were unsuccessful, and a solo 130-mile journey by car in the early 1900s, which ran the risk of mechanical incident, seems highly impractical. This rumor, however, is not insignificant, for it reflects the town's association of her mobility with self-sufficiency. Isabelle recalls other childhood stories about the château's history, some incidental, such as a particular room where Maupassant slept while supposedly visiting La Vaudère. Regrettably, many anecdotes have since faded from her memory. She has mused with me about starting a blog for citizens of Parigné-l'Évêque to share rumors about La Vaudère that have circulated over the decades. This blog would undoubtedly elicit a good deal of traffic; since beginning this project, many "Parignéens" have been eager to share with me what knowledge they have about the local "celebrity." Alain Maury, for example, spoke to me at length by phone about the Crapez family. His father, Pierre, had been a close friend of La Vaudère's grandson, Jean.[30] Alain represents a rare living connection to La Vaudère's son: he had once met Fernand and Léopoldine Crapez in Parigné-l'Évêque as a child shortly after the 1944 liberation.

If my pilgrimage to Parigné-l'Évêque has confirmed anything, it is about the interconnectedness that lies at the heart of this project. In uncovering La Vaudère's forgotten history, I have stumbled upon new stories that are indicative of the far reach of literary history. Beyond the archives of national libraries and institutions, some of my most valuable sources for reconstructing La Vaudère's life have been the people that I encountered in my pilgrimages. And these connections have worked in both directions. In recounting her own childhood at the château and revisiting the places that profoundly marked her, Anne-Charlotte has experienced the power of La Vaudère's memory in present day: "Je découvre la force de l'endroit grâce à Jane." Through our enlightening discussions, I recognize that like the embalmed cadavers of her relatives, La Vaudère's legacy has been preserved through the château property and transmitted through its inhabitants and their stories. It is my hope that this study—and those that follow—may do the same.

NOTES

INTRODUCTION

1. La Vaudère and Théo-Critt, *Confessions*, 63.

2. Statistics, though impossible to verify to the exact number, unequivocally reflect these record figures. In 1894, author Octave Uzanne calculated that over 2,100 women were producing works in fiction, poetry, journalism, or pedagogy. By 1907, the year before La Vaudère's death, the periodical *Je sais tout* estimated that women were responsible for 20 percent of the year's literary production (up from 4 percent from two decades earlier). Uzanne, *La femme à Paris* and *Je sais tout*, September 15, 1907, quoted in Bertrand-Sabiani and Leroy, *Vie littéraire*, 264–65.

3. Examples of anthologies include Barbey d'Aurevilly's *Les bas-bleus* (1878), Henri Carton's *Histoire des femmes écrivains de la France* (1886), Paul Jacquinet's *Les femmes de France: Poètes et prosateurs* (1886), and Jules Bertaut's *La littérature féminine d'aujourd'hui* (1909).

4. Fuster, "Notes parisiennes," 1, original emphasis.

5. The details that follow were recorded in 1908 by La Vaudère's notary, Pierre-Marie Moreau (Archives nationales, Département du minutier central des notaires de Paris, étude CXI).

6. Garval, *Cléo de Mérode*, 4.

7. Rachilde, "*Florifières*," 547, and "*Idylle saphique*," 781.

8. See, for example, Holmes, "Daniel Lesueur," and Mesch, "Husbands."

9. Palacio, "Postérité," 197, 202.

10. On La Vaudère's correspondence with Zola about this play, see Viveiros's "Lettres inédites."

11. Mesch, *Having It All*, 152; Cosnier, *Dames*, 207.

12. Bélilon, "Chronique féministe," 2.

13. For example, works such as Mary Louise Roberts's *Disruptive Acts* (2002), Rachel Mesch's *Hysteric's Revenge* (2006), Juliette Rogers's *Career Stories* (2007), and Adrianna Paliyenko's *Genius Envy* (2016) are representative of the increasing effort to amplify women writers' voices from the Belle Époque that have since been lost or silenced.

14. Scholarship continues to evolve alongside new methodologies and models for understanding gender difference. For example, though Marc de Montifaud's and Rachilde's names have traditionally appeared alongside those of nineteenth-century women writers, Mesch has recently reexamined their unconventional gender expression through modern narratives of transgender identity (*Before Trans*).

15. Articles and book chapters about La Vaudère include Joëlle Prungnaud's

Gothique et décadence (pages 223–32); Geneviève de Viveiros's "Lettres inédites" and "Jane de la Vaudère ou l'éclectisme littéraire"; Guy Ducrey's "Jane de la Vaudère: La science et le sang"; Michela Gardini's "Jane de la Vaudère sous le signe de l'occultisme"; Rachel Mesch's "Husbands, Wives and Doctors"; Anne Linton's "Mutating Bodies"; and my own "Jane de La Vaudère and Maupassant" and "Feminine Copy."

16. Coincidentally, Lyane lives at La Vaudère's former Place des Ternes address, which has inspired the research for her novel.

17. Farge, *Goût*, 121.

CHAPTER 1

1. In these pages, I refer to La Vaudère as "Jeanne" during her childhood and adolescent years. It was not until the late 1880s that she established the persona of Jane de La Vaudère, and I adopt this name accordingly.

2. Located near the Luxembourg Garden, parts of the rue d'Enfer were demolished shortly after Jeanne's birth with the construction of the boulevard Saint-Michel. The sections that remained of the rue d'Enfer were later renamed rue Henri-Barbusse and avenue Denfert-Rochereau, and are located in today's fifth and fourteenth arrondissements.

3. Jeanne Scrive's reconstituted birth and baptism certificates can be viewed on microfilm at the Archives de Paris (reference 5MI1 / 941, 942).

4. The Scrive family has even inspired works of historical fiction, such as Anne Mémet-Scrive's 2010 homage *La légende des Scrive: Le roman d'une grande famille lilloise* (Ravet-Anceau).

5. See, for example, *Dispositions hygiéniques à prendre pour l'armée d'Orient* (1854), *Esquisse historique et philosophique des maladies qui ont sévi sur les soldats de l'armée d'Orient* (1856), and *Relation médico-chirurgicale de la campagne d'Orient* (1857).

6. For a biographical account of Gaspard Scrive's military service and advancement to chief medical officer, see Des Cilleuls, "Souvenir de Scrive."

7. Guy Ducrey has mused over a possible psychoanalytic interpretation of Gaspard's presence in La Vaudère's corpus. For a discussion of the ambivalent and ubiquitous figure of the doctor in her fiction, see his article "Jane de la Vaudère," 153–56. Though a psychoanalytic reading is not my intention here, it may be worth noting that Marie Scrive, La Vaudère's sister, would later marry a man nearly thirty years her senior.

8. La Vaudère recounted these details of childhood in an article appearing in *Gil Blas* in 1901 ("'Jane de la Vaudère'").

9. Like La Vaudère's birth certificate, the related records of the Justice of the Peace of the Canton de Sceaux were destroyed during the Paris Commune. La Vaudère's marriage contract from 1875 references the court case on multiple occasions.

10. Mme. Louis Maurecy, "Ceux qui croient," 228. I discuss this interview in greater depth in chapter 2.

11. Ibid.

12. *Pères Ratisbonne*, 151.

13. Ibid., 228, 229.

14. Ibid., 230.

15. Ibid., 233. For a recounting of these events, see ibid., 233–45.

16. I extend my appreciation to the Notre-Dame de Sion archivist Céline Hirsch Poynard for communicating the information that follows.

17. A few months later, on November 16, 1871, Marie married the military doctor Jean-Baptiste Victor Joseph Dauvais de Gérardcourt. Nearly thirty years her senior, Dauvais de Gérardcourt lived on the boulevard du Montparnasse, a few blocks from both Sophie Debonte's residence and the convent.

18. The *Figures contemporaines tirées de l'album Mariani* were a series of advertisements for the vin Mariani, a popular coca wine invented by the chemist Angelo Mariani. To boost his sales, Mariani solicited hundreds of endorsements from public figures like artists, actors, and politicians. Over the course of three decades, he printed fourteen volumes of testimonials, and each featured a brief biography and portrait of the participating celebrity. Like all of the biographical notices in Mariani's albums, La Vaudère's is unsigned. However, excerpts from her profile later appeared in Théodore Cahu's piece on La Vaudère for the *Revue illustrée* (June 15, 1904), suggesting that he may have also been the author here.

19. "Jane de la Vaudère," *Figures contemporaines.*

20. Notre-Dame de Sion faced a similar fate with the wave of secular laws that were passed at the turn of the twentieth century. According to Chantal Paisant, the 1901 and 1904 laws led to the temporary closing of seven schools of the Notre-Dame de Sion congregation, including the campus in Paris (*Exil*, 352–53).

21. The digitized marriage certificate or "acte de mariage" from April 29, 1875, can be viewed online via the Archives départementales de la Sarthe: http://archives.sarthe.fr/f/etatcivil/tableau/?&debut=200 (commune Le Mans, cote 5Mi 191_354–55, page 69, no. 122).

22. This extremely detailed document can be found at the Archives départementales de la Sarthe (4 E 194/201).

23. The inventory appears in the marriage contract cited above.

24. As stipulated in the marriage contract.

25. Like La Vaudère's marriage certificate, Fernand's "acte de naissance" has been digitized by the Archives départementales de la Sarthe: http://archives.sarthe.fr/f/etatcivil/tableau/?&debut=200 (commune Le Mans, cote 5Mi 191_364–65, page 18, no. 70).

26. Cahu, "Jane de la Vaudère."

27. "Jane de la Vaudère," *Figures contemporaines.*

28. "Échos," 1.

29. La Vaudère was one of several contemporary "Jeannes" to adopt an English pseudonym for a career in the arts: Jane Avril (1868–1943), cabaret dancer; Jane Dieulafoy (1851–1916), archeologist and writer; Jane Misme (1865–1935), journalist; Jane Catulle Mendès (1867–1955), poet; and Jane Vieu (1871–1955), singer (with whom La Vaudère collaborated).

30. Tout-Paris, "Bloc-notes," 2.

31. Doucet, "Rapport." I am grateful to Marie-Claire Chatelain from the Service des prix littéraires of the Académie française for her generous help in locating this report.

32. La Vaudère, preface to *Victor*, 5–6.

33. La Vaudère and Hugo appear to have met on at least one occasion. The Médiathèque Louis-Aragon in Le Mans contains an 1879 edition of *Notre-Dame de Paris* dedicated to "Jane Scrive" and signed by Hugo, a rare remnant of her personal library.

34. Hawthorne, *Rachilde*, 81–82.

35. Her letters are part of the SDGL collection at the Archives nationales in Pierrefitte-sur-Seine, just outside of Paris. The reference for La Vaudère's dossier is 454AP/431. Additionally, the current office of the SDGL at the Hôtel Massa in Paris contains the original records of the committee deliberations and past issues of the *Chronique de la Société des gens de lettres*, an internal periodical that reported on the activities of the SDGL and legal rulings concerning literary property. The discussion that follows is based on research in these two collections.

36. Gordon de Genouillac's report on La Vaudère's candidacy for admission (March 21, 1891, Archives nationales, Pierrefitte-sur-Seine). According to the committee deliberations from March 23, fifteen members voted against her application and three voted in its support (SDGL archives at the Hôtel Massa).

37. Archives nationales, Pierrefitte-sur-Seine.

38. Félix Jahyer's report from 1894 (Archives nationales, Pierrefitte-sur-Seine). The committee deliberations from March 19, 1894, indicate that she was admitted as "sociétaire" with a 15-2 vote (SDGL archives at the Hôtel Massa).

39. In her article "Lettres inédites," Viveiros transcribes La Vaudère's letters to Zola and discusses her involvement with the SDGL.

40. Chincholle, "Autour," 2. Zola was convicted and sentenced to one year in prison; he fled to London in July and returned to Paris in June 1899.

41. *Chronique de la Société des gens de lettres* (SDGL archives at the Hôtel Massa).

42. Rip, "Candidatures féminines," 3.

43. Rip, "Dernière réunion," 2.

44. Ibid.

45. "Assemblé Générale," 108–9.

46. "Jane de la Vaudère," *Figures contemporaines*; Cahu, "Jane de la Vaudère."

47. For a thorough outline of the legal and social discourses behind the divorce question throughout nineteenth-century France, see White, *French Divorce Fiction*.

48. Mansker, *Sex, Honor and Citizenship*, 104.

49. In an 1897 editorial for *La presse*, La Vaudère condemned these two stipulations of the Loi Naquet, which she felt were particularly favorable to husbands. See chapter 5 for a detailed discussion of her piece "Du divorce."

50. White, *French Divorce Fiction*, 76.

51. Ledermann, "Divorces," 339. Ledermann provides useful tables and graphs of divorce statistics and their demographics in France through 1947.

52. Mansker, *Sex, Honor and Citizenship*, 100–101.

53. White, *French Divorce Fiction*, 35.

54. This document may be consulted at the Archives de Paris (DU5 1082).

55. Interestingly, Gaston's father had led a similar life. In 1856, Gaston's mother, Estelle Emmanuelle Huet, was granted a "séparation de corps et de biens" from her husband on the grounds of adultery. Like his son, Victor Crapez had been living with his mistress for a number of years at the time of the hearing. The summary of the hearing can be consulted at the Archives départementales de la Sarthe (1 U 986).

56. Fernand Crapez's military registry or "fiche matricule" has been digitized by the Archives départementales de la Sarthe and can be accessed by his last name: http://archives.sarthe.fr/r/23/-matricules-militaires.

57. La Vaudère's file is located in the Archives nationales's Département du minutier central des notaires de Paris (Moreau, étude CXI).

58. See, for example, the covers of her texts *Les mousseuses* (1901), *La mystérieuse* (1902), and *L'amazone du roi de Siam* (1902). To see La Vaudère's illustrations from *Lulu*, see chapter 2 of this study.

59. These collaborative works include: *Les trois mousmés* (1898, unpublished), an operetta with Champsaur, under the name Jean Scrive; *Confessions galantes* (1905), an epistolary novel with Cahu (Théo-Critt); *Dupont sera élu!* (1906), a theatrical comedy with Derys (Sedry); and *Piège d'amour* (1905), a lyric fantasy with Vieu.

60. Many of the novels that Atamian illustrated formed La Vaudère's "Orientalist" or "fantasy" corpus that featured exoticized, often brutal, depictions of the Far East. There were numerous editions of these novels, and it is not always clear which edition(s) contained Atamian's work. The following texts were each illustrated by Atamian, but their dates are approximate: *Le harem de Syta* (1904); *L'amante du pharaon* (1905); *L'élève chérie* (1908); *La porte de félicité* (1908); *La vierge d'Israël* (1908); *Le mystère de Kama* (1910, 10th ed.). Steinlen's and Kirchner's contributions are easier to track: they illustrated *Les frôleurs* (1899) and *La cité des sourires* (1907), respectively.

61. Viveiros reports some of these figures ("Lettres inédites," 233). For comparison, Viveiros notes that the average print run for

novels in 1900 was around eleven thousand copies.

62. Rachilde, "*Sataniques*," 342. Rachilde reviewed a number of La Vaudère's works for the *Mercure de France*, though rarely favorably. See Rachilde's "*Demi-sexes*," "*Sang*," "*Frôleurs*," "*Mousseuses*," "*Mystère*," "*Androgynes*," "*Guescha*," "*Porte*," and "*Sorcière*."

63. La Vaudère mentions her portrait with Nadar in an undated letter that is part of the René Laruelle collection at the BnF. Thank you to Mathilde Huet for bringing this letter and La Vaudère's Lenthéric cosmetics advertisement to my attention.

64. This correspondence was likely related to a letter that she wrote the previous week discussing advertising pricing with the newspaper.

65. This clipping appeared in the January 16 issue; La Vaudère's letter was likely written between January 17 and 19.

66. La Vaudère's "acte de décès" can be consulted online at http://archives.paris.fr/s/4/etat-civil-actes/? (décès, 17th arrondissement, year 1908, acte number 1870). This Georges Roux must not be confused with the illustrator George Roux (1853–1929), who was fifty-four at the time of her death.

67. "Nécrologie," 235. The article erroneously reported that she died at age forty-five instead of fifty-one. It was not uncommon for La Vaudère to lie about her age (see chapter 2).

68. "Madame Jane de la Vaudère," 2.

69. Butterfly, "Paris l'été."

70. As recorded in 1908 by La Vaudère's notary, Pierre-Marie Moreau (Archives nationales's Département du minutier central des notaires de Paris, étude CXI). La Vaudère had known Belmontet for some time, though the nature of their relationship is unclear. In a letter from January 18, 1897, she mentioned organizing a dinner with the mayor of Saint-Cloud (author's personal collection). Unfortunately, I have found no additional references to Deturmény and cannot speculate on his affiliation with La Vaudère.

71. The handwriting of this inventory is at times illegible, but the names of the works appear to read as follows (a question mark indicates illegibility): *Pantins tragiques*, *Le spectre*, *Le feu follet*, *Mlle de Fontanges*, *Sylviane*, *La maison Moses*, *Le secret de Salhante* (?), *Mes ennemis*, *Le beau Marcellus*, *L'amour en cage*, *Bulle de savon*, *Madame Laurence*, *La hausse et la baisse*, *Pour un être*, *Combats d'amour*, *Le droit d'aimer*, *Plus on est de fous*, *Frégate* (?), *Les legances* (?), *Le cention de Bibis* (?).

72. While many of these manuscripts may have been works in progress, a selection of these titles had previously appeared in the press of the period. *Le droit d'aimer* was originally published as a novel in 1895 and is the only work in the inventory that showed no signs of being adapted for the theatre. The three-act *Madame Laurence* was first published in the late 1890s (publisher unknown). *Le beau Marcellus* was printed in three installments in *La presse* on February 18, March 3, and March 10, 1899. As of 1907, La Vaudère had arranged a production of her Japanese play, *Pantins tragiques* (unpublished), with the Mévisto theatre for the following year (Mortier, "Courrier"). It is unclear whether this production ever occurred, though it was never mentioned in the press after 1907. The Archives and Manuscripts collection at the BnF contains a letter from La Vaudère to Auguste Mévisto, the theatre director, in which she proposes the actress Bertile Leblanc for a role in the production (reference MNn-37[321]).

73. Clarens, "Dans le monde."

74. La Vaudère's SDGL file at the Archives nationales in Pierrefitte-sur-Seine contains Fernand's contract, which Cahu forwarded to the organization.

75. The marriage certificate is located in the Archives de la Vendée in La Roche-sur-Yon.

76. "Nécrologie," 235.

77. For reference, the plot is located in Division 8, line 1 East, tomb 9 South.

78. According to these records, La Vaudère's burial occurred in two phases. On July 29, the day of the ceremony, her body was placed in a temporary tomb, not uncommon for the time. On August 5, it was permanently moved to the family plot (https://archives.paris.fr/s/24/cimetieres-ra/?, Montparnasse cemetery, Scrive, 1908).

79. "Secrétariat," 2042.

CHAPTER 2

1. Rochetal, "Chronique."

2. Ibid.

3. Ibid.

4. Roberts, *Disruptive Acts*.

5. On Durand, see Roberts, *Disruptive Acts*, especially chapters 2 and 3.

6. Rochetal, "Chronique."

7. Les Treize, "Nos échos," 2.

8. Marcus, *Drama of Celebrity*, 3–4.

9. La Vaudère's command over her public persona stretched beyond the literary milieu, and she frequently lied about her age in court records and family genealogical documents. On October 23, 1903, La Vaudère appeared before the Tribunal de première instance du département de la Seine for a case involving the periodical *La vie en rose*. The records state that La Vaudère was thirty-nine years old at the time, "se disant née le 15 avril 1864." Actually born in 1857, she had misrepresented her age by seven years. This document may be consulted at the Archives de Paris, D1U6 839.

10. Roberts, *Disruptive Acts*, 104.

11. For an in-depth examination of the gendering of nineteenth-century literary genres (especially lyric poetry), see Schultz, *Gendered Lyric*. In her study of women poets and gendered conceptions of genius in the nineteenth century, Paliyenko also provides a useful overview of scientific and literary discourses on female intellect and creative expression. See her *Genius Envy*, particularly chapters 1–2.

12. Jean de Gourmont, *Muses*, 237–38.

13. Tout-Paris, "Bloc-notes," 2.

14. Ibid.

15. Ibid., original emphasis.

16. Ibid.

17. Ibid.

18. Rubempré, "Courrier de Paris," 75.

19. Ibid.

20. "Librairie," 3.

21. Séché, *Muses françaises*, vol. 2, 323.

22. Ibid.

23. Ibid.

24. Sénéchal, "*Demi-sexes*," 570.

25. Ibid.

26. Ibid.

27. Ibid., 571, 570.

28. Ibid., 570.

29. Pontaillac, "Nos échos," 1.

30. Senner, "Scène," 3. It is uncertain if this production ever took place.

31. Bauer, "Livres," 2.

32. Ryner, *Massacre*, 1.

33. Representative examples include Honoré Daumier's 1844 series of caricatures for *Le Charivari* and Jules Barbey d'Aurevilly's 1878 anthology *Les bas-bleus*.

34. Ryner, *Massacre*, 4.

35. Ibid., 4–5.

36. In 1893, under the pseudonym "Hunedell," Georges de Peyrebrune (née Mathilde-Marie Georgina Élisabeth de Peyrebrune) published a short story in *Le Figaro* parodying the demonization of female intellectuals. In "Jupiter et les 'bas-bleus,'" dozens of renowned women writers appear before Jupiter to endorse their aesthetic and philosophical influences. While many highlight their indispensable contributions, others like La Vaudère occupy more ambivalent roles as amateurs dabbling in literary pursuits: "Beaucoup de mondaines, qui sont de mon avis, ne dédaignent pas de glisser leur fine jambe, au moins une fois, en passant, par caprice, dans le symbolique 'bas-bleu.' Telle commet un joli roman, comme [. . .] Jane de la Vaudère" (Peyrebrune, "Jupiter," 1). La Vaudère's inclusion in this category suggests an uncertainty about her place among the

great female figures of the time. This may be due to the story's publication date, which coincided with the early years of La Vaudère's career. For a study of the figure of the *bas-bleu* in Peyrebrune's works, see Larson, "'Elle n'est pas un "bas-bleu".'"

37. Ryner, *Massacre*, 14–15.

38. Ibid., 209.

39. Ibid., 15.

40. Ibid., 16.

41. Ibid., 16.

42. La Vaudère, "Protestations," 2.

43. Ibid.

44. The novel was later published under the title *Folie d'opium*, also through Méricant.

45. Stableford, "Introduction," xxii.

46. "Androgynes, roman passionnel," *Revue du cercle militaire*, 559.

47. "'Androgynes,'" *Le journal*, 2.

48. Potinier, "Coulisses," 4.

49. Lorrain also published his play the following year in his collection *Quatre femmes en pièces*. An earlier version of this work first appeared in *Le journal* on May 20, 1897. Simply called *Bas-bleu*, the original play made no mention of *Les hermaphrodites* or "Mme de la Crapaudère" (see discussion of "Mme de la Crapaudère" that follows).

50. Lorrain, "Mme de Larmaille," 2.

51. La Vaudère, *Androgynes*, 49–50, my emphasis.

52. Roberts, *Disruptive Acts*, especially chapters 2 and 3.

53. These novels include *Trois fleurs de volupté* (1900); *Le mystère de Kama* (1901); *L'amazone du roi de Siam* (1902); *Les courtisanes de Brahma* (1903); *Le harem de Syta* (1904); *La guescha amoureuse* (1904); *L'amante du pharaon* (1905); *La porte de félicité* (1905); *La sorcière d'Ecbatane* (1906); *La vierge d'Israël* (1906); *La cité des sourires* (1907); *Les prêtresses de Mylitta* (1907); and *Le rêve de Mysès* (1907).

54. A selection of these photographs was reprinted in Théodore Cahu's 1904 article for the *Revue illustrée*, which I discuss below.

55. Many thanks to Elizabeth Emery for sharing her thoughts on the Exposition. For a discussion of Mérode's evolving fame in France and across the Atlantic, see Garval's *Cléo de Mérode.*

56. Garval, *Cléo de Mérode*, 130–31.

57. Ibid., 131.

58. I extend my gratitude to Michael Garval for bringing these details to my attention.

59. Champsaur, "Princesse," 2.

60. Ibid.

61. "*Mystère de Kama*," *Saturday Review*, 628.

62. "Jane de la Vaudère," *Revue du Nivernais*, 279.

63. Bethléem, *Romans*, 134.

64. Brisson, "Divers," 253.

65. Laborde, "'Amazone,'" 2.

66. "*Prêtresses de Mylitta*," 2.

67. Edwards, *Soleil*, 231–32.

68. Ibels, "Enquête," 115.

69. Grivel, "Roman," 153.

70. Ibid., 154.

71. Les Treize, "Nos échos," 2.

72. This was not La Vaudère's only collaboration with Champsaur. As previously noted, Champsaur and La Vaudère (under the name Jean Scrive) cowrote a Japanese-themed operetta entitled *Les trois mousmés* in 1898. Pauvert-Raimbault suggests that Champsaur and La Vaudère had an intimate relationship, though she provides no support for this ("Champsaur," 25). They were, however, likely friends. The collection at the Musée de Tessé in Le Mans contains Antoine Bourdelle's sculpture of Champsaur's wife, which was probably in La Vaudère's possession at some time in her life. Before his death, Fernand Crapez bequeathed this work to a friend, Pierre Maury, whose daughter donated it to the museum in 2013. Pierre Maury also donated a painting by Denys Van Alsloot and Hendrick de Clerck, *La mort d'Adonis*, that he had received from Fernand. Dating from around 1620, this painting was likely passed down by La Vaudère to her son. I extend

my appreciation to museum director François Arné for this information.

73. It is entirely possible that La Vaudère provided additional illustrations to the novel. However, only three images bear her discernible signature, and Champsaur supplies no information linking individual illustrations to the artists named on the cover page.

74. The text for La Vaudère's first illustration highlights Lulu's seductive silhouette:

> Son corps gracile, tanagréen, est photographié en maillot, sans autre voile que des roses, des guirlandes de coroles. Et toutes ces fleurs, au contour de la chair de Lulu, semblent des bouches amoureuses, baisant au cou, aux lèvres, aux boutons des seins, l'adorable aux cheveux en houppe. Une branchette vient mourir au milieu d'elle, masque le retrait d'amour, que caressent les pétales parfumés d'une rose hardie, comme déléguée par les autres roses, et pâmée de tous leurs désirs. (240–41)

La Vaudère's second illustration depicts a kiss between a cross-dressing Lulu and a famous female Spanish vocalist:

> Une fantaisie. Lulu, en torero, tout brodé d'or. Il n'est pas seul, le galant éphèbe d'Espagne. Lucita Cillero, la chanteuse nouvelle qui, avant les danses lumineuses, se fait applaudir au Casino de Paris, dans ses chansons et ses tarentelles, Lucita Cillero, en costume de l'île de Capri, debout, une main sur la hanche, sourit dans un baiser qui joint leurs deux bouches—fleur sur fleur—et fait se frôler les deux corps voluptueux et souples, adorablement mièvres, comme ces groupes anciens de Saxe dont raffolent les amateurs des grâces d'antan. (242)

The portrayal of Lulu on a bicycle underscores the mobility and autonomy of the modern woman:

> Des affiches annonçaient une marque de bicyclettes, des affiches américaines très longues, encadrées de branche noires et torses de pommier où les feuillages et les fruits éclataient en vert cru, orangés, dorés et rouges. Au centre,—dans un paysage en perspective rapide, des maisons, des toits au lointain,—sur une route en pente, Lulu dévale, penchée sur son guidon: une Lulu aux cheveux rouges, à béret quadrillé de brun et de noir, la taille souple sous un jersey noir et le boléro léger. Des souliers mordorés, des bas quadrillés, noir sur brun, perdus dans une culotte bouffante. En exergue: *Cycles Lulu*. (243–44)

75. See Bazile ("Lulu s'affiche") for an intriguing analysis of the visual, literary, and cultural intertextuality of the novel. Without naming La Vaudère directly, she illustrates the aesthetic parallels of her drawing for "Cycles Lulu" and Théophile Steinlen's *Motocylces Comiot* poster advertisement from 1899.

76. Like La Vaudère, Champsaur had been suspected of plagiarism on multiple occasions. Though she stops short of labeling it as such, Pauvert-Raimbault contends that in writing *Lulu*, Champsaur drew inspiration from Huysmans's 1884 novel *À rebours* and its discussion of Gustave Moreau's *Salomé* (Pauvert-Raimbault, "Champsaur," 25). Jean de Palacio has demonstrated that these same episodes influenced La Vaudère's novels *Les courtisanes de Brahma*, *L'amazone du roi de Siam*, and *Le mystère de Kama*, which each incorporated passages copied verbatim from Huysmans's work (Palacio, "Postérité," 197–202).

77. Champsaur, "Princesse," 2.

78. La Vaudère, "Poupée japonaise," 1.

79. Lyons's comprehensive *Readers and Society* traces scientific and religious discourses about reading and the demographics of literacy in nineteenth-century France.

80. Emery, *Photojournalism*, 124.

81. Ibid., 148–49.

82. As noted in the previous chapter, sections of this article first appeared in the profile of La Vaudère for the 1902 volume

of *Figures contemporaines tirées de l'Album Mariani.*

83. Cahu, "Jane de la Vaudère."

84. Atamian illustrated *Le harem de Syta* (1904); *L'amante du pharaon* (1905); *L'élève chérie* (1908); *La porte de félicité* (1908); *La vierge d'Israël* (1908); and the tenth edition of *Le mystère de Kama* (1910).

85. Emery, *Photojournalism*, 59.

86. Fouquières, *Mon Paris*, 19.

87. Emery, *Photojournalism*, 86.

88. Maurecy, "Ceux qui croient," 227–28.

89. For more on mediumism in La Vaudère's corpus, see chapter 5.

90. Maurecy, "Ceux qui croient," 228. This was not the only time that the enigmatic La Vaudère was tied to the occult. In Liane de Pougy's *Les sensations de Mlle de la Bringue*, she appeared as "Vande de la Janère" and participated in a shocking satanic ritual that celebrated bestiality, incest, and cannibalism. Curiously, Pougy depicted her alongside her friend (and rumored lover) Félicien Champsaur ("Félicité Saurien de Champs"). I extend my gratitude to Courtney Sullivan for her expertise on this *roman à clef.* In her study on the courtesan novel, Sullivan considers the allegorical implications of this exaggerated episode: "One wonders whether all these Belle Époque celebrities really attended such an event or whether the cavalcade of demi-monde personnages at a 'sabbat' serves as a metaphor for the entire debauched world of this turn-of-the-century social group" (Sullivan, *Evolution*, 54).

91. Cahu, "Jane de la Vaudère."

92. Ibid.

93. This same photo appears in Alphonse Séché's *Les muses françaises: Anthologie des femmes-poètes* (1908).

94. Mesch, *Having It All*, chapter 2.

95. Thank you to Michael Scrive for sharing his insight on La Vaudère's clothing.

96. Emery, "Maison," 65.

97. Kerley, *Uncovering*, 95.

98. "Mme Marguerite Durand," *Femina*, cover.

99. Zarmanian, "Quand les femmes," 251.

100. See, for example, André Germain's *La bourgeoisie qui brûle* (1951), which recounts this episode. I am grateful to Michael Scrive for this reference. On a related note, in his chronicles on Belle Époque Paris, André de Fouquières imagines La Vaudère's legacy in the company of Deslandes and the patroness Luisa Casati: "Jane de La Vaudière [*sic*] mériterait que son nom s'inscrivît au côté de ceux d'une baronne Deslandes et d'une marquise Casati dont les mémorialistes entretiennent la légende" (*Mon Paris*, 18).

CHAPTER 3

Sections of this chapter are based on two previously published articles: "Jane de La Vaudère and Maupassant: A New Appreciation of Plagiarism," *L'érudit franco-espagnol* (2016), and "The Feminine Copy: Travel and Textual Reproduction in Jane de la Vaudère's *Les demi-sexes*," in "Women and Traveling," special issue, ed. Catherine R. Montfort and Christine McCall Probes, *Women in French Studies* 7 (2018): 225–40.

1. Ryner, *Massacre*, 251.

2. Chadoqueau, "Maupassant plagié," 69, original emphasis.

3. Maurevert, *Livre*, 300.

4. Palacio, "Postérité," 202.

5. Due to their sheer abundance, it is impossible to identify all of the texts that La Vaudère integrated into her Orientalist corpus. Here, with the help of online search engines, I provide an abridged list that will give readers a sense of the frequency of her plagiarism (and perhaps encourage further study). In her novel *Le mystère de Kama* (1901), La Vaudère copies extensively from Éliphas Lévi's *Histoire de la magie* (1860). *L'amante du pharaon* (1905) integrates Ernest Bosc's *Isis dévoilée* (1897) and Gustave Le Bon's *Les premières civilisations* (1889). In *La sorcière d'Ecbatane* (1906), she

reproduces passages from Lévi's and Le Bon's works referenced here, as well as Léon Denis's *Après la mort: De la philosophie des esprits* (1893) and Gaston Maspero's *Histoire ancienne des peuples de l'Orient* (1878).

6. *Rien qu'amante!* (1894) includes passages from Paul Bourget's *André Cornélis* (1886); Alfred de Musset's *La confession d'un enfant du siècle* (1836); and Honoré de Balzac's *Gobseck* (1830), *Le lys dans la vallée* (1836), and *La femme de trente ans* (1842). In *Le droit d'aimer* (1895), La Vaudère again draws from Balzac's *Le lys dans la vallée*, as well as Edmond and Jules de Goncourt's *Charles Demailly* (1868); Dr. Henry Maudsley's *Le crime et la folie* (1874); and Dr. Théodule-Armand Ribot's *Les maladies de la personnalité* (1885). *Ambitieuse* (1896) features excerpts from Adolphe Belot's *Deux femmes: L'habitude et le souvenir* (1873); Maxime Du Camp's *Mémoires d'un suicidé* (1855); Théophile Gautier's *Voyage en Espagne* (1845); and Benjamin Constant's *Adolphe* (1816). *Le sang* (1898) contains sections from Auguste Villiers de L'Isle-Adam's *Contes cruels* (1883); Pierre Loti's *Le roman d'un enfant* (1890); and Émile Zola's *La faute de l'Abbé Mouret* (1875) and *Le rêve* (1888).

7. In addition to the works discussed in this chapter, La Vaudère's *L'amuseur* (1900) incorporates passages from Maupassant's *Une vie* (1883). *Le peintre des frissons* (1907) incorporates passages from *Bel ami* (1885).

8. "De ci, de là," 204.

9. To my knowledge, there is no concrete evidence that La Vaudère and Maupassant were ever in contact with one another. However, it is worth noting that both writers published various works with Ollendorff, including *Notre cœur* and *Les demi-sexes*, and it is likely that their paths crossed before Maupassant's death in 1893. Most curious, perhaps, is that no editor at Ollendorff recognized or disapproved of the similarities between the two novels. I wish to thank Marlo Johnston for her gracious correspondence and help with this matter.

10. Notions of authors' rights continually evolved throughout the eighteenth and nineteenth centuries, as evidenced by the numerous legislative developments that addressed intellectual property and literary reproduction. The revolutionary law of 1791, for example, specifically granted dramatists property rights over the theatrical representation of their works. In 1793, the Convention expanded the law to include the reproduction of texts appearing in print and increased the duration of protection from five to ten years after the author's death. Throughout the nineteenth century, the laws continued to evolve, and by 1866, authors' rights were protected for fifty years postmortem. In 1886, shortly before the publication of *Notre cœur*, France signed the Berne Convention treaty, an international copyright agreement recognizing authors' rights in all signatory countries (a total of 168 today). For a detailed account of the legal history of authors' rights in France since the fifteenth century, see Latournerie, "Petite histoire."

11. Maurel-Indart, *Plagiat*, 203.

12. For a compelling anthology of essays on postmodern approaches to plagiarism across the disciplines, see Buranen and Roy, *Perspectives on Plagiarism*.

13. Halbert, "Poaching and Plagiarizing," 111.

14. Anne Linton notes that *Les demi-sexes* was inspired by the scandal of doctors La Jarrige and Boisleux, whose 1897 trial exposed a network of underground abortionists throughout Paris ("Mutating Bodies," 583). She reads the novel's final vilification of the voluntary *ovariotomie* in the context of nineteenth-century anxiety about modern medicine and reproductive surgery. For an additional analysis of the ambivalent role of medicine in *Les demi-sexes*, see Mesch, "Husbands."

15. "La Sicile" was originally published in *La nouvelle revue* in 1886 and has since been reprinted in *En Sicile*, a collection of Maupassant's travel memoirs. The collection includes his 1890 essay "La côte italienne,"

traces of which are also found in La Vaudère's descriptions. All of my references are taken from this edition.

16. Finn provides a detailed account of the medical literature of the time and discusses the scientific, social, and moral implications of the procedure ("Female Sterilization," 27–32).

17. Offen, "Depopulation," 658.

18. Finn, "Female Sterilization," 27.

19. La Vaudère, *Demi-sexes*, 45.

20. Ibid., 48, my emphasis.

21. Ibid., 20.

22. Ibid., 193.

23. Ibid., epigraph, line 14.

24. Maupassant, *En Sicile*, 97.

25. Ibid., 99, 100.

26. La Vaudère, *Demi-sexes*, epigraph, line 3; Maupassant, *En Sicile*, 97, my emphasis.

27. La Vaudère, *Demi-sexes*, epigraph, line 6.

28. Additionally, La Vaudère's "La Vénus de Syracuse" sonnet was published two other times. It appeared in the October 25, 1902, issue of *La lanterne* and in the 1905 novel *Confessions galantes*, cowritten with Théodore Cahu (alias Théo-Critt).

29. La Vaudère, *Demi-sexes*, 242.

30. Ibid., 231, original emphasis.

31. Ibid., 238–39.

32. Maupassant, *En Sicile*, 36.

33. La Vaudère, *Demi-sexes*, 246.

34. Maupassant, *En Sicile*, 45–46.

35. Finn, "Female Sterilization," 32.

36. Examples of similarly themed novels from the period include Émile Zola's *Nana* (1880); Catulle Mendès's *La première maîtresse* (1887); Pierre Louÿs's *La femme et le pantin* (1898); and Octave Mirbeau's *Le jardin des supplices* (1899), to name just a few. For a comprehensive study of the figure of the *femme fatale* in late nineteenth-century fiction, see Dottin-Orsini's *Cette femme*.

37. Maupassant, *Notre cœur*, 59.

38. Ibid., 76.

39. Ibid., 160.

40. On the figure of the malicious lesbian in nineteenth-century French literature, see Waelti-Walters, *Damned Women*. For a detailed study of lesbianism in Decadent fiction, see Albert, *Saphisme et décadence*. Though focused solely on male authors, Schultz's *Sapphic Fathers* provides a compelling discussion of the literary and medical discourses of lesbianism in the nineteenth and twentieth centuries.

41. La Vaudère, *Demi-sexes*, 190–91.

42. Maupassant, *Notre cœur*, 80–81.

43. La Vaudère, *Demi-sexes*, 189–90.

44. Maupassant, *Notre cœur*, 80.

45. La Vaudère, *Demi-sexes*, 190.

46. Ibid., 193.

47. Maupassant, *Notre cœur*, 179.

48. La Vaudère, *Demi-sexes*, 194–95.

49. Maupassant, *Notre cœur*, 148–49.

50. Ibid., 160.

51. La Vaudère, *Demi-sexes*, 253.

52. Maupassant, *Notre cœur*, 229–30.

53. Ibid., 120.

54. Mesch, "Husbands," 99.

55. Maupassant, *Notre cœur*, 162.

56. Ibid., 182.

57. Ibid., 182–83.

58. Randall, *Pragmatic Plagiarism*, 221.

CHAPTER 4

1. See, for example, Day, *Mummy's Curse*; Fleischhack, *Narrating*; Parramore, *Reading*.

2. Fleischhack, *Narrating*, 213–27.

3. Thank you to Frédéric Maget of the Société des amis de Colette and to Jean-Luc Pehau-Ricau of the Moulin Rouge for confirming my suspicions on this matter.

4. Delilia, "Spectacles" (1906), 5.

5. George-Michael, "Marquise de Morny," 3.

6. Delilia, "Spectacles" (1907), 5.

7. See, for example, Lucey's discussion of the sensationalized publicity for *Rêve d'Égypte*, its reception in aristocratic circles, and the subsequent scandal at the Moulin Rouge (*Never Say I*, especially chapter 3).

8. Delilia, "Spectacles" (1906), 5.

9. Delilia, "Spectacles" (1907), 5.

10. The storylines of both *Le rêve de Mysès* and *Rêve d'Égypte* revolve around a dream sequence. Fleischhack identifies sleep as a convenient trope in mummy fiction to depict a mummy's mystical powers: "[Sleep] allows for the literary creation of a world in which supernatural events can occur without the reader having to question their actuality. Through sleep, two alternative realities are created: the real world of which the sleeper is unaware during sleep and a dream world in which supernatural events or occurrences are not necessarily questioned" (*Narrating*, 213).

11. This letter may be consulted at the archives of the Société des auteurs et compositeurs dramatiques (SACD), Paris.

12. No records of La Vaudère's submission or correspondence have been found at the Moulin Rouge, the Théâtre des Bouffes Parisiens, or L'Olympia.

13. The archivists at the SACD have generously communicated the contents of this procès-verbal with me.

14. "Théâtres," 3. On January 7, *Gil Blas* also reported on this "constant par huissier," suggesting that La Vaudère's appearance at the Tribunal civil de la Seine may have been as early as January 6.

15. As confirmed by the Archives de Paris, the Archives nationales at Pierrefitte-sur-Seine, and the Bibliothèque-musée de l'Opéra.

16. La Vaudère, *Peintre*, 16.

17. Ibid.

18. Ibid., 22.

19. Ibid., 15.

20. Ibid., 146.

21. Ibid.

22. Ibid., footnote 1.

23. The January 5 report by the newspaper *L'intransigeant* provides the following account of the notable audience members at the Moulin Rouge: "On rencontrait les personnalités les plus en vue du Tout-Paris: MM. le marquis de Castellane, Périvier, Henri Rochefort, Pédro Gailhard, Jacques de Fouquières, Albert Flamant, Xavier Roux, Alfred Delilia, Pierre Mortier, Paul Fugère, Joachim Gasquet, Lusciez, Trébor, Paul Iribe, Timmory, etc., Mmes Otéro, Liane de Pougy, Suzanne Derval, Lilian Greuze, tant d'autres encore que l'on se serait cru à une fête essentiellement 'mondaine'" (Beaudu, "Théâtre," 3).

24. La Vaudère, *Peintre*, 168.

25. Ibid., 188.

26. Quoted in Bonal's and Remy-Bieth's *Colette intime*, 116. Colette eventually resumed the performance of *Rêve d'Égypte* in Nice in March 1907. However, the show at the Théâtre des Capucines incorporated one major difference: Missy was replaced by Georges Wague in the role of the savant.

27. La Vaudère contributed to similar works of this kind, providing the preface to C. Klary's *La photographie du nu* (1902), a selection of photographs and essays defending the artistic merits of nude photography.

28. See Viveiros's article "Albert Méricant" for a historical overview of the publishing house.

29. Edwards, *Soleil*, 388.

30. Indeed, such works were relatively new to Méricant. The previous year, Méricant printed an advertisement for Guy de Téramond's *Une courtisane grecque* (1906), which he heralded as the first novel in his catalog to be illustrated by nude photography (cited by Viveiros, "Albert Méricant," 203).

31. Lucey cites Pierre Louÿs's 1896 novel *Aphrodite* as a quintessential literary example (*Never Say I*, 136).

32. La Vaudère's contract with Tallandier for *L'amante du pharaon* is dated March 12, 1904, and may be consulted at the Institut mémoires de l'édition contemporaine (IMEC) at the Abbaye d'Ardenne. This, to my knowledge, is the only conserved contract between La Vaudère and any of her editors.

33. Dobson ("Sleeping Beauties") teases out an intriguing thematic link between the trope of the sleeping female mummy, common to fin-de-siècle "mummy fiction,"

and the sleeping beauty of the classic fairy-tale genre whose awakening depends on a gallant onlooker.

34. La Vaudère, *Amante*, 63. The corresponding passage from *Le rêve de Mysès* reads as follows:

> Pourtant, la mort ne se présentait pas à l'esprit du prêtre avec son cortège de douleur et d'épouvante. Comme tous les hommes de sa caste, il la jugeait bienfaisante et réparatrice. L'inerte momie, toute raidie dans ses bandelettes, avec la fixité de son regard d'émail dans son masque d'or, n'éveillait en lui aucune répulsion. Il se plaisait dans la solennité des sarcophages, le mystère des chambres de granit où sommeillait l'âme des défunts.
>
> Toute l'architecture égyptienne, à l'image des pensées de l'homme, ne s'inspirait, d'ailleurs, que d'un songe funèbre. Les pyramides, les obélisques, les pylônes, les colonnes immenses représentaient une vague forme humaine: celle du cadavre enlinceulé dans ses bandelettes. L'Egyptien [*sic*] ne pensait qu'à la résurrection et ne travaillait que pour l'éternité. (112–15)

35. La Vaudère, *Amante*, 99. The corresponding passage in *Le rêve de Mysès* reads as follows:

> La substitution d'un personnage de marque était chose grave, que l'on punissait sévèrement dans la classe sacerdotale. Cette fraude, cependant, s'accomplissait fréquemment, grâce au mystère qui entourait les pratiques de l'embaumement.
>
> Le mort n'étant montré aux familles que recouvert de son masque et enveloppé de ses bandelettes, il était aisé de le faire disparaître, et des corps d'esclaves occupaient, parfois, des sarcophages princiers.
>
> Nul n'était autorisé à défaire les visages d'or ou d'ivoire qui recouvraient les traits véritables, ni à dérouler les bandelettes des bras et des jambes, aussi, arrivait il [*sic*], parfois, qu'un grand dignitaire emmaillotté de toile grossière, cousue à larges points, vint [*sic*], après un séjour plus ou moins prolongé dans le "natron," prendre sa place anonyme dans les caveaux publics.
>
> Les jeunes mortes, violées par les embaumeurs, étaient livrées aux crocodiles sacrés. (11–12)

36. La Vaudère, *Amante*, 237.

37. La Vaudère, *Rêve de Mysès*, 77.

38. Le Bon, *Premières civilisations*, 428–29.

39. La Vaudère, *Amante*, 103.

40. La Vaudère, *Rêve de Mysès*, 19–20.

41. Le Bon, *Premières civilisations*, 354–55.

42. La Vaudère, *Amante*, 101–2.

43. La Vaudère, *Rêve de Mysès*, 19.

44. Bosc, *Isis dévoilée*, 191–92.

45. In addition to those discussed here, there are a plethora of other passages common to both *Le rêve de Mysès* and *L'amante du pharaon*. Readers interested in further pursuing a comparative analysis may wish to consult the following passages and page numbers: *L'amante du pharaon*, 74, *Le rêve de Mysès*, 126–27; *L'amante du pharaon*, 107, *Le rêve de Mysès*, 16; *L'amante du pharaon*, 109, *Le rêve de Mysès*, 23; *L'amante du pharaon*, 113, *Le rêve de Mysès*, 24; *L'amante du pharaon*, 117, *Le rêve de Mysès*, 27; *L'amante du pharaon*, 235, *Le rêve de Mysès*, 67; *L'amante du pharaon*, 248, *Le rêve de Mysès*, 75; *L'amante du pharaon*, 256, *Le rêve de Mysès*, 80; *L'amante du pharaon*, 279, *Le rêve de Mysès*, 107.

46. I wish to thank bioanthropologist and mummy expert Dr. Dario Piombino-Mascali for his help in identifying these signs. Curiously, by midcentury, the efficacy of chemical injection in embalming techniques rendered the invasive craniotomy unnecessary.

47. Carol's comprehensive *L'embaumement* examines the techniques of body conservation and shifting cultural attitudes about death in nineteenth-century France. I express my gratitude to Carol for her

assistance in contextualizing the embalmed remains of La Vaudère's family members.

48. Carol, *L'embaumement*, 20–21. For a discussion of embalming practices in France and Italy during the Middle Ages, see Marinozzi, "Embalming Art."

49. Cahu, "Jane de la Vaudère." Not all depictions of the chapel were this romanticized. In his memoirs fifty years later, André de Fouquières exaggerated the morbid eccentricity of the writer and her surroundings: "Les paysans ne la rencontraient guère car elle ne sortait presque pas de son parc, et la 'dame' les plongeait dans l'effroi. [. . .] Et puis, dans la chapelle du château, il y avait ces deux cercueils où reposaient, embaumés, les corps des parents de la chatelaine [*sic*], visibles sous un couvercle de verre . . . On disait que chaque nuit, un flambeau au poing, elle allait poursuivre un colloque muet avec ses morts" (*Mon Paris*, 20).

50. La Vaudère, *Rêve de Mysès*, 35.

51. Ibid., 127.

52. Ibid., 128.

53. I owe my thanks to Melanie Hawthorne for inquiring about this potential play on words. Alas, this appears to be a coincidence, as records from the SACD indicate that La Vaudère had already chosen a title for her pantomime well before Missy's production at the Moulin Rouge.

54. *The Dream of Mysès* appears in the same volume as *The Double Star and Other Occult Fantasies* (2018). *Pharaoh's Lover* appears in the volume with *Syta's Harem* (2020).

CHAPTER 5

1. Drevet, "Jane de la Vaudère," 81; Bélilon, "Chronique féministe," 2.

2. La Vaudère and Théo-Critt, *Confessions*, 63.

3. Nineteenth-century scholars who are familiar with La Vaudère have mostly written about *Les demi-sexes*. See, for example, Mesch ("Husbands"); Linton ("Mutating"); and Larson ("Jane" and "The Feminine," which are also the basis for chapter 3 of this book). *Les demi-sexes* is now accessible to Anglophone readers, thanks to a translation by Snuggly Books.

4. Offen's comprehensive volume *Debating the Woman Question in the French Third Republic, 1870–1920* provides historical accounts of debates around womanhood.

5. The bimonthly *La citoyenne*, founded by Hubertine Auclert, was in circulation from 1881 to 1891 and was predominantly interested in French women's suffrage and full citizenship under the Civil Code. Clotilde Dissard directed *La revue féministe*, which ran from 1895 to 1897 and promoted a brand of feminism based on motherhood and the complementarity of the sexes. Perhaps most influential was Marguerite Durand's *La fronde*, an entirely women-run newspaper that covered a variety of women's issues and featured articles by the era's most prominent activists (Madeleine Pelletier, Jeanne Chauvin, Nelly Roussel, and Clotilde Dissard, to name a few).

6. The Congrès international du droit des femmes was held in Paris in 1878 and inaugurated a series of conferences hosted by the capital city. The Congrès français international du droit des femmes, the Congrès féministe international, and the Congrès international de la condition et des droits des femmes took place in Paris in 1889, 1896, and 1900, respectively. According to popular anecdote, journalist Marguerite Durand became committed to feminist activism after attending the 1896 congress while on assignment for *Le Figaro* (she founded *La fronde* just a year later).

7. La Vaudère, "Ève nouvelle," 2.

8. See Perry, "Memorializing," for the historical background of the Woman's Building and its prominence at the Tennessee Exposition.

9. La Vaudère, "Exposition," 2.

10. Ibid. La Vaudère's predictions proved wrong: in December 1897, just months later, women obtained the right to bear

witness to legal acts, and in 1907, wives gained lawful control over their earnings.

11. La Vaudère, "Exposition," 2.

12. Offen traces the origin of the word "feminism" to 1882, when Hubertine Auclert used it in an open letter published in her newspaper *La citoyenne*. Alexandre Dumas *fils* is often credited for first incorporating the neologism in his deeply misogynist work *L'homme-femme* (1872), but it was Auclert who seems to have first applied its modern usage (Offen, *Debating*, 158–60). For more on the word's origins and usage, see Offen, "On the French" and "Defining."

13. See Offen, *Debating*, 189–90, on the portrayal of the American "new woman" in the French imagination in the years following the Chicago Exposition.

14. La Vaudère, "École," 2.

15. Ibid.

16. Ibid.

17. Ibid.

18. Ibid.

19. Offen, "Defining."

20. La Vaudère, "Femmes," 1.

21. Ibid., original emphasis.

22. Bélilon, "Chronique féministe," 2.

23. Ibid.

24. Grandfort, "Causerie," 2.

25. Intérim, "Chronique des livres," 2.

26. La Vaudère, "Protestations," 2.

27. Ibid.

28. Ibid., original emphasis.

29. Ibid. It is unclear whom La Vaudère was referencing here. The "plus beau succès dramatique" of the time was perhaps Edmond Rostand's *Cyrano de Bergerac*, which had premiered in Paris in 1897 and was still running in the spring of 1899. Rostand's wife, poet Rosemonde Gérard, had helped finance the production by contributing a substantial sum from her dowry. Widespread rumors suggested that Gérard had also written scenes of the play, which may explain La Vaudère's allusion. In his biography of Rostand, Pierre Espil recalls, "J'ai souvent entendu dire, dans l'entourage des Rostand, que sa femme était pour beaucoup dans *Cyrano de Bergerac* et même qu'elle aurait entièrement écrit la fameuse scène du balcon, point culminant de l'œuvre" (*Edmond Rostand*, 94).

30. La Vaudère, "Protestations," 2.

31. La Vaudère, *Amuseur*, 242.

32. Champsaur, "Princesse," 2.

33. La Vaudère, "Révolution," 273.

34. See Wilkins, "Paris International," for a discussion of the conference's proceedings, attendees, and their representation by the contemporary press. Her article also features a useful historic outline of feminism in nineteenth-century France.

35. La Vaudère, "Revolution," 274.

36. Ibid., 278.

37. Ibid., 277.

38. Ibid., 280, my emphasis.

39. For more on the French depopulation crisis in the context of feminism(s), see Offen, "Depopulation." Offen contends that relational feminism appealed most to nationalist and pronatalist campaigns because it tactfully coupled feminist efforts with the politics of motherhood.

40. La Vaudère, "Revolution," 282.

41. La Vaudère and Théo-Critt, *Confessions*, 24 and 159, respectively. For more on "La Vénus de Syracuse," see chapter 3.

42. Ibid., 15, my emphasis.

43. Ibid., 63.

44. In an overtly misogynistic review of *L'amuseur* in 1900, Drevet reproached La Vaudère for what he considered a simplistic and vilifying depiction of masculinity: "Le féminisme de la Vaudère est de qualité inférieure; séduite par une utopie insane, elle n'en a vu que le principe fondamental, qui est aussi le but à atteindre, et n'a nullement cherché à discuter les théories et les faits qui prétendent la réaliser: elle ne voit en l'homme qu'un ennemi à détruire, alors que les théories féministes les plus vraisemblables, les mieux raisonnées, voudraient au contraire faire de l'homme *l'allié* de la femme et établir la société nouvelle et féministe sur cette alliance"

("Jane de la Vaudère," 81, original emphasis).

45. La Vaudère and Théo-Critt, *Confessions*, 294.

46. See Offen's "Defining" for more on relational and individualist feminisms.

47. The quotation "Père, je veux divorcer" appears in La Vaudère's *L'amuseur*, a tragic novel about a woman's attempt to escape the patriarchal bonds of marriage. La Vaudère, *Amuseur*, 142.

48. La Vaudère, "Vierges," 3. The following year, in response to an inquiry on the institution of marriage, La Vaudère shared these reflections with Jean Joseph-Renaud, who published them in the form of a letter in his double volume *La faillite du mariage et l'union future* (1899).

49. La Vaudère, "Vierges," 3.

50. Stewart, *Health and Beauty* (especially chapter 5).

51. See Offen, *Debating*, 416–26, for a discussion of this issue in feminist circles.

52. Accampo, *Blessed*, 61.

53. La Vaudère, "Vierges," 3.

54. La Vaudère and Théo-Critt, *Confessions*, 316.

55. This reasoning recalls a passage from La Vaudère's 1896 novel *Ambitieuse* that links a woman's sexual education with her marital fidelity: "Maintenues dans une éducation obscure et fausse, jetées brutalement au milieu de la vie, sans aucune préparation, sans aucun avertissement, elles connaissent, tout à coup, l'amour et la maternité qui les laissent plus faibles et plus souffrantes. Puis, irritées par une direction compressive et rarement bienveillante, elles se révoltent, sans oser encore obéir aux mouvements spontanés de leur conscience et de leur cœur qu'on leur impute à crime. Enfin, elles risquent leur renom, leur tranquillité, leur vie, parfois, lorsque les passions trop longtemps combattues se déchaînent en elles, avec l'irrésistible puissance du mal" (134–35).

56. La Vaudère, "Vierges," 3.

57. Mesch, "Husbands."

58. Cryle, "Terrible Ordeal." Cryle's article provides an illuminating reading of medical and literary constructions of the wedding night at the turn of the twentieth century.

59. Dr. Rhazis, *L'initiation amoureuse, ou L'art de se faire aimer et de plaire* (1909), 32. Quoted by Cryle, "Terrible Ordeal," 46.

60. Adler, *Secrets*, 33.

61. For example, in La Vaudère's and Cahu's *Confessions galantes*, Arlette reproduces letters from two convent friends who recount in detail the rapes of their wedding night. The first recalls, "Il écarta les couvertures, se jeta sur moi, et, malgré mes efforts et mes prières, me prit brutalement. Je crus à un assassinat et poussai un grand cri. De mes deux bras crispés, je tâchai d'écarter le monstre qui me rudoyait, me brisait, me déchirait jusque dans les fibres les plus profondes, les plus secrètes de mon être!" (249). The second friend suffered a similar encounter, despite her resistance against her husband: "Je luttai de nouveau, dégrisée tout à coup, en proie à une terreur sans nom. Ma résistance exaspérait son désir qui se faisait violent, presque cruel. Malgré mes plaintes, il me serrait brutalement, me meurtrissait, enfonçait ses ongles dans ma chair" (288). In *L'amuseur*, the female protagonist's mother links marital rape to insufficient sexual education, which she claims leaves young women vulnerable to the sexual aggression of husband: "Il faut qu'une fille ne sache rien pour être digne de l'homme qui sait tout," she remarks. "On la livre sans défense au seigneur et maître qui, d'ailleurs, lui fera durement payer cette ignorance qu'il a exigée" (59).

62. La Vaudère, "Divorce," 2.

63. Pedersen's *Legislating* (especially chapter 2) provides a detailed summary of feminist debates and campaigns on divorce reform (including divorce by mutual consent).

64. For an interdisciplinary study of the legal and cultural debates on adultery in

early nineteenth-century France, see Mainardi, *Husbands*.

65. La Vaudère, "Divorce," 2.

66. Mesch, *Before Trans*, 126–27, 189.

67. In describing his doctrine, Kardec preferred the term "spiritisme" to "spiritualisme" because it placed an emphasis on reincarnation and communication with spirit phenomena (*Livre*, iii). La Vaudère also employed the term "spiritism" in her related writing and I will do so here.

68. Kardec, *Livre*, 345, original emphasis.

69. Zarmanian, *Créatrices*, 133.

70. Mme. Louis Maurecy, "Ceux qui croient," 228.

71. Tromp, "Queering."

72. Gardini, "Jane de la Vaudère," 283.

73. In the last decades of the nineteenth century, feminist spiritists like Olga de Bézobrazow and Lucie Grange used their influential platforms to advocate for marital and educational reforms to benefit women (Sharp, *Secular*, 169–70).

74. Edelman, *Voyantes*, 81–82. Through exhaustive archival research, Edelman's study uncovers female mediums and healers in nineteenth-century France who were prominent figures in spiritist circles and popular culture.

75. La Vaudère, "Spiritisme," 2.

76. La Vaudère, "Pièce," 3.

77. La Vaudère, *Sorcière*, xi.

78. As the novel unfolds, La Vaudère includes uncited passages from works by Gustave Le Bon, Éliphas Lévi, Gaston Maspero, and Guy de Maupassant (and likely others).

79. Adam, "Conceptions," 1. Adam reproduces many of these passages in his work *La morale de l'amour*, published in 1907.

80. La Vaudère, "Réponse," 2.

81. "Les femmes," 3.

82. La Vaudère, "Réponse," 2.

83. Ibid.

84. He recounts his practice of automatic writing or "l'écriture spirite" in Jules Bois's *L'au-delà et les forces inconnues*, 1902.

85. I am grateful to Michael Scrive for this reference and for his assistance in fleshing out the contextual nuances of La Vaudère's editorial.

86. Tromp, "Queering," 91 and 96.

CHAPTER 6

1. La Vaudère, "Automobiles," 2.

2. Ibid.

3. Ibid.

4. "Chauffeuse" was first published in 1898 in *La presse* and then republished in 1902 in *La lanterne* under the title "Teuf-teuf." It was also included in La Vaudère's short-story collection *Les mousseuses* (1901).

5. La Vaudère, "Chauffeuse," 2.

6. Ibid.

7. La Vaudère, "Soleil," 115–16.

8. Buisseret, "Femmes," 51.

9. La Vaudère, *Panne*, 205–6. This work originally appeared in 1905 in La Vaudère's *Pour le flirt!*, a collection of dialogues subtitled "saynètes mondaines."

10. La Vaudère, *Panne*, 198–99.

11. Ibid., 200.

12. In a notable point of convergence, Georges de Peyrebrune associates La Vaudère with the Duchesse in her short story "Jupiter et les bas-bleus" (referenced in chapter 2). Published in 1893, in the early stages of La Vaudère's career, the story classifies the two women as socialites who, on a whim, try their hand at writing.

13. Scharff, *Taking*, 26.

14. Labadie-Lagrave, "Pourquoi," 10.

15. Buisseret, "Femmes," 49.

16. "2e Exposition," 1.

17. Souvestre, "Circuit," 1.

18. Souvestre, "Coupe," 3.

19. Buisseret, "Femmes."

20. Néret's and Poulain's *Art, la femme et l'automobile* offers a stunning sampling of Belle Époque posters, paintings, and sculptures representative of the woman/automobile iconography.

21. As the case of Violette Morris (1893–1944) has shown, anxieties around

female drivers' clothing continued to manifest in the decades that followed. Morris, a champion race car driver and exceptional athlete, frequently dressed in men's clothing. In order to more comfortably race cars, she also had a voluntary mastectomy, which further eliminated signifiers of femininity. When she refused to give up her pants for feminine attire, the Fédération féminine sportive de France (FFSF) prohibited her from participating in the 1928 summer Olympics. In response, Morris sued the FFSF for damages but lost. For an in-depth discussion of the trial, see chapter 9 of Bard's *Histoire politique*.

22. Scharff, *Taking*, 15–16.

23. Clasti, "Vierge," 223.

24. Ibid.

25. Cahu, "Jane de la Vaudère."

26. Her 1895 novel *Le droit d'aimer* is perhaps the most blatant example: the "Château de la Vénerie," badly mismanaged by the protagonist's in-laws, falls into ruins. While her husband depletes her dowry on his mistress, the protagonist successfully restores it from debts.

27. Trubek, *Skeptic's Guide*, 12.

28. The content and quotations in this section are taken from an interview that I conducted with Anne-Charlotte.

29. Hawthorne, *Finding*, 96.

30. Following Jean's death in 1940, Pierre, a doctor, regularly looked in on Fernand and Léopoldine Crapez and provided free medical care to them for the remainder of their lives. In exchange, they offered him a selection of artistic works that Fernand likely inherited from La Vaudère and that Pierre later donated to the Musée de Tessé in Le Mans.

JANE DE LA VAUDÈRE: A COMPREHENSIVE BIBLIOGRAPHY

The works compiled here represent La Vaudère's published poetry, novels, short stories, theatrical works, editorials, and prefaces that she provided for other works. Some of the novels and short stories that appeared in volume form were also published in periodicals (sometimes under different titles). In the interest of space, I have not included bibliographic details for the serial versions of these works. Many of the journals that printed her editorials, short stories, and poems have been digitized and can be consulted on Gallica (Gallica.bnf.fr). Despite its size, this list is likely not complete, and the poems or short stories that were neither preserved nor digitized are extremely difficult to locate. Nonetheless, this bibliography reflects the breadth of La Vaudère's writing production and can serve as a guide for future reading.

POETRY COLLECTIONS

Les heures perdues. Paris: Lemerre, 1889.
L'éternelle chanson. Paris: Ollendorff, 1890.
Minuit. Paris: Ollendorff, 1892.
Évocation. Paris: Ollendorff, 1893.
Les baisers de la chimère (?)
Les cigales d'amour (?)

NOVELS

Mortelle étreinte. Paris: Ollendorff, 1891.
Rien qu'amante! Paris: Ollendorff, 1894.
Le droit d'aimer. Paris: Ollendorff, 1895.
Ambitieuse. Paris: Ollendorff, 1896.
Les demi-sexes. Paris: Ollendorff, 1897.
Les sataniques. Paris: Ollendorff, 1897.
Le sang. Paris: Ollendorff, 1898.
Les frôleurs. Paris: Ollendorff, 1899.
L'amuseur. Paris: Ollendorff, 1900.
Trois fleurs de volupté. Paris: Flammarion, 1900.
Le mystère de Kama. Paris: Flammarion, 1901.
L'amazone du roi de Siam. Paris: Flammarion, 1902.
Les androgynes. Paris: Méricant, 1903. (published later under the title *Folie d'opium*)
Les courtisanes de Brahma. Paris: Flammarion, 1903.
L'expulsée. Paris: Flammarion, 1903.

La guescha amoureuse. Paris: Flammarion, 1904.
Le harem de Syta. Paris: Méricant, 1904.
L'amante du Pharaon. Paris: Tallandier, 1905.
Confessions galantes (with Théo-Critt, pseud. Théodore Cahu). Paris: Méricant, 1905.
La porte de félicité. Paris: Flammarion, 1905.
L'invincible amour! Paris: Méricant, 1906.
La sorcière d'Ecbatane. Paris: Flammarion, 1906.
La vierge d'Israël. Paris: Méricant, 1906.
La cité des sourires. Paris: Librairie des publications modernes, 1907.
Le jardin du péché. Paris: Méricant, 1907.
Le peintre des frissons. Paris: Flammarion, 1907.
Les prêtresses de Mylitta. Paris: Méricant, 1907.
Le rêve de Mysès. Paris: Librairie d'art technique, 1907.
Le crime d'aimer. Paris: Méricant, 1908.
L'élève chérie. Paris: Bibliothèque générale d'édition, 1908.
Sapho, dompteuse. Paris: Méricant, 1908.
Les audacieux. Paris: Méricant, 1909.

SHORT-STORY COLLECTIONS

L'anarchiste. Paris: Ollendorff, 1893.
Les mousseuses. Paris: Flammarion, 1901.
La mystérieuse. Paris: Flammarion, 1902.

THEATRICAL WORKS

Le modèle: Comédie en 1 acte. Paris: Lemerre, 1889.
Madame Laurence: Pièce en trois actes. (1890s)
Pour une nuit d'amour!: Drame en 1 acte. Paris: Ollendorff, 1898. (based on Émile Zola's story)
Victor Hugo: Grande scène dramatique. Paris: Librairie théâtrale, 1904.
Pour le flirt!: Saynètes mondaines. Paris: Flammarion, 1905.
Dupont sera élu!: Comédie électorale en 1 acte. Paris: Ondet, 1906.
Mademoiselle de Fontanges: Pièce en 4 actes, en vers. Paris: Méricant, 1909.

POEMS APPEARING IN PERIODICALS

"La Tour Eiffel." *Gil Blas*, May 24, 1889.
"Printemps." *Paris-croquis*, June 8, 1889.
"Chanson." *Le supplément*, August 23, 1898.
"Papiers de verre: Colère de l'oncle." *La presse*, November 5, 1898.
"C'est la dépopulation!" *Gil Blas*, November 24, 1898.
"Livres d'hiver." *Le supplément*, January 9, 1902.
"Le chemin des amandiers." *Le supplément*, February 8, 1902.
"Madrigal." *Le supplément*, February 22, 1902.
"Chanson des baisers." *Le supplément*, March 20, 1902.
"Un nid." *Le supplément*, April 12, 1902.
"Avril fleuri." *Le supplément*, April 29, 1902.
"Mon étang." *Le supplément*, August 21, 1902.
"Ivresse." *Le supplément*, October 14, 1902.
"La Vénus de Syracuse." *Le supplément*, October 15, 1902.
"Souvenir." *Le supplément*, November 8, 1902.
"Sultanes." *Le supplément*, December 2, 1902.
"Premiers baisers: Triolets." *Le supplément*, December 11, 1902.
"Angoisse de l'attente." *Le supplément*, January 22, 1903.
"Le yacht." *Le supplément*, August 15, 1907.
"Parfum." *Le supplément*, August 22, 1907.
"D'une courtisane." *Le supplément*, October 1, 1907.
"Après la pluie." *Le supplément*, December 26, 1907.
"L'hiver." *Le supplément*, February 13, 1908.

SHORT STORIES APPEARING IN PERIODICALS

"Le pardon." *Le Figaro*, December 1, 1894.
"Philtre de beauté." *La nouvelle revue* (July–August 1896): 610–11.

"Royauté morte!" *La nouvelle revue*, March 15, 1897.
"Contes rapides: Opérée!" *La presse*, March 29, 1897.
"Contes rapides: Sauts d'obstacles." *La presse*, April 5, 1897.
"Contes rapides: Sermons de Carême." *La presse*, April 8, 1897.
"Contes rapides: Les rameaux." *La presse*, April 16, 1897.
"Contes rapides: Juvénilité." *La presse*, April 29, 1897.
"Contes rapides: Pour ta fête. . . ." *La presse*, May 21, 1897.
"Contes rapides: Les fraises." *La presse*, May 29, 1897.
"Contes rapides: Débutante!" *La presse*, June 2, 1897.
"Contes rapides: Nuit de juin." *La presse*, June 9, 1897.
"Contes rapides: Un amour sérieux." *La presse*, June 18, 1897.
"Contes rapides: Une révolution." *La presse*, June 23, 1897.
"Contes rapides: Lucette." *La presse*, July 12, 1897.
"Contes rapides: En wagon." *La presse*, July 20, 1897.
"Contes rapides: Jardin d'amour." *La presse*, August 6, 1897.
"Contes rapides: Dompteuse." *La presse*, August 13, 1897.
"Contes rapides: Sur la plage." *La presse*, August 21, 1897.
"Contes rapides: La pêche." *La presse*, August 28, 1897.
"Contes rapides: Le départ." *La presse*, September 7, 1897.
"Contes rapides: Les yeux." *La presse*, September 23, 1897.
"Contes rapides: Claudie." *La presse*, October 24, 1897.
"Contes rapides: Devant les chats." *La presse*, October 29, 1897.
"Contes rapides: Le sanglier." *La presse*, November 17, 1897.
"Contes rapides: L'accident." *La presse*, November 27, 1897.
"Contes rapides: Un fou." *La presse*, December 8, 1897.
"Contes rapides: Les dernières roses." *La presse*, December 19, 1897.
"Contes rapides: Roseline." *La presse*, December 24, 1897.
"Contes rapides: La foi." *La presse*, December 27, 1897.
"Contes rapides: La fête des roses." *La presse*, January 18, 1898.
"Contes rapides: Un début." *La presse*, January 29, 1898.
"Contes rapides: Quête à domicile." *La presse*, February 6, 1898.
"Contes rapides: L'amant." *La presse*, February 13, 1898.
"Contes rapides: Pour être aimé." *La presse*, March 10, 1898.
"Contes rapides: Adultère." *La presse*, March 27, 1898.
"Contes rapides: Concours hippique." *La presse*, April 16, 1898.
"Contes rapides: Nouveau tarif." *La presse*, April 27, 1898.
"Contes rapides: Pour en être." *La presse*, May 5, 1898.
"Contes rapides: À triplette." *La presse*, May 12, 1898.
"Contes rapides: Nouveau jeu." *La presse*, May 21, 1898.
"Contes rapides: Entre amants." *La presse*, June 28, 1898.
"Contes rapides: Chauffeuse." *La presse*, July 27, 1898.
"Contes rapides: Monsieur, Madame. . . ." *La presse*, November 11, 1898.
"Contes rapides: Au cabaret." *La presse*, December 10, 1898.
"Contes rapides: Cambrioleur!" *La presse*, December 17, 1898.
"Contes rapides: Sauvetage." *La presse*, December 27, 1898.
"Contes rapides: Soleil d'hiver." *La presse*, February 1, 1899.
"Contes rapides: La preuve." *La presse*, February 12, 1899.
"Le beau Marcellus: Les conseils d'une mère I." *La presse*, February 18, 1899. (Part I)

"Le beau Marcellus: Déception II." *La presse*, March 3, 1899. (Part II)
"Le beau Marcellus: Confidences III." *La presse*, March 10, 1899. (Part III)
"Protestations: La femme." *La presse*, April 6, 1899.
"À vol d'oison: L'hippique." *La presse*, April 12, 1899.
"Idylles: Léo et Julie." *La presse*, November 3, 1899.
"Arabesques: L'amour gelé." *La presse*, December 31, 1899.
"Contes inquiétants: Parfum." *La presse*, January 17, 1900.
"Contes inquiétants: Les yeux." *La presse*, January 21, 1900.
"Conte javanais: Les bédayas." *La presse*, March 2, 1900.
"Contes inquiétants: Polygamie." *La presse*, March 22, 1900.
"Dans une étoile." *La presse*, March 28, 1900. (Part I)
"Dans une étoile." *La presse*, March 29, 1900. (Part II)
"Dans une étoile." *La presse*, March 30, 1900. (Part III)
"Dans une étoile." *La presse*, March 31, 1900. (Part IV)
"Dans une étoile." *La presse*, April 2, 1900. (Part V)
"Conte de paques: L'œuf rouge." *La presse*, April 14, 1900.
"Contes d'exposition: Un bon ami." *La presse*, May 10, 1900.
"Contes d'exposition: Au chinois." *La presse*, June 1, 1900.
"Conte graphologique: Un crime." *La presse*, July 1, 1900.
"Fantasia: Un roi." *La presse*, February 18, 1901.
"Fantasia: Dans le ciel." *La presse*, March 12, 1901.
"Fantasia: Fin de carême." *La presse*, March 17, 1901.
"Fantasia: Les rayons x." *La presse*, March 28, 1901.
"Fantasia: Vernissage." *La presse*, May 2, 1901.
"Cambrioleur!" *Le supplément*, September 21, 1901.
"Opérée!" *Le supplément*, October 5, 1901.
"Un bon ami." *Le supplément*, October 24, 1901.
"Le prétendant." *Le supplément*, November 19, 1901.
"Sapho." *Le supplément*, December 3, 1901.
"En loterie." *Le supplément*, December 16, 1901.
"Un divorce." *Le supplément*, December 17, 1901.
"Débutante!" *Le supplément*, January 14, 1902.
"Le suiveur." *Le supplément*, January 30, 1902.
"L'entraînement." *Le supplément*, March 1, 1902.
"Un ange!" *Le supplément*, March 27, 1902.
"Juvénilité." *Le supplément*, May 8, 1902.
"L'amazone du roi de Siam." *Le supplément*, June 12, 1902. (excerpt)
"Aymienne." *Le supplément*, June 24, 1902.
"Un roi." *Le supplément*, July 8, 1902.
"Pour ta fête . . . ." *Le supplément*, August 2, 1902.
"Teuf-Teuf." *Le supplément*, August 5, 1902.
"Ninoche." *Le supplément*, August 12, 1902.
"Heureux ménages!" *Le supplément*, August 28, 1902.
"Le sermon du père Frumence." *Le supplément*, September 23, 1902.
"La grande vie." *La vie en rose*, October 19, 1902. (published later in *Le supplément*, January 29, 1903)
"Confetti." *Le supplément*, November 4, 1902.
"Les yeux." *Le supplément*, November 15, 1902.
"Volupté rouge." *Le supplément*, December 18, 1902.
"Le premier pas." *Le supplément*, January 6, 1903.
"L'escapade." *Le supplément*, February 19, 1903.
"La belle Houséini." *Le supplément*, April 4, 1903.
"Sayameda." *Revue illustrée*, November 15, 1904.

"Quête à domicile." *Le supplément*, March 3, 1906.
"Pomponnet." *Le supplément*, July 13, 1907.
"Plaisir!" *Le supplément*, September 7, 1907.
"La preuve." *Le supplément*, September 28, 1907.
"Chat-Myen." *Le supplément*, December 21, 1907.
"Le remède." *Le supplément*, February 4, 1908.

EDITORIALS APPEARING IN PERIODICALS

"Tauromachie: Les joies de l'arène." *La presse*, September 16, 1896.
"On rentre!: Les victimes du baccara." *La presse*, September 23, 1896.
"Les automobiles de l'avenir: La roulette d'agrément." *La presse*, October 1, 1896.
"Sur le caractère russe: L'esprit généralisateur." *La presse*, October 7, 1896.
"La foule: Celle des bons et des mauvais jours." *La presse*, October 14, 1896.
"Automne: Journées grises." *La presse*, October 24, 1896.
"La maison maudite: Sorciers et envoûteurs." *La presse*, November 1, 1896.
"Hommes de génie et névropathes: Une enquête." *La presse*, November 5, 1896.
"La chasse: Bourgeois et gentilshommes." *La presse*, November 13, 1896.
"Un banquet d'honneur: Étoiles et nébuleuses." *La presse*, November 19, 1896.
"Les spéculateurs: L'amour du jeu." *La presse*, November 26, 1896.
"Les deux salons: Venise à Paris." *La presse*, December 3, 1896.
"Les sans ovaires." *La presse*, December 9, 1896.
"Une pièce nouvelle: Magnétisme et sortilèges." *La presse*, December 16, 1896.
"Les amants de Venise: Le plus aimé." *La presse*, December 24, 1896.
"Le livre et le théâtre: Auteurs et comédiens." *La presse*, December 30, 1896.
"Un burnous: Petit projet de costume." *La presse*, January 6, 1897.
"Dépopulation: Trop heureux!" *La presse*, January 13, 1897.
"Danse macabre: Petites expériences." *La presse*, January 20, 1897.
"Révélations posthumes: De l'amour." *La presse*, January 27, 1897.
"Du divorce: Réformes nécessaires." *La presse*, February 7, 1897.
"La censure russe: Nos hommes de lettres." *La presse*, February 13, 1897.
"Spiritisme: Hier et aujourd'hui." *La presse*, February 17, 1897.
"Livrets d'opéra: La prose tue le vers!" *La presse*, February 25, 1897.
"Une exposition: Pour le féminisme." *La presse*, March 4, 1897.
"Symbolisme: Une pièce nouvelle." *La presse*, March 11, 1897.
"À l'école des beaux-arts: L'admission des femmes." *La presse*, March 19, 1897.
"Vierges modernes: Le krach du mariage." *La presse*, October 27, 1898.
"Réponse à M. Paul Adam: Royauté!" *La presse*, February 5, 1899.
"À vol d'oison: Vénus de Syracuse." *La presse*, April 6, 1900.

MUSIC LYRICS

"Le portrait de ma cousine: Confidence!" A. Tallien de Cabarrus. Paris: Éditions Henri Tellier, 1891.
"Sérénade du baiser." A. Tallien de Cabarrus. Paris: Éditions Henri Tellier, 1892.
"Chant-rayon-amour!" Pompilio Sudessi. Paris: L. Bathlot-Joubert, 1892.
"Tout aime!" Pompilio Sudessi. Paris: L. Bathlot-Joubert, 1892.
"Parfums mouillés!" Georges Marietti. Paris: E. Gallet, 1895.
"En valsant: Aveu." A. Tallien de Cabarrus. Paris, 1898.
"Comme nos cœurs battaient bien." A. Tallien de Cabarrus. Paris, 1899.

"Heure d'aimer!" Daniel Sergey. Sénart: Paris, 1904.

Piège d'amour: Fantaisie-lyrique en 1 acte. Jane Vieu. Hachette: Paris, 1905.

"Ensorceleuse!" Jane Vieu. Hachette: Paris, 1907.

PREFACES

Preface to *La photographie du nu*, by C. Klary (Paris: C. Klary, 1902).

Preface to *Mes hauts faits d'armes*, by Paul Franz Namur (1899).

WORKS CITED

"2e Exposition Internationale de l'Automobile et du Cycle à Lille." *L'auto-vélo*, March 28, 1901.

Accampo, Elinor. *Blessed Motherhood, Bitter Fruit: Nelly Roussel and the Politics of Female Pain in Third Republic France.* Baltimore: Johns Hopkins University Press, 2006.

Adam, Paul. "Conceptions fausses." *Le journal*, January 28, 1899.

Adler, Laure. *Secrets d'alcôve: Histoire du couple de 1830 à 1930.* Paris: Hachette, 1983.

Albert, Nicole G. *Saphisme et décadence dans Paris fin-de-siècle*. Paris: Martinière, 2005.

"'Les androgynes.'" *Le journal*, September 11, 1903.

"Les androgynes, roman passionnel, par Jane De La Vaudère." *Revue du cercle militaire* 20 (May 16, 1903): 559.

"Assemblé Générale du 8 avril 1900." *Chronique de la Société des gens de lettres*, May, 1900.

Bard, Christine. *Une histoire politique du pantalon.* Paris: Seuil, 2010.

Bauer, B. "Les livres." *La presse*, June 14, 1898.

Bazile, Sandrine. "Lulu s'affiche—Affiches et intertextualité dans Lulu Roman clownesque (1901) de Félicien Champsaur. *Image [&] Narrative* 20 (December 2007). http://www.imageandnarrative.be/inarchive/affiche_findesiecle/bazile.htm.

Beaudu, Edouard. "Le théâtre." *L'intransigeant*, January 5, 1907.

Bélilon, Camille. "Chronique féministe." *La fronde*, August 19, 1898.

Bertrand-Sabiani, Julie, and Géraldi Leroy. *La vie littéraire à la Belle Époque.* Paris: Presses universitaires de France, 1998.

Bethléem, Louis. *Romans à lire et romans à proscrire.* 6th ed. Lille: Romans-Revue, 1914.

Bonal, Gérard, and Michel Remy-Bieth. *Colette intime*. Paris: Éditions Phébus, 2004.

Bosc, Ernest. *Isis dévoilée ou l'égyptologie sacrée.* Paris: Chamuel & Cie., 1891.

Brisson, Adolphe. "Divers." *Les annales politiques et littéraires*, April 19, 1903.

Buisseret, Alexandre. "Les femmes et l'automobile à la Belle Époque." In "Circulations," edited by Catherine Bertho Lavenir. Special issue, *Le mouvement social* 192 (July–September 2000): 41–64.

Buranen, Lise, and Alice M. Roy, eds. *Perspectives on Plagiarism and Intellectual Property in a Postmodern World.* Albany: SUNY Press, 1999.

Butterfly. "Paris l'été." *Gil Blas*, July 30, 1908.

Cahu, Théodore. "Jane de la Vaudère." *Revue illustrée*, June 15, 1904.

Carol, Anne. *L'embaumement, une passion romantique.* Ceyzérieu: Champ Vallon, 2015.

Chadoqueau, Patrick. "Maupassant plagié." *Histoires littéraires* 16 (October–December 2003): 69.

Champsaur, Félicien. *Lulu.* Paris: Librairie Charpentier et Fasquelle, 1901.

———. "Une princesse d'art." *Le journal,* July 23, 1901.

Chincholle, Charles. "Autour de l'audience." *Le Figaro,* February 16, 1898.

Clarens, Juliette. "Dans le monde." *Comœdia,* January 22, 1908.

Clasti. "La vierge d'Israël par Jane de la Vaudère." *Le carnet de la femme,* October 15, 1906.

Cosnier, Colette. *Les dames de* Femina*: Un féminisme mystifié.* Rennes: Presses universitaires de Rennes, 2009.

Cryle, Peter. "'A Terrible Ordeal from Every Point of View': (Not) Managing Female Sexuality on the Wedding Night." In "Feminine Sexual Pathologies in Nineteenth- and Early Twentieth-Century Europe," edited by Peter Cryle and Lisa Downing. Special issue, *Journal of the History of Sexuality* 18, no. 1 (January 2009): 44–64.

Day, Jasmine. *The Mummy's Curse: Mummymania in the English-Speaking World.* New York: Routledge, 2006.

"De ci, de là." *La province nouvelle* 18 (October 1897): 204.

Delilia, Alfred. "Spectacles et concerts." *Le Figaro,* December 30, 1906.

———. "Spectacles et concerts." *Le Figaro,* January 3, 1907.

Des Cilleuls, J.-M. "Le souvenir de Scrive." *Revue du service de santé militaire* 104, no. 6 (1936): 1075–109.

Dobson, Eleanor. "Sleeping Beauties: Mummies and the Fairy-Tale Genre at the *Fin de Siècle.*" *Journal of International Women's Studies* 18, no. 3 (2017): 19–34.

Dottin-Orsini, Mireille. *Cette femme qu'ils disent fatale.* Paris: Grasset, 1993.

Doucet, Camille. "Rapport sur les concours de l'année 1891." Speech, Paris, November 19, 1891. Académie française. http://www.academie-francaise.fr/rapport-sur-les-concours-de-lannee-1891.

Drevet, Laurent. "Jane de la Vaudère: *L'amuseur.*" *La chronique des livres* 1, no. 1 (June–December 1900): 80–81.

Ducrey, Guy. "Jane de la Vaudère: La science et le sang." In "Décadents méconnus," edited by Guy Ducrey and Hélène Védrine. Special issue, *Cahiers de littérature française* 7–8 (2009): 144–60.

"Échos." *Le Figaro,* March 23, 1889, 1.

Edelman, Nicole. *Voyantes, guérisseuses et visionnaires en France, 1785–1914.* Paris: Albin Michel, 1995.

Edwards, Paul. *Soleil noir: Photographie et littérature des origines au surréalisme.* Rennes: Presses universitaires de Rennes, 2008.

Emery, Elizabeth. "La Maison Langweil and Women's Exchange of Asian Art in Fin-de-siècle Paris." In "Cultural Exchange and Creative Identity: France/Asia in the Nineteenth and Early Twentieth Centuries," edited by Aimée Boutin and Elizabeth Emery. Special issue, *L'esprit créateur* 56, no. 3 (2016): 61–75.

———. *Photojournalism and the Origins of the French Writer House Museum (1881–1914).* Farnham: Ashgate, 2012.

Espil, Pierre. *Edmond Rostand, une vie.* Anglet: Éditions du Mondarrain, 1998.

Farge, Arlette. *Le goût de l'archive.* Paris: Éditions du Seuil, 1989.

"Les femmes ont-elles une âme?" *Revue spirite* 9, no. 1 (January, 1866): 1–5.

Finn, Michael. "Female Sterilization and Artificial Insemination at the French Fin de Siècle: Facts and Fictions." *Journal of the History of Sexuality* 18, no. 1 (2009): 26–43.

Fleischhack, Maria. *Narrating Ancient Egypt: The Representation of Ancient Egypt in Nineteenth-Century and Early-Twentieth-Century Fantastic Fiction.* Frankfurt: Peter Lang, 2015.

Fouquières, André de. *Mon Paris et ses Parisiens.* Vol. 2, *Le quartier Monceau.* Paris: Éditions Pierre Horay, 1954.

Fuster, Charles. "Notes parisiennes: La littérature féminine & la passion." *L'événement*, January 5, 1897.

Gardini, Michela. "Jane de la Vaudère sous le signe de l'occultisme." In *La littérature en bas-bleus*, vol. 3, *Romancières en France de 1870 à 1914*, edited by Andrea Del Lungo and Brigitte Louichon, 279–90. Paris: Éditions Classiques Garnier, 2017.

Garval, Michael. *Cléo de Mérode and the Rise of Modern Celebrity Culture.* Farnham: Ashgate, 2012.

Georges-Michel. "La Marquise de Morny au Moulin Rouge." *Gil Blas*, December 30, 1906.

Gourmont, Jean de. *Muses d'aujourd'hui.* Paris: Mercure de France, 1910.

Grandfort, Manoël de. "Causerie littéraire." *La fronde*, June 15, 1898.

Grivel, Charles. "Le roman mis à nu par la photographie, même." In "L'imaginaire photographique," edited by Daniel Grojnowski and Philippe Ortel. Special issue, *Romantisme* 105 (1999): 145–55.

Halbert, Debora. "Poaching and Plagiarizing: Property, Plagiarism, and Feminist Futures." In *Perspectives on Plagiarism and Intellectual Property in a Postmodern World*, edited by Lise Buranen and Alice M. Roy, 111–20. Albany: SUNY Press, 1999.

Hawthorne, Melanie. *Finding the Woman Who Didn't Exist: The Curious Life of Gisèle d'Estoc.* Lincoln: University of Nebraska Press, 2013.

———. *Rachilde and French Women's Authorship: From Decadence to Modernism.* Lincoln: University of Nebraska Press, 2001.

Holmes, Diana. "Daniel Lesueur and the Feminist Romance." In *A "Belle Epoque"? Women in French Society and Culture, 1890–1914*, edited by Diana Holmes and Carrie Tarr, 197–210. New York: Berghahn Books, 2006.

Ibels, André. "Enquête sur le roman illustré par la photographie." *Mercure de France*, January 1898.

Intérim. "Chronique des livres." *La fronde*, October 24, 1901.

"Jane de la Vaudère." In *Figures contemporaines tirées de l'Album Mariani*, vol. 7. Paris: Librairie Henri Floury, 1902.

"'Jane de la Vaudère.'" *Gil Blas*, February 27, 1901.

"Jane de la Vaudère—*L'amazone du roi de Siam.*" *Revue du Nivernais* 5 (1900–1901): 279.

Joseph-Renaud, Jean. *La faillite du mariage et l'union future.* Paris: Flammarion, 1899.

Kardec, Allan. *Le livre des esprits.* 15th ed. Paris: Didier et cie., 1867.

Kerley, Lela F. *Uncovering Paris: Scandals and Nude Spectacles in the Belle Époque.* Baton Rouge: Louisiana State University, 2017.

Klary, C. *La photographie du nu.* Paris: C. Klary, 1902.

Labadie-Lagrave, G. "Pourqoui les femmes ne savent pas conduire les automobiles." *Les annales*, July 1, 1906.

Laborde, B. de. "'L'amazone du roi de Siam.'" *Gil Blas*, May 29, 1902.

Larson, Sharon. "'Elle n'est pas un "bas-bleu," mais un écrivain': Georges de Peyrebrune's Woman Writer." *Nineteenth-Century Contexts* 40, no. 1 (2018): 19–31.

———. "The Feminine Copy: Travel and Textual Reproduction in Jane de la Vaudère's *Les Demi-sexes.*" In "Women and Traveling," edited by Catherine R. Montfort and Christine McCall Probes. Special

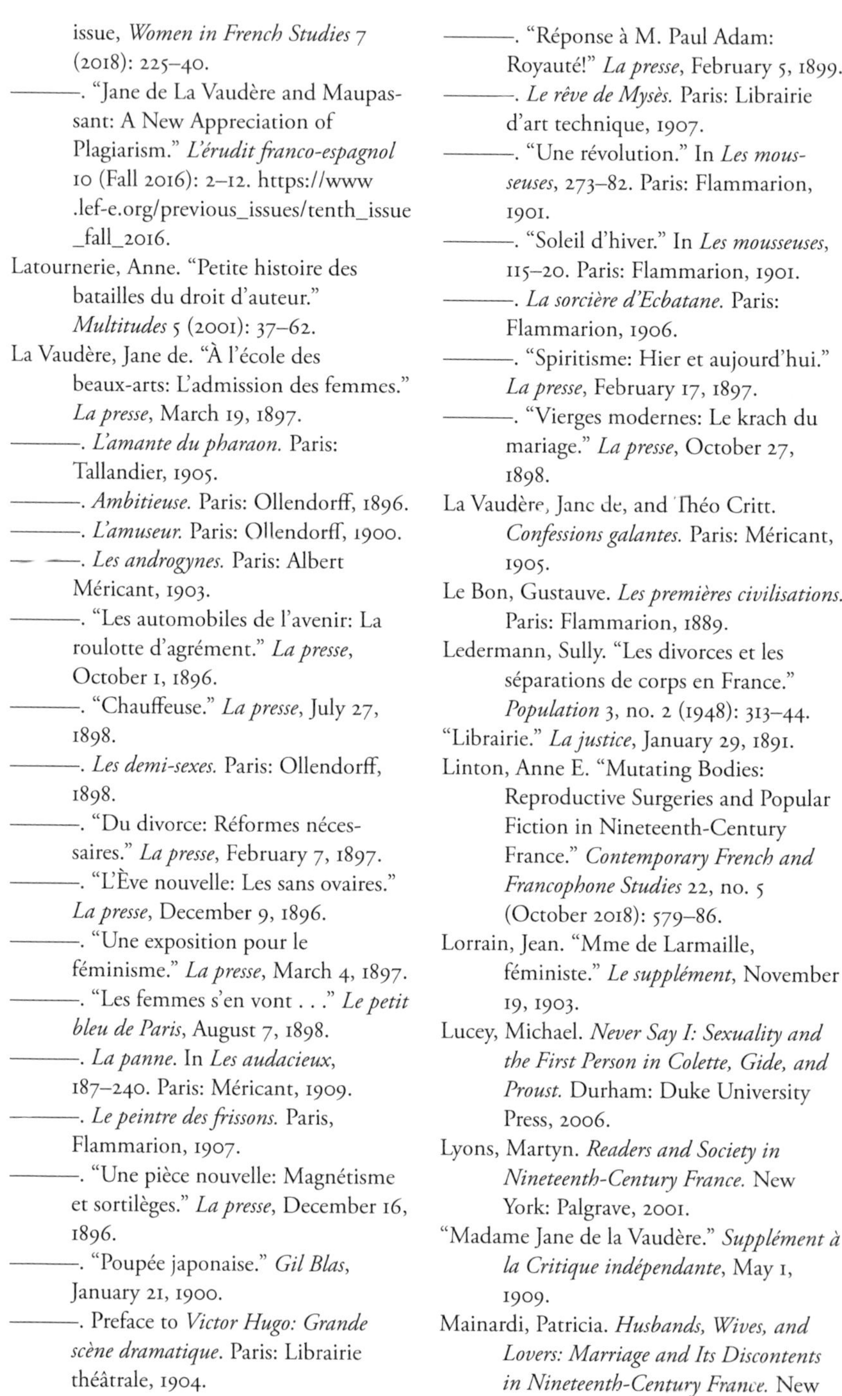

issue, *Women in French Studies* 7 (2018): 225–40.

———. "Jane de La Vaudère and Maupassant: A New Appreciation of Plagiarism." *L'érudit franco-espagnol* 10 (Fall 2016): 2–12. https://www.lef-e.org/previous_issues/tenth_issue_fall_2016.

Latournerie, Anne. "Petite histoire des batailles du droit d'auteur." *Multitudes* 5 (2001): 37–62.

La Vaudère, Jane de. "À l'école des beaux-arts: L'admission des femmes." *La presse*, March 19, 1897.

———. *L'amante du pharaon.* Paris: Tallandier, 1905.

———. *Ambitieuse.* Paris: Ollendorff, 1896.

———. *L'amuseur.* Paris: Ollendorff, 1900.

———. *Les androgynes.* Paris: Albert Méricant, 1903.

———. "Les automobiles de l'avenir: La roulotte d'agrément." *La presse*, October 1, 1896.

———. "Chauffeuse." *La presse*, July 27, 1898.

———. *Les demi-sexes.* Paris: Ollendorff, 1898.

———. "Du divorce: Réformes nécessaires." *La presse*, February 7, 1897.

———. "L'Ève nouvelle: Les sans ovaires." *La presse*, December 9, 1896.

———. "Une exposition pour le féminisme." *La presse*, March 4, 1897.

———. "Les femmes s'en vont . . ." *Le petit bleu de Paris*, August 7, 1898.

———. *La panne.* In *Les audacieux*, 187–240. Paris: Méricant, 1909.

———. *Le peintre des frissons.* Paris, Flammarion, 1907.

———. "Une pièce nouvelle: Magnétisme et sortilèges." *La presse*, December 16, 1896.

———. "Poupée japonaise." *Gil Blas*, January 21, 1900.

———. Preface to *Victor Hugo: Grande scène dramatique.* Paris: Librairie théâtrale, 1904.

———. "Protestations: La femme." *La presse*, April 6, 1899.

———. "Réponse à M. Paul Adam: Royauté!" *La presse*, February 5, 1899.

———. *Le rêve de Mysès.* Paris: Librairie d'art technique, 1907.

———. "Une révolution." In *Les mousseuses*, 273–82. Paris: Flammarion, 1901.

———. "Soleil d'hiver." In *Les mousseuses*, 115–20. Paris: Flammarion, 1901.

———. *La sorcière d'Ecbatane.* Paris: Flammarion, 1906.

———. "Spiritisme: Hier et aujourd'hui." *La presse*, February 17, 1897.

———. "Vierges modernes: Le krach du mariage." *La presse*, October 27, 1898.

La Vaudère, Jane de, and Théo Critt. *Confessions galantes.* Paris: Méricant, 1905.

Le Bon, Gustauve. *Les premières civilisations.* Paris: Flammarion, 1889.

Ledermann, Sully. "Les divorces et les séparations de corps en France." *Population* 3, no. 2 (1948): 313–44.

"Librairie." *La justice*, January 29, 1891.

Linton, Anne E. "Mutating Bodies: Reproductive Surgeries and Popular Fiction in Nineteenth-Century France." *Contemporary French and Francophone Studies* 22, no. 5 (October 2018): 579–86.

Lorrain, Jean. "Mme de Larmaille, féministe." *Le supplément*, November 19, 1903.

Lucey, Michael. *Never Say I: Sexuality and the First Person in Colette, Gide, and Proust.* Durham: Duke University Press, 2006.

Lyons, Martyn. *Readers and Society in Nineteenth-Century France.* New York: Palgrave, 2001.

"Madame Jane de la Vaudère." *Supplément à la Critique indépendante*, May 1, 1909.

Mainardi, Patricia. *Husbands, Wives, and Lovers: Marriage and Its Discontents in Nineteenth-Century France.* New Haven: Yale University Press, 2003.

Mansker, Andrea. *Sex, Honor and Citizenship in Early Third Republic France.* Basingstoke: Palgrave Macmillan, 2011.

Marcus, Sharon. *The Drama of Celebrity.* Princeton: Princeton University Press, 2019.

Marinozzi, Silvia. "The Embalming Art in the Modern Age: The Mummies of Caroline, Letizia and Joachim-Napoleon Agar as Examples of Funerary Rites in the Napoleonic Empire." *Nuncius* 27 (2012): 309–29.

Maupassant, Guy de. *En Sicile.* Bruxelles: Éditions Complexe, 1993.

———. *Notre cœur.* Edited by Marie-Claire Bancquart. Paris: Gallimard, 1993.

Maurecy, Mme. Louis. "Ceux qui croient au merveilleux: Chez Mme Jane de la Vaudère." *L'écho du merveilleux* 227 (June 15, 1906): 227–28.

Maurel-Indart, Hélène. *Du plagiat.* Paris: Presses universitaires de France, 1999.

Maurevert, Georges. *Le livre des plagiats.* Paris: Fayard, 1922.

Mesch, Rachel. *Before Trans: Three Gender Stories from Nineteenth-Century France.* Stanford: Stanford University Press, 2020.

———. *Having It All in the Belle Epoque: How French Women's Magazines Invented the Modern Woman.* Stanford: Stanford University Press, 2013.

———. "Husbands, Wives and Doctors: Marriage and Medicine in Rachilde, Jane de La Vaudère and Camille Pert." In "State of the Union: Marriage in Nineteenth-Century France," edited by Masha Belenky and Rachel Mesch. Special issue, *Dix-neuf* 11, no. 1 (November 2008): 90–104.

"Mme Marguerite Durand et sa lionne 'Tigre.'" *Femina*, April 1, 1910.

Mortier, Pierre. "Courrier des théâtres." *Gil Blas*, July 16, 1907.

"*Le mystère de Kama.*" *Saturday Review of Politics, Literature, Science, and Art*, November 16, 1901.

"Nécrologie." *Chronique de la Société des gens de lettres*, August, 1908.

Néret, Gilles, and Hervé Poulain. *L'art, la femme et l'automobile.* Paris: E. P. A., 1989.

Offen, Karen. *Debating the Woman Question in the French Third Republic, 1870–1920.* Cambridge: Cambridge University Press, 2018.

———. "Defining Feminism: A Comparative Historical Approach." *Signs* 14, no. 1 (Autumn 1988): 119–57.

———. "Depopulation, Nationalism, and Feminism in Fin-de-Siècle France." *American Historical Review* 89, no. 3 (June 1984): 648–76.

———. "On the French Origin of the Words Feminism and Feminist." *Feminist Issues* 8, no. 2 (Fall 1988): 45–51.

Paisant, Chantal. *De l'exil aux tranchées, 1901/1914–1918: Le témoignage des sœurs.* Paris: Éditions Karthala, 2014.

Palacio, Jean de. "La postérité d'*À rebours* ou le livre dans le livre." In *Figures et formes de la décadence*, Deuxième série, 194–202. Paris: Séguier, 2000.

Paliyenko, Adrianna. *Genius Envy: Women Shaping French Poetic History, 1801–1901.* University Park: Penn State University Press, 2016.

Parramore, Lynn. *Reading the Sphinx: Ancient Egypt in Nineteenth-Century Literary Culture.* New York: Palgrave Macmillan, 2008.

Pauvert-Raimbault, Dorothée. "Champsaur, Mirbeau et Rimbaud." *Cahiers Octave Mirbeau* 17 (2010): 22–39.

Pedersen, Jean Elisabeth. *Legislating the French Family: Feminism, Theater, and Republican Politics, 1870–1920.* New Brunswick: Rutgers University Press, 2003.

Les Pères Ratisbonne et Notre-Dame de Sion. Paris: Beauchesne, 1931.

Perry, Elisabeth Israels. "Memorializing the 1897 Tennessee Centennial Woman's Building." In *Gendering the Fair: Histories of Women and Gender at World's Fairs*, edited by T. J. Boisseau and Abigail M. Markwyn, 149–65. Urbana: University of Illinois Press, 2010.

Peyrebrune, Georges de (Hunedell, pseud.). "Jupiter et les bas-bleus." *Le Figaro*, December 2, 1893.

Pontaillac. "Nos échos." *Le journal*, July 30, 1897.

Potinier. "Les coulisses." *Le supplément*, April 23, 1903.

Pougy, Liane de. *Les sensations de Mlle de Bringue.* Paris: Albin Michel, 1904.

"*Les prêtresses de Mylitta.*" *Le journal*, July 23, 1907.

Prungnaud, Joëlle. *Gothique et décadence: Recherches sur la continuité d'un mythe et d'un genre au XIXe siècle en Grande-Bretagne et en France.* Paris: Honoré Champion, 1997.

Rachilde. "*Les androgynes*, par Jane de la Vaudère." *Mercure de France*, July 1903, 179–80.

———. "*Les demi-sexes*, par Jane de la Vaudère." *Mercure de France*, September 1897, 523.

———. "*Les florifières*, par Camille Pert." *Mercure de France*, May 1898, 547.

———. "*Les frôleurs*, par Jane de la Vaudère." *Mercure de France*, September 1899, 781.

———. "*La guescha amoureuse*, par Jane de la Vaudère." *Mercure de France*, August 1904, 475–76.

———. "*Idylle saphique*, par Liane de Pougy." *Mercure de France*, December 1901, 781–82.

———. "*Les mousseuses*, par Jane de la Vaudère." *Mercure de France*, August 1901, 492.

———. "*Le mystère de Kama*, par Jane de la Vaudère." *Mercure de France*, December 1901, 782.

———. "*La porte de Félicité*, par Jane de la Vaudère." *Mercure de France*, May 1905, 413.

———. "*Le sang*, par Jane de la Vaudère." *Mercure de France*, July 1898, 231.

———. "*Les sataniques*, par Jane de la Vaudère." *Mercure de France*, August 1897, 342.

———. "*La sorcière d'Ecbatane*, par Jane de la Vaudère." *Mercure de France*, April 15, 1906, 569.

Randall, Marilyn. *Pragmatic Plagiarism: Authorship, Profit, and Power.* Toronto: University of Toronto Press, 2001.

Rip, Georges. "Les candidatures féminines." *Le Figaro*, March 27, 1900.

———. "La dernière reunion." *Le Figaro*, April 7, 1900.

Roberts, Mary Louise. *Disruptive Acts: The New Woman in Fin-de-Siècle France.* Chicago: University of Chicago Press, 2002.

Rochetal, Albert de. "Chronique graphologique: Jane de La Vaudère." *Revue illustrée*, June 15, 1904.

Rubempré. "Courrier de Paris." *L'univers illustré*, February 13, 1892.

Ryner, Han. *Le massacre des amazones: Études critiques sur deux cents bas-bleus contemporains.* Paris: Chamuel, 1899.

Scharff, Virginia. *Taking the Wheel: Women and the Coming of the Motor Age.* Albuquerque: University of New Mexico Press, 1999.

Schultz, Gretchen. *The Gendered Lyric: Subjectivity and Difference in Nineteenth-Century French Poetry.* West Lafayette: Purdue University Press, 1999.

———. *Sapphic Fathers: Discourses of Same-Sex Desire from Nineteenth-Century France.* Toronto: University of Toronto Press, 2015.

Séché, Alphonse. *Les muses françaises: Anthologie des femmes-poètes.* Vol. 2, *XXe siècle.* Paris: Louis-Michaud, 1908.

"Secrétariat d'État à la Guerre." *Journal officiel de l'État français*, June 11, 1942.

Sénéchal, Georges. "Les *demi-sexes*, par Jane de la Vaudère." *La nouvelle revue* 107 (July–August 1897): 570–71.

Senner, Gaston. "La scène." *La presse*, September 1, 1897.

Sharp, Lynn L. *Secular Spirituality: Reincarnation and Spiritism in Nineteenth-Century France.* Lanham: Lexington Books, 2006.

Souvestre, Pierre. "Le circuit européen." *L'auto*, March 29, 1906.

———. "La coupe du 'Matin.'" *L'auto*, August 1, 1906.

Stableford, Brian. Introduction to *The Demi-Sexes and The Androgynes*, by Jane de la Vaudère, translated by Brian Stableford. Snuggly Books, 2018.

Stewart, Mary Lynn. *For Health and Beauty: Physical Culture for Frenchwomen, 1880s–1930s.* Baltimore: Johns Hopkins University Press, 2001.

Sullivan, Courtney. *The Evolution of the French Courtesan Novel: From de Chabrillan to Colette.* London: Palgrave Macmillan, 2016.

"Théâtres." *Le temps*, January 8, 1907.

Tout-Paris. "Bloc-notes parisien: Femmes poètes." *Le gaulois*, July 3, 1890.

Les Treize. "Nos échos." *L'intransigeant*, April 21, 1911.

Tromp, Marlene. "Queering the Séance: Bodies, Bondage, and Touching in Victorian Spiritualism." In *Handbook of Spiritualism and Channeling*, edited by Cathy Gutierrez, 87–115. Boston: Brill, 2015.

Trubek, Anne. *A Skeptic's Guide to Writers' Houses.* Philadelphia: University of Pennsylvania Press, 2011.

Viveiros, Geneviève de. "Albert Méricant: Éditeur innovateur de la Belle Époque (1897–1928)." *Revue française d'histoire du livre* 136 (2015): 193–206.

———. "Jane de la Vaudère ou l'éclectisme littéraire." *Passées sous silence: Onze femmes écrivains à relire*, edited by Patrick Bergeron, 173–86. Valenciennes: Presses universitaires de Valenciennes, 2015.

———. "Lettres inédites de Jane de la Vaudère à Émile Zola: De la Société des Gens de Lettres à *Pour une nuit d'amour!*" *Cahiers naturalists* 81 (2007): 231–42.

Waelti-Walters, Jennifer. *Damned Women: Lesbians in French Novels.* Montreal: McGill-Queen's Press, 2000.

White, Nicholas. *French Divorce Fiction from the Revolution to the First World War.* London: Modern Humanities Research Association and Maney Publishing, 2013.

Wilkins, Wynona H. "The Paris International Feminist Congress of 1896 and Its French Antecedents." *North Dakota Quarterly* 43, no. 4 (Autumn 1975): 5–28.

Zarmanian, Charlotte Foucher. *Créatrices en 1900: Femmes artistes en France dans les milieux symbolistes.* Paris: Éditions Mare & Martin, 2015.

———. "Quand les femmes entrent en piste! Domptage et émancipation féminine au passage du XIXe au XXe siècle." *Horizons/théâtre* 10–11 (2017): 240–58.

INDEX

Italicized page references indicate illustrations. Endnotes are referenced with "n" followed by the endnote number.